The Emancipation of Angelina Grimké

Sarah M. Grimké

Angelina Grimké Weld

Theodore D. Weld

THE EMANCIPATION
OF ANGELINA GRIMKÉ

by KATHARINE DU PRE LUMPKIN

The University of North Carolina Press
Chapel Hill

Copyright © 1974 by
The University of North Carolina Press
All rights reserved
Manufactured in the United States of America
ISBN 0-8078-1232-3
Library of Congress Catalog Card Number 74-8914

3/4/82

Library of Congress Cataloging in Publication Data

Lumpkin, Katharine Du Pre, 1897-
  The emancipation of Angelina Grimké.

  Bibliography: p.
  1. Grimké, Angelina Emily, 1805-1879.   I.   Title.
E449.G865L85   322.4'4'0924 [B]   74-8914
ISBN 0-8078-1232-3

Contents

Foreword

A more unlikely social background could hardly be imagined than the one from which Angelina Grimké came to become a leading woman figure in nineteenth-century movements for the emancipation of slaves and of her own sex. She was born February 20, 1805, to a family of wealth and high station. Her South Carolina home was in the City of Charleston, a place where family name was expecially revered, and she never ceased to hold the name of Grimké high. John Faucheraud Grimké, her father, was Oxford educated, a distinguished lawyer, and a state supreme court judge. Several of her brothers became well-known professional men, learned in the law and highly regarded. Formal higher education was not available to a woman, though Angelina was self-educated to a high degree. She came of a people who were owners of many slaves. Her family lived in the city but drew their wealth from a plantation two hundred miles distant. Angelina saw little of the Grimké slaves, except for those who served the household on Charleston's East Bay. It is true that she saw slaves by the hundreds on Charleston's streets and those who served in the stately homes of relatives and friends. Thus what Angelina knew was luxury and ease, as these were made possible by ample means and numerous slaves, although as matters turned out she was far from protected from sights, sounds, and experiences that would come to haunt her life.

There were many children in the Grimké family, fourteen in all, with the three who died in childhood. Angelina was the fourteenth child. Of the eleven living children, only two among them turned actively against slavery—Angelina and a middle child named Sarah, who was twelve years older. Sarah, from the first, was Angelina's mentor and became a strange and dubious kind of catalytic agent at times of major crisis for Angelina. At no time was this clearer than when Angelina was confronted with the clear-cut issue: could she continue to condone human slavery? Not that Sarah put the matter directly; it was put by certain Friends whom Sarah knew in her Philadelphia Friends Meeting. Angelina met the slavery issue head-on, with consequences that Sarah never dreamed could ensue.

The years that preceded Angelina's career, beginning around the time she came of age, are rich in materials from Angelina's and Sarah's letters and diaries. There are also letters from their mother, Mary Smith Grimké and, at certain times, from others. Thus the record is full, explicit, revealing, and so extensive that only significant portions can be given. Of course all of the documents contribute to the author's knowledge of Angelina's development, motives, and character.

Since her early twenties Angelina Grimké had felt the pressures of her great potential gifts and the urgings of her ambitious nature, and these she expressed in perhaps the only terms open to a woman of her time and place. She experienced conversion, a religious upheaval that demanded a full and complete commitment. While in that day it was not at all unusual for a female—girl or woman—to experience conversion and become more religious in her devotion to her church, the conversion customarily brought no change in her traditional female functions. On the contrary, Angelina's experience was unusual. In the language of her day, she, a woman, felt called to some great mission, but at the time she did not know where the call would lead her. The conviction that she was meant to do important work never left Angelina in the ensuing years, though she rarely expressed what she sensed it was that drove her on—the need to use her powers and to have them be of use—and when she spoke of freedom this was part of what she meant.

It was more than mere chance that the antislavery movement became for Angelina the means and symbol of her "mission." When she settled in Philadelphia in late 1829, antislavery groups throughout the North and Middle West were moving ever closer to a merger of their members.[1] The founding convention met in late 1833 in Philadelphia, and from this time on, all through the 1830s, the American Anti-Slavery Society was a vigorous, vociferous, controversial force that was confronted by an ever-rising hostile opposition. The more it was attacked, the more unyielding grew its principles—"abolition of slavery," "immediate emancipation." Many of the leaders were of outstanding qualities, men of various vocations, all of deep commitment, who, while they came to differ, remained devoted to abolition, and, in these first years, their differences were muted. With very few exceptions, they were religious people, so the abolition movement was religiously motivated. The leaders practiced prayer, they used churches for their meetings, and they called on fellow Christians to be consistent in their beliefs and to condemn human slavery as a sin in God's eyes. The number of abolitionist publications showed a rapid increase: Garrison's paper, the *Liberator*, was founded in the early thirties; the *Emancipator* was the official organ of the Anti-Slavery Society; tracts poured from the presses as the decade went on, with a wide distribution in local societies; abolitionist speakers began to move from place to place, meeting ever-growing interest and often violent hostility. Within the movement, the 1830s were a creative time—stimulating, exciting, and full of hope for the converted, who felt the thrill of belonging to this company of men and women so committed to a noble human cause.

By 1834 Angelina was awakened, and in the antislavery movement she recognized her "call." In fact, as she began, she was merely a member of a small, local female antislavery society. The fact that her name became notorious within a matter of months is one of the more remarkable features of her career. Thenceforth she was swept into uncharted seas, in which, despite her womanhood and the time and place, she found the power somehow to steer a clear direction.

One strong force in the abolition movement came to Angelina's aid at this crucial time, and it is not too much to surmise that it was an essential element. This was the company of "female" abolitionists. The American Anti-Slavery Society was composed of men and women, although the women, it must be said, were in an auxiliary position. At least they were in the men's eyes, a fact that came to light in highly vocal terms once the question of woman's status became acute within the movement—an issue, be it said, that Angelina and Sarah Grimké, more than any others, helped to precipitate. In the mid-1830s many women's groups existed, usually called Female Anti-Slavery Societies. They were active and vocal, but they were separate from the men's organizations. At the founding convention in 1833, there were only men delegates; women had no vote. A few well-known women were allowed in the hall. Lucretia Mott, a noted Hicksite Quaker minister and an outstanding abolitionist in Philadelphia and beyond, was permitted the floor to say a few words. Among the most active of the women's abolitionist groups were those in Philadelphia, New York, and Massachusetts, though there were many local societies throughout the East and Middle West. These women gave of their energies in wide-ranging activities: they circulated petitions urging Congress to act; they sold antislavery tracts and subscriptions to their papers; they arranged public meetings to hear antislavery speakers; when a slave escaped and his case came before a northern court, they aroused public indignation for fear the fugitive would be returned to his slavery. Even at their own gatherings, hostile mobs sometimes would gather. These women expected danger and were known for their courage.

Angelina's career did not trace a smooth course. It began, in sudden burst, with her incredible crusade. By late 1836 her direction was apparent—to become a platform lecturer for the abolition cause. At first she did not know the greatness of her powers or what it meant to her to give them full expression as she labored in a "high and holy cause." She was swift to embrace her second "human right," freedom for woman as well as for the slave, though clearly, during this period, she merely "practiced equal rights," while she gave without stint for abolition of slavery. Her brilliant intellect and phenomenal voice found full expression by early 1838 as her "mission" reached its peak in great public triumphs. The full story of her amazing speaking journeys was recorded at the time in rich and full detail. Candid documents, once scattered, were somehow preserved, including full accounts from Angelina's own pen. Nor were press and pulpit silent concerning these notorious women. For Sarah Grimké had come to Angelina's side, become an abolitionist, joined her on the public platform, and also become a vocal advocate of woman's rights.

Angelina was married in May 1838. Theodore Weld was a leading abolitionist who might have become a matchless figure in the abolition movement, but that time had passed by the wedding day. Angelina was thirty-three, Weld less than two years older. Angelina had expected to continue her "public life," a fact well known to her closer friends whose support had upheld her in her tumultuous crusade: Lydia Maria Child, Maria Chapman, Anna Weston, Abby Kelley, all well known as fearless abolitionists and spirited advocates of woman's freedom. In fact Angelina did not continue in public work. For at least a dozen years she remained aloof, an inexplicable withdrawal to the friends who knew her well. Weld had often said that he approved her public work and believed in woman's right to be treated as an equal. Considerable mystery has surrounded these intervening years, and Angelina herself offered no explanation. She offered none even after she emerged and engaged once more in public activity. Again, there are documents that indicate what occurred in this home of hidden struggles. Chiefly these are letters written by Angelina, her husband Weld, and her sister Sarah, who lived with the Welds from the day of their marriage until her death at eighty-one.

Perhaps no period of Angelina Grimké's life has more to say than these years of withdrawal. In no respect is her life more a mirror of her age and of subsequent times, for that matter, than in the painful, unrelenting conflicts and frustrations that she could not escape because she was a woman. In the day-to-day impact of person on person, she often failed to sense the subtle pressures to conform (pressures that often came in very strange guises), and she could not fully realize how pervasively effective were the laws and customs that treated woman as inferior. At no time was her drive for emancipation clearer, as she dealt with the obstacles, both within and without, that throughout this period she feared might defeat her.

Angelina took up her work again as she returned to activities in behalf of her causes. All was not as before; she was somehow changed, though the records of these years show beyond any doubt that if anything she was even more steadfast, more unyielding, as she continually upheld her principles of human freedom. This last, long period brought a different kind of triumph from the one she had known in her first great crusade.

Acknowledgments

Some twenty years ago I began my research on Angelina and Sarah Grimké. I had first learned of the Grimké sisters while I was reading extensively in southern social and economic history in preparation for writing my autobiographical study, *The Making of a Southerner*.* Merle Curti, at the time professor of history at Smith College, suggested that the Grimkés might be the subject of my next writing project, and I shall always be grateful to him for making the suggestion. A few years later my research on the Grimkés was underway.

Although most of my primary materials on Angelina Grimké and those associated with her were gathered in the 1950s, I have continued my research on into the 1970s. As matters turned out, I was obliged to wait until my retirement from college teaching to write *The Emancipation of Angelina Grimké*, but the extensive firsthand materials that I had accumulated were never far from my attention. I had not only many notebooks covering my research, but also some portions of the manuscript materials on microfilm, and a good many printed documents from the period in photostat. During these past years I have many times reviewed what I have collected, so when it came to the final writing I had a sense of close familiarity with the firsthand materials.

The Making of a Southerner (1947; reprint ed., Westport, Conn.: Greenwood Press, 1971).

In carrying on my research I have worked in many libraries, and I am mindful of the assistance and advice of so many staff members in these institutions that it would be impossible to name more than a few.

The principal manuscript collection of Angelina Grimké Weld and Sarah M. Grimké is in the Weld-Grimké Collection in the William L. Clements Library of the University of Michigan, Ann Arbor. I spent several periods of time in this library and wish to express my very great appreciation to Howard H. Peckham, the director, for the opportunities afforded me as I carried on my research. Also I wish to say how greatly I am indebted to William S. Ewing, formerly curator of manuscripts, for his never-failing help and invaluable advice. I also wish to thank Mrs. Georgia Haugh, now curator of rare books, for the generous help she has given me recently.

I spent a substantial amount of time in a number of other libraries. The Boston Public Library had much to offer, especially in the Department of Rare Books and Manuscripts, where the Anna Weston and the William Lloyd Garrison manuscripts had many items of interest to me; I quote from manuscript materials by courtesy of the Trustees of the Boston Public Library. I also used this library's extensive collection of nineteenth-century newspapers, including antislavery papers. The Oberlin College Library collection of antislavery materials was especially helpful for publications of the period, as was the Samuel J. May antislavery collection in Cornell University Library. I have made use of the Library of Congress on a number of occasions, searching in the Manuscripts Division for Grimké letters, examining volumes in the rare book collection, and spending many hours in the collection of nineteenth-century newspapers. I am indebted to the Library of Congress Prints and Photographs Division for furnishing me with the photographs of Angelina Grimké, Sarah Grimké, and Theodore D. Weld which are found in this book.

Among the libraries where I spent short but rewarding periods, I wish to mention the following: the George Arents Research Library for Special Collections at Syracuse University, with its Gerrit Smith Collection, where I found some valuable letters from both Angelina and Sarah Grimké to Gerrit Smith; the Howard University Library, where Mrs. Dorothy Porter was of much help to me; Fisk University Library, where I explored various antislavery materials; Haverford College Library, especially the periodicals and books relating to the Society of Friends; The Massachusetts Historical Society Library in Boston with its manuscript materials on the Grimkés; also the Pennsylvania Historial Society Library in Philadelphia with its manuscripts dealing with the Grimkés. I made a visit to Lincoln University in Pennsylvania and its library to learn of the university's history and to inquire about material touching on Angelina Grimké's visit in 1868.

In all of the libraries and other institutions in which I have searched for material, the staff members have been unfailingly generous with their time and of great help as I carried on my research. I wish I knew how to pay adequate tribute to all of them.

In my bibliography I mention my interview of several hours with Angelina Weld Grimké, daughter of Archibald H. Grimké, who spoke with much pleasure of being Angelina's namesake. Although Miss Grimké died a number of years ago, I cannot refrain from expressing deep gratitude for the unique opportunity afforded me of talking with her, for the letters and other materials of her father's that she shared with me, and for her perceptive comments on some of the people who had touched Angelina Grimké's life.

In conclusion, I wish to express my great appreciation to Mrs. Preston H. Pumphrey and Professor Dwight L. Dumond for permission to quote material from the following published work: Gilbert H. Barnes and Dwight L. Dumond (eds.), *Letters of Theodore Dwight Weld, Angelina Grimké Weld, and Sarah Grimké, 1822-1844*, 2 vols. (1934; reprint ed., New York: Da Capo Press, 1970). Copyright © 1934 by the American Historical Association. Copyright renewed, 1962, by Dwight L. Dumond and Elizabeth B. Pumphrey. Material quoted with the permission of the copyright owners.

Katharine DuPre Lumpkin

The Emancipation of Angelina Grimké

I. Of Violence and Discord

"Mother is perfectly blind to how miserably she has brought us up. . . . She rules slaves and children with a rod of fear!"
ANGELINA GRIMKÉ, *Diary, 1828.*

"God is a God of order! & cannot approve of violence and discord."
MARY S. GRIMKÉ, *slaveholder of Charleston, in a letter to her abolitionist daughters, June 16, 1839.*

1.

Dread of the work house reached back to early memory, though for a while Angelina could not have told what went on there. She was a child of seven or eight when a kind of comprehension forced its way into her consciousness. Mary Grimké was not one to permit her children to move in circles other than the elite; hence it might seem strange to find a Charleston first-family in close proximity to so unseemly a place. But for one thing the work house had once been something else: witness how the name "sugar house" had clung to it; for another, in the Charleston of the early nineteenth century, it appears that old families lived where it pleased them, especially if their homes had been in the family for generations.[1] Nina, the family name for Angelina, sometimes went on foot to visit a playmate who lived on a street near the building.[2] As her feet led her by those ugly brick walls, she said she had heard "screams" and, inquiring of her friend, was "often" given accounts of what the screams meant. One can guess at the scene, recapture its aura: the two little girls in a child's pleasant bedroom playing, then listening to faint eerie sounds that came floating through the windows from the old "sugar house," and whispering, as little girls do, forbidden things that repel and fascinate.

When Angelina, as a child, had learned of the work house and passed its drab walls, shivering at the "screams," what clung to her mind could scarcely be termed knowledge; it was something so shadowy, so vaguely remote. She could have been aware that some slaveowners sometimes used the work house to have slaves punished, whether by the lash, the paddle, or the treadmill. Her first direct knowledge came when she was about twelve. This, like her earlier memory, was recorded in later years when, as an abolitionist, she described what slavery meant.[3]

The school Angelina attended was highly regarded, and to it "nearly all the aristocracy" sent their daughters. A man and wife of "superior education" conducted it. This couple, it appears, owned a few slaves to do the household work of their establishment. One of these slaves was a young boy about Angelina's age, who was called into the schoolroom one day to open a window. His head had been shaved, and he was so "dreadfully crippled" that he could "hardly walk across the room"; on his face Angelina saw a "heartbroken look." The school girls knew what had happened to the boy —that he had come from the "sugar house," where he had been whipped. Angelina, remembering, said she "fainted away."

She went on to tell of another school slave, the mulatto seamstress. Angelina soon learned—was she listening for it now, reluctantly impelled to seek out the young seamstress, busy at her sewing, where she sat on her low stool on a rear piazza?—that this slave woman had been sent to the work house more than once. "She often told [me] secretly, how cruelly she was whipped when they sent her to the work house." From this time on, when Angelina passed those walls, her limbs, she wrote, would hardly sustain her.[4]

These experiences of slavery were but the first of many that sooner or later Angelina made known. Some that she recalled were of the work house, some had happened in friends' houses, and others within the walls of her own home. A number of these experiences she recorded in her diary once it began—she was twenty-one at the time of her first entry—in October 1826. If all this disturbing knowledge meant what it seems to mean, a recurring fear of violence in the treatment of slaves, then it suggests that Angelina, unlike most slave-owners' children, was not impervious to the grosser aspects of the system. Not that Angelina was then rejecting slavery. She lived with it and accepted it until well into her twenties.

The signs are clear that sometime in her childhood Angelina began to feel an estrangement from her mother, a feeling that persisted for a good many years and was openly expressed to certain members of her family.

Most of what is known of the mother, Mary Grimké, is found in the letters and diaries of Sarah and Angelina and in the letters that the mother wrote to them. The greater part of what was written (in the papers that were preserved) came out of a time when conflict and tension were apparent in the relationship between mother and daughter. Hence, while there is evidence of what the mother was like, how she spent her days, what she deeply valued, and how she spoke and felt when she was challenged on slavery, the image that emerges in Angelina's story may be a warped picture, overclouded by emotion.

Mary Smith Grimké came of Charleston's elite. She was a fit wife for John Faucheraud Grimké, a man who ranked high in the city's aristocracy. Mary Grimké could claim descent from distinguished Carolinians, among them Thomas Smith, a landgrave of Carolina.[5] She was known as a woman who took great pride in family name.

The mother lived a life filled with duties. Overburdened was the way she described her days,[6] nor could her husband's wealth do much to ease her responsibilities. Never since her marriage had she known much leisure. She had married at twenty, and John, her first child, was born ten months later. Within twenty years she had borne fourteen children. Three died, two in infancy, and while these losses themselves must have taken a great toll, there still remained eleven to be reared. Angelina was her youngest child.[7]

Mary Grimké's duties mounted as the years went by. Of first importance was the management of her large household. In general she oversaw the rearing of her children: her children must be clothed and in the height of fashion, given Grimké standards, which meant materials to purchase and slave seamstresses to supervise, though sometimes she would "put out" the tailoring for the male members of the family. Yet the slave always came between her and the care of each young child. She had a slave "mauma" and several nursemaid helpers; and when nursery days were over, she had assistance still, since each child was given a slave servant. The number of slaves in the Grimké household can only be surmised by comparison with similar homes.[8] The house was very large, a handsome Georgian structure, its three stories rising above a street-level basement. The spacious rooms were numerous, the furnishings luxurious. It required many servants to man such a dwelling: cook, kitchen helpers, butler and footman, "mauma" and nursemaids, chambermaids, waitingmaids, male members' body servants, coachman and stable boys, seamstresses, "washers," and even slave children, once they were old enough for various little tasks. These were not the only slaves the Grimkés owned. The principal wealth of the father, Judge Grimké, lay in his plantation and his numerous slaves there. But "Bellemont"—as the country place was called—was distant from Charleston, in the Carolina "upcountry" on the edge of Union County.[9] Mary Grimké had no responsibility for the slaves on the plantation; her duties lay in managing the Charleston household. Not only must the household slaves be fed and clothed, their manners and morals overseen to some degree, and decisions made when she thought they should be punished, but there was also the never-ending, thankless task of keeping them busy with the work of the household. Her "People," as she called them, could be trusted just so far; her eye must be ever and always on the slave.[10]

With all this, Mary Grimké was a leader in the manner a lady was expected to lead. She was "devout," all testified to it, and she leaned heavily on strict Episcopalian teaching, the creed, and man's "duty towards God," as this was set down in the Book of Common Prayer. Also, Charleston had its Ladies Benevolent Society, and Mary Grimké was "foremost in benevolent enterprises," thus fulfilling the other duty laid down in her prayer book, her duty to her "neighbor," Charleston's white poor. Somehow she found time to visit the needy, the destitute sick, the sinful woman prisoner, and she expected her daughters to conform to this practice as they grew old enough to join her missions of mercy.

Time also had to be found for another weighty duty, the social obligations of a Charleston "first family." Angelina more than once described the high estate from which she came, the small "elite" of the wealthier class. Once her diary began in the late 1820s, it frequently referred to her mother's entertaining and to her own and her brothers' social life.[11] Mary Grimké was a leader in this elite society, a position she held by right of birth and marriage, and also by the power of her pride and condescension. Even her own children often found her unapproachable.[12]

Mary Grimké's preoccupation with her full, absorbing life may be a chief reason that she seemed inaccessible; it may have helped to raise the barrier that Angelina felt, indeed was aware of before she reached her teens. One memory of this time Angelina called up long years later, well after her marriage, in writing to her husband of the problems of family life, and the tone was charged with excessive emotion, as if that early trauma could still give pain.[13] Judge Grimké was ill at the time of this event, and the decision was taken, most certainly by the mother, to place her youngest child in that fateful academy in which Angelina was to gain firsthand knowledge of the work house. The reasons for the step were obvious enough. The mother had no time for her youngest child, weighed down as she was by distressing anxiety and her duties of supervising both household and children. When her children were young, a slave "mauma" was in charge; not so when her daughters stood on the threshhold of their teens. A young girl must be trained for her social position. The school Angelina attended was not distant from her home. While apparently she was sent somewhat earlier than usual, how can one account for the child's feelings of acute deprivation? Thirty years later Angelina could term it being "violently wrenched." She could write to her husband, "I felt so troubled," "cried so bitterly" at being "torn from the bosoms to which my heart clung," and was "made to become independent of those props which my childish heart so deeply needed." The family called her distress "foolish weakness"—the words an echo surely of the mother's stern tones. This stirred Angelina's pride, and she felt she would be "miserable" if she did not make "great effort" to "wean" herself from that "dependence that each member of a family ought to feel . . . on all the others." Angelina at the time felt her mother had failed her in forcing on her an unfeeling separation.

It was Angelina's fate to find a substitute mother, her sister Sarah, who was twelve years older. Sarah, it appears, was a lonely child, full of vague, hidden fears, and she no doubt sought to banish these by finding people who would love her. Very probably she too had found her mother wanting, but the case was different with her father. Sarah spoke of him as strict, prudent, economical, perhaps remote, and possessing high standards of conduct and character. As his children grew older, he showed concern for their upbringing, and he had singled out Sarah as a favorite among his daughters. Sarah had responded with devotion and adoration. Her needs and affections were deeply focused on her father. Angelina's advent was a memorable time for Sarah. Apparently she told the story directly to Catherine Birney who, in her 1885 biography of the sisters, quoted Sarah freely, often using Sarah's words.[14] Sarah announced that she wished to be Angelina's godmother. Her parents were amazed at this strange request. To the mother, especially, it made no sense. She dismissed Sarah's notion as a "childish whim" and objected to it on grave grounds, the duties of a sponsor, the heavy obligations. The latter meant a great deal to Mary Grimké, for whom baptism by Episcopal rite was a requisite condition for the soul's salvation: a sponsor must be surety for the helpless infant. But Sarah felt driven—this was how she later told it—by the "yearning tenderness of a mother" toward this baby or, as she also said, by "mysterious affinity." She waged a daily, unremitting campaign, pleaded, wept, argued, prayed—without a doubt making certain that her family knew she prayed. When her father said she was too young, she argued sensibly that she would not be too young when her vows must be fulfilled. So Sarah came to stand at the font in old St. Philip's, renouncing "the Devil and all his works, the vain pomp and glory of the world . . . the sinful desires of the flesh," all these on behalf of her baby sister "Nina." And having done it—she told it this way—she slipped apart, shut herself in her room, and fell on her knees, tears coursing down her cheeks. She prayed to be made worthy of her task, she prayed for help to "guide my precious child," she prayed to be good so that her own life would always be a blessing to this little sister.

It can be imagined with what childish fantasies twelve-year-old Sarah regarded her new baby sister. For what developed reflected Sarah's principal attachment, the one to her father that she so strained to enhance, the only one that apparently brought her some feeling of safety in a threatening world. What Sarah did was to adopt Angelina, to absorb her as her own, so that as years passed, by the time the youngest was emerging from the nursery and the mother would have begun to replace the slave "mauma," Angelina was markedly clinging to Sarah, showing preference for Sarah, even calling Sarah "mother." She sometimes still called Sarah "mother" as late as her mid-twenties.

Here then was the beginning of Sarah's special claims that would haunt Angelina through all her days. There is an 1828 letter of Angelina's that bears on its face the story of these years. Angelina was twenty-three when she wrote, still living in Charleston, although absent from home. The letter opens "Dear Mother" yet remarks further on, "I think I shall write to Mother tomorrow." The letter is bewildering in another regard, since, throughout the pages that begin "Dear Mother," Angelina speaks freely from her inmost thoughts, something she never could do with her real mother. The frayed and yellowed sheet had been folded and addressed, as was the custom then, on the back of the letter, so the name of the addressee is there to be read. The "Dear Mother" of the letter is none other than Sarah. There is another letter, perhaps more revealing, this one written some six months later. Angelina opened this letter to her sister, "Thou art Dearest my best beloved." Sarah was the "mother," the "best beloved."[15] Mary Grimké would have found this very odd; it might have wounded her pride, not to say her mother love. Also it might have made her more withdrawn than ever, since she would hardly have wished to become a rival of her daughter. Hence the overburdened mother would not have stood in the way, not in Angelina's early years and, as it turned out, not in the later years. Mary Grimké was at hand, but she was busy, distracted, hard to find when her youngest reached out for reassurance. This is not to suggest that Sarah ever assuaged Angelina's painful sense of estrangement from her mother, as is amply shown in ensuing years, but Angelina had felt the pull of Sarah's warm and hovering love and had given herself up to be Sarah's child.

2.

In 1811 Angelina's family was faced with a grave and unexpected crisis. Despite his great prestige, Judge Grimké was threatened with impeachment as a state supreme court judge. The charges and complaints, as given in the Charleston press, implied that the judge was an imperious man, almost arrogantly secure as to the rightness of his judgments and sometimes inconsistent in interpreting the law. The accounts suggested that he had made enemies. The Committee on Impeachment could not agree, so the House of Representatives was asked to vote on each article, and most of the votes were disturbingly close.[16]

The mother was the pivotal figure in the home during these weeks, as she was to be again after Judge Grimké's death in 1819. Perhaps the traits in her mother that Angelina found hardest to bear were Mary Grimké's main strength at this time—the tight reserve, the unyielding pride, the stern sense of duty that would let nothing sway her. She was not fond of weaklings, and demanded of her children conduct worthy of their name. It is easy to picture her throughout these weeks, pointedly adhering to her accustomed rounds, more especially to every normal public appearance, whether on the streets, in the drawing room, or in her pew on Sundays at St. Philip's. Nearly thirty years later she wrote Angelina thoughts that may have come into focus at this time: "The evils of life you must share with others, for God has not promised to exempt his Children from these; but he will enable them to face them; & he will sanctify all their crosses to them."[17]

Angelina was only six at the time of the attempted impeachment of her father, but she was sensitive and intelligent. She would have felt the family tensions and perchance remembered the lesson this experience drove home—what was expected of a Grimké in upholding the family name. So ingrained was the feeling that when she was thirty years of age, and in turn brought disgrace on the family name when overnight she became a notorious abolitionist, she at first voiced grief and even shame. "Blushing and confusion of face were mine, and I thought the walls of a prison would have been preferable to such an exposure." She placed her finger directly on the wound. "To have my name, not so much my name as the name of Grimké, associated with that of the despised Garrison, seemed like bringing disgrace on my *family*, not myself alone. I felt as though the name had been tarnished in the eyes of thousands who had before loved and revered it."[18]

Judge Grimké was acquitted and remained on the court, but the consequences of this crisis were far-reaching for Angelina. It appears that the father's health had been undermined, for the judge began to decline not long thereafter. For some years he suffered a lingering illness, and this meant that his wife must assume heavier burdens and that she was more than ever absorbed and remote.

Sarah also became hard to reach. At sixteen Sarah had entered grand society, at eighteen she experienced a religious conversion, but soon she returned to her feverish social rounds. Preoccupied with society or religion in these years, Sarah was out of touch. When the father grew feeble, Sarah devoted her life to him, her energies and affections caught up in his needs. More than ever, Sarah had no time for Angelina and remained inaccessible for a number of years.[19]

It may be that the Grimké home was more rigidly pious than other Charleston homes of similar wealth and station.[20] Mary Grimké imposed certain formal duties on her children: attendance at St. Philip's at her side; confirmation when the appropriate age arrived; personal devotions in their private chambers; and attendance at daily family prayers. Once the mother was in charge, family prayers became mandatory for all under her roof, children and servants alike. At twelve years of age a child was ripe for confirmation, but Angelina reached and passed this normal time. Her mother was troubled, how disturbed can be guessed from the steps she took and the time at which she took them. Judge Grimké lay ill in 1818, and in August 1819, his end came. It was during the course of these distracted months that the mother asked the rector to talk to Angelina.[21]

Confirmation, of course, was a public event, and all St. Philip's would have known and wondered when each year the bishop came for the laying on of hands, and Angelina Grimké remained in her pew. This sorely tried Mary Grimké, nor was the mother's concern merely for appearances. She was a woman of dogmatic beliefs, and in her eyes confirmation was not only a religious duty but a necessity for the soul's salvation. The rector reported that Angelina had said she could not make the vows the prayer book required, even when he assured her it was "only a form." Angelina argued that she was in a state of doubt and that with her "feelings and views" what they were to go through the form "would be a lie."

To her family and the rector, Angelina's rebellion was a dangerous symptom, and they warned the child that such stubborn disrespect toward home and church was an "ominous sign" of a "mental instability" that boded ill. In later years, her husband told this story, stressing this girlhood incident as a sign of Angelina's mental independence, an early precursor of her later strong convictions. It may have been the latter in a rudimentary sense. The incident surely marked a widening of the breach with her mother. Perhaps Mary Grimké's authority was impaired when this observant child experienced momentarily the helplessness of adults in dictating her beliefs. Sarah's influence also must have played a part. Sarah, after all, was Angelina's godmother. It was Sarah, according to the tenets of the church, who, when the appropriate age had been reached, should teach her godchild the church's beliefs and bring the child for the laying on of hands, but Sarah, at this time, was enmeshed in fears and doubts. On this occasion convention triumphed.[22] Angelina's refusal turned out to be short-lived, and within a year or two she was confirmed, although, as time soon showed, she remained disaffected.

Angelina was fourteen when her father died, so her mother's rule was the one she chiefly knew. This was true during the crucial years of her early teens, the time of her stormy adolescence, and the fateful period of her young womanhood. Outwardly Angelina lived the usual life of a Grimké daughter who, at the appropriate age, took her expected place in Charleston's select society. Catherine Birney[23] reports that Angelina grew up a "gay, fashionable girl," possessing "personal beauty," high spirits, wit, charm, and unusual qualities of "mind and heart" and that men were drawn to her—there were many "admirers." And she spoke of Angelina's "brilliant intellect."* Presumably Catherine Birney gained her knowledge from Sarah; she was a pupil of both sisters at Eagleswood School and became their good friend. Several glimpses of Charleston social life can be found in diaries of the sisters, though they are scattered and incidental: how society alternated between city and plantation, when the heavy social seasons were at their height, and how the Grimké sons and daughters went the rounds of houses with their

---

*Was Angelina Grimké a "beautiful" woman? This reference to her beauty is only one of many from persons who knew her well, especially in the 1830s when she was a public figure. Yet published photographs of her give no hint of personal beauty or even of vitality and attractiveness of expression. There must have been good reason for the use of the term. Conceivably, she was simply not a photogenic person. More probably the explanation is a deeper one. Anglina once described Theodore Weld, the man she was to marry in 1838, in terms that might have been applicable to herself. She had known Weld only briefly when she was writing to her close friend, Jane Smith, about him: "At first sight there was nothing remarkable to me in his appearance & I wondered whether he really was as great as I had heard, but as soon as his countenance became animated by speaking I found it was one which portrayed the noblest quality of heart & head." It seems probable that Angelina's countenance was transformed in the moment in which her inner qualities found expression.

dances, house parties, and other entertainments. Angelina once used the words, "before I was serious" in referring to those years of busy social pursuits; and, on one occasion—she was by then an abolitionist—she gave a swift pen-picture of her family's way of life: one filled with "politics, field sports, races, speculations, journeys, visits, company, literary pursuits."[24] Angelina's diary, in the late 1820s, many times mentioned "tea" as a social occasion: friends had "come to tea," her aunt was "in for tea," her mother had guests "for tea." Frederika Bremmer, in her 1850 visit to Charleston, was a guest in several wealthy homes and once described "tea" where she was staying, explaining that "dinner" was served at three and "tea" in the evening. She called this evening hour "the flower of the day."

> Then the lamps are lighted in the beautiful drawing rooms, and all are summoned to tea. Then is Mrs. W. H. seated on the sofa . . . with the great tea-table before her loaded with good things; then small tea-tables are placed about (I always have my own little table . . .) and the lively little negro boy, Sam [a slave] carries round the refreshments. Then come in almost always three or four young lads, sons of neighboring friends of the family, and a couple of young girls also, and the young people dance gaily and gracefully to the piano. I generally play an hour for them, either waltzes or quadrilles. Strangers [meaning visitors] in the meantime, call and take their leave.[25]

While Angelina for a time played her normal part in the circles of Charleston's fashionable society, it appears that all the while she was plagued by deep disquiet that resulted from more than the lack of closeness to her mother. To Angelina her home was an unhappy place, full of stresses and strains that disturbed and confused her, and she felt that her mother was the source of what was wrong.

Angelina was not the only Grimké child to complain of the mother and the conditions of the home. In her early twenties she recorded a conversation that had just taken place with her two sisters, Mary and Eliza.[26] Sarah was not present; she was then living in Philadelphia. The "deplorable state of the family" was the theme. The sisters were complaining of "the servants being rude" and always doing "very much as they pleased," of the food being served cold, and the home at loggerheads, and the lack of order and discipline everywhere in the house. While Angelina had not yet turned against slavery, it had come to be her way to excuse the shortcomings of the slaves. "I tried to convince them that the servants were just what the family was . . . not at all more rude and selfish and disobliging . . . and how could they expect the servants to behave, when they had such examples continually before them." Eliza admitted that all this was true. Mary, however, would not condemn herself, though she acknowledged the "sad state" the family was in. It was Mary who added the all-revealing words that the mother was the one "altogether to blame." Angelina's own disaffection welled up and spilled from her pen as she wrote. "Mother is perfectly blind," she exclaimed, "as to the miserable way in which she has brought us up." Mary Grimké, of course, felt put upon, and it is small wonder that she was sometimes heard to exclaim (Angelina faithfully recorded the words), "I am tired of being blamed for everything."[27]

This was not all that disturbed Angelina. Well before the time that she rejected slavery, she felt that Grimké slaves were grossly mismanaged, sometimes to the point of harsh, unfeeling treatment. When she wrote of these conditions, she was an abolitionist, but scattered entries in her diary before she turned against slavery and a few stories that she recounted from her girlhood years suggest that the conditions, as she later told of them, were printed on her memory, although apparently, at the time, she was not conscious of real distress but only of a continuing, uneasy disquiet.

She spoke of her memories of separation by force and was made especially miserable by the plight of slave children, their fate entirely determined by the will of the owner. She told of what went on in her own home, that of a city family with a distant plantation. Sometimes children of the Charleston houseservants were taken from their mothers and sent to the plantation, the better to make use of both mother's and child's services; and sometimes children of plantation field hands were brought to the city to be taught houseservants' work—in either case the mother-child tie was broken, and the child was treated as a mere chattel.

Angelina was plagued for years by the servants' lack of comforts: no bed or bedding, they must sleep on the floor; no table on which to eat, just a tin plate and a spoon; no lights in their quarters, nor firewood—unless they found it; seamstresses required to work after dark in winter in "cold entries" by stair-case lamps, with light so poor they must stand up to see their work; and children kept on duty through the long winter evenings, "sitting on the stair-case in a cold entry," to be at the family's beck and call, "to snuff candles or hand a tumbler of water, or go on errands from one room to another."[28]

Her mother, she felt, was often callous and unfeeling, a belief that persisted for years in a particular conflict over the mother's personal maid. This dispute began before Angelina became an abolitionist. Cindie had been married for a good many years to a slave husband, they were "tenderly attached," and yet the maid, as Angelina told it, had been required to sleep in the mistress's bedroom on a pallet on the floor. Mary Grimké said the woman was a most faithful servant, and she depended on Cindie for her personal comforts, to dress and undress her, to bring her meals, to brush her hair, all the usual services; but in particular she needed Cindie near her bed at night, for she was growing old. The story of Cindie was in a published account, but no names were mentioned, just a "certain mistress" who "told a friend of mine." However, anonymity is swept aside by a sharply resentful letter, written in 1838, from Mary Grimké to her distant daughters. "Poor Cindie!" the mother's letter scornfully exclaimed, "has several times been mentioned [in your letters] as an object of compassion because she was separated from her *husband* [day and night]; Let me make you easy on this account, for she has long since replaced him; consequently as old as I am, I sleep entirely by myself, so that should I be ill in the night, I might probably suffer until morning—But it is my desire to have it so."[29]

Punishment of slaves especially disturbed Angelina and not merely the dread prompted by the shadowy work house. Physical punishment was employed in her own home and was remembered with distress and revulsion. Angelina once told her husband of a time in her girlhood when she risked her elders' wrath because a slave had been thrashed till her back was lacerated, and Angelina had slipped out by night to the slave quarters to bathe the woman's wounds with a soothing lotion.

Angelina's fear of slave mistreatment became focused on her brother Henry, but at the same time he was especially dear to her. Under Mary Grimké's rule, Henry became the male authority since he was the elder of the two sons still at home, and Henry was a man of extreme and sudden rages. Angelina came to dread his harsh punishment of the slaves. Once her journal was begun, entries often mentioned her precipitate retreat to her own chamber to shut out the sounds of Henry, in his bedroom, angrily thrashing his man-servant John.[30] In an 1839 published account, she wrote of Henry anonymously: "I heard another man of equally high standing say that he believed he suffered far more than his waiter did whenever he flogged him, for he felt the *exertion* for days afterward, but he could not let his servant go on in the neglect of his business, it was *his duty* to chastise him. . . . He broke a large stick over the back of a slave." Henry, it seems certain, was responsible for the condition of Stephen, the Grimké butler who became a family cause célèbre. While in the published account she again mentioned no names, later letters to her mother made the case clear. "And at another time [he broke] the ivory butt-end of a long coach whip over the *head* of another [slave]. This last was attacked with epileptic fits some months after, and has ever since been subject to them, and occasionally to violent fits of insanity."

The mother, it appears, excused Henry's rages, defending him when her daughter criticized and justifying his loss of self-control. Angelina, on her part, found one excuse; it was her mother, she insisted, who was really to blame, in her complacent acceptance of the white master's right to use any means he chose to control his slaves. She cited what were presumably her mother's words: "I heard the mother of this man say it would be no surprise to her, if he killed a slave some day, for, when transported with passion, he did not seem to care what he did."[31]

In those tumultuous years while she was still at home and before she had turned her back on slavery, she heaped guilt on her mother, blaming Mary Grimké for much that seemed amiss. In particular she blamed her mother for the fears within herself and the widespread fear she sensed among their slaves. "Mother," she once exclaimed in unrelieved condemnation, "rules slaves and children with a rod of fear."[32] While these early memories, intermingled as they were with her sense of deep estrangement, cannot give an accurate picture of her mother or her home, it is evident that what Angelina felt and saw had a disaffecting influence on her as she grew up under slavery.

In the early summer of 1822 a certain free black man, Denmark Vesey, a carpenter by trade, was secretly organizing an extensive slave revolt. The plot was uncovered in May of that year when slave informers revealed it to their masters. Arrests of more than a hundred slaves followed, Vesey himself was soon apprehended, trials were held, and thirty-seven black men, most of them slaves, were hanged between June and August 1822.[33]

Angelina was seventeen early that year. She was at home in Charleston when the plot was first uncovered, the trials held, the first slaves hanged, and Vesey himself swung from the gallows. Apparently she left no record of what she knew and felt at that time. She had not yet begun her journal. Sarah also was in Charleston for a long visit home, and although her diary was at hand she wrote nothing of it.

It can only be imagined what these frightening days meant to Angelina, the Grimké family, their neighbors and friends, and slaveholders everywhere. For the facts were not suppressed, as had frequently been the case in earlier threatened slave revolts; they were published abroad by both press and official report. There can be no doubt that there was terrible alarm from the moment the first vague rumors spread until the first arrests were made, the spies were set to work, hundreds of slave names poured in, and witnesses at the trials made assertion that six thousand slaves, some said nine thousand, were in the plot. Of course rumor and fantasy were at work, since whites were so outnumbered by their many slaves: there were sixty thousand slaves in the district of Charleston, twenty thousand whites to confront the threat, and in addition there were some four thousand free Negroes.[34] Many slaves were concentrated in homes of wealth. Angelina at one time voiced her irritation at never being alone, never being able to wait on herself, because slaves intervened in every act of daily life. It is certain that at the time of the Denmark Vesey plot, slaveholders looked at these chattels with considerable apprehension.

Even though Angelina wrote nothing at the time to indicate what she felt and heard and thought during those months of slave trials for "intended insurrection," how could she wipe it from her memory as though it had never happened? Perhaps she supposed that she had left it all behind once her world seemed reasonably safe again, but a time came when she showed that she remembered. Once she had become an abolitionist, she sent back to Charleston for a full copy of the official report. Moreover, she later showed the effect on her beliefs of this first-hand experience of a threatened slave revolt. Thirteen years afterward, in 1835, in her historic letter to William Lloyd Garrison which launched her directly into the antislavery movement, she voiced belief and hope in the use of peaceful means by which slaves would be set free without resort to violence. "At one time I thought this system would be overthrown in blood. . . . But hope gleams across my mind that our [abolition-ists'] blood will be spilt, instead of the slaveholders' . . . for of all things I desire to be spared the anguish of seeing our beloved country desolated with the horrors of a servile war."[35]

If Sarah had lived at home and remained unchanged, Angelina's disaffection towards her mother and her home might have been somewhat diminished, with what consequences to her life it would be hard to guess. Sarah's outgoing warmth and protective presence for years had been a refuge for her beloved youngest sister. But Sarah underwent a drastic change that caused her to leave home in her intense search for God. For many years she was turned in on herself. Her diary is complete and full for these years, beginning in 1819, at the time her father died. On its pages she set forth, day by day, her anguished mental conflicts. Angelina could not know what was happening to her sister, but she could feel that Sarah was different and often inaccessible.

The change began for Sarah with a religious crisis[36] when she was in her early twenties and Angelina nine or ten. She experienced a conversion in two episodes, one of them abortive, the other more prolonged. First she rejected the fashionable life, returned to its old pleasures once more, and deserted it again in the hope of being "saved." She felt guilt at her backsliding, relating how "more vain," "more trifling" she was, "more than ever coveting admiration as the chief end." At last, as she said, "a merciful Providence inter-vened," visiting a painful illness on her father and, in the end, re-claiming his erring child.

The father's long illness and eventual loss caused Sarah's greatest trauma. She accompanied him to Philadelphia to consult a Quaker physician. She was his only nurse and remained alone with him in the weeks he lay dying. While he had always been her main under-girding, in her mind he now became lifted up, idealized, and adored. "From the high and gifted character of the man of this world, he became fashioned in the Likeness of Christ."

It so chanced that kind Quakers befriended Sarah while she waited in Philadelphia after her father's death. On shipboard re-turning home, she met other Friends, among them Israel Morris whom she saw much of. He was a prominent Quaker and a man of means who, with his wife and children, lived outside Philadelphia. Throughout these weeks Sarah bore her grief well, but not so when finally she reached home.

For more than a year, so her record makes plain, Sarah had experienced a prolonged mental crisis. The very terms she used show her critical mental state: "sunk in melancholy," "dreariness indescribable," "settled despondence," "desolation, suffering, wormwood and gall." No tears would come, she said, no prayers would well up in her, she felt herself to be an "empty void."

In her search for God, Sarah turned to Quaker writings. There had been some correspondence with Israel Morris, and Sarah soon became obsessed with the belief that God was calling her to become a Quaker. While she admired her Quaker friends, the thought of being one appalled her. Even so, she felt driven to attend Charleston's Friends Meeting. There in the small plain house of worship, overcome by the silence and inner fears, Sarah heard her God command that she rise to make public declaration of submission to His will. She could not force herself to do so and left, her lips sealed. From that day on she felt misery and guilt. She was certain that she had "sinned" and that God would make her pay. "Satan desireth to have me so that he may sift me as wheat. Lord, save me or I perish!"

In much the same spirit Sarah left her people in 1821 and sailed for Philadelphia, there to begin the life of a Quaker. A sister, Anna Grimké Frost, accompanied Sarah. Mrs. Frost was a widow with an inadequate income and a small child to support. She soon established a small private school in Philadelphia, which she continued to operate for many years. Sarah did not make her home with Mrs. Frost, as might be expected, but stayed in the Israel Morris home. After a few months she went to live with Israel's sister, Catherine Morris, a devout and strict Quaker, where she remained until the 1830s.

In the next few years, Sarah underwent the change from a Charleston Episcopalian of the highest social circles, a slaveholder's daughter accustomed to luxury, to a Quaker of strict belief and practices.

After her departure in 1821 Sarah returned home several times for visits, and Angelina could not fail to sense the change in her sister, still so beloved and whom she still called "Mother." There was a period when the two corresponded very little, but by the mid-1820s the old relationship had been reestablished. Letters of this period reflect their renewed closeness: "dear Mother," "dearest Mother," "my precious child."

Although her doubts were not all dispelled, Sarah's change was now complete, which is not to say that she was always dour. On occasion her old good spirits would break through—she once noted in her diary, "today I talked and laughed too much"—and her warm, friendly nature often showed itself. But she was now a Quaker in all respects—demeanor, language, dress, attitudes, and beliefs. By her Quaker friends, she was looked upon as humble, self-effacing and unselfish, strict in Quaker standards, sound in Quaker doctrine, and regarding her religion as the purest and best. She was full of good works toward the sick, the needy, and outcasts who were prisoners in Philadelphia's jails. She now believed that holding slaves was a sin in God's eyes, though in these years she had rarely spoken of it; it was simply a tenet of her Quaker beliefs.

While this person was not the Sarah that Angelina had once known, Angelina now viewed her sister as a devout, noble woman, who had sacrificed many earthly pleasures in her yearning for perfection in her service to her God. Angelina did not know, until Sarah revealed it on a long visit home in 1827, of the years of mental anguish that lay behind Sarah's change or of the bitter loneliness that Sarah had come to feel.

3.

In the course of her life Angelina Grimké changed her religious affiliation several times, and no changes were more fateful than those she made in the 1820s. Yet while she was inconstant towards religious institutions, she never seemed to question her deep reliance on religion, as though nothing of prime importance to her religious life was altered. She evidently drew another lesson from these first changes—a strong skepticism towards all man-made institutions when they stood between her and the dictates of her conscience.

Initially Angelina had to break away from her strictly conventional religious upbringing. Belonging as she did to the Episcopal church, she was shut off by barriers of considerable resistance which were comprised of beliefs and established sacred customs. As it happened, during the years in which she was growing up, evangelical religion was a spreading influence. From 1800 on it was taking strong hold throughout the southern states, with so much vital force that the religious movement of this period has sometimes been called the "second great awakening." While the seaboard states did not experience the striking phase that occurred in the western South, especially in Kentucky, where the protracted revivals of the "camp meeting" type found their first expression, evangelicalism was advancing rapidly everywhere. Methodist and Baptist preachers began to draw larger followings, until throughout the slave states these denominations became the dominant religious force among the masses of people. Not only was this true for the poorer farming whites and the less well-to-do in the towns, but these churches also attracted many slaveholders and some of the more prosperous city dwellers. The Presbyterian church had no such mass following, but its evangelists were prominent at the outset of the movement and continued to be a factor, especially in urban areas.

Periodic "revivals" became the principal means for increasing the sway of evangelical religion. Although revivals were more usual among Methodists and Baptists, some of the great revival preachers were of the Presbyterian faith. Theodore Weld, whom Angelina Grimké married, was converted in the 1820s by Charles Grandison Finney, an eminent Presbyterian educator and revivalist. Although doctrinal differences were significant and divisive, there was a generally common language among the evangelical sects which was used to express the urgent message voiced by their preachers: "salvation of souls," "sinners, repent," "eternal damnation," "everlasting life," and the steps to be taken—"repentance," "conversion," with a public "acceptance of Jesus Christ." Commonly conversion meant a renunciation of certain worldly pleasures—dancing, card playing, theater, frivolity—but what made the movement spread was the urgency of its message, it evangelistic fervor, and the personal commitment required of the converted.

If the experiences of Angelina, Sarah, and Mary Grimké were indicative of the currents that were moving in their city in the first decades of the 1800s, then the evangelical spirit was certainly at work in Charleston, stronghold though it was of the Anglican church. Indeed, something similar had happened earlier, dating back to the Charleston of more than seventy years before. Frederick Bowes tells at length of the impact on the city of the unorthodox Anglican minister, the Reverend Charles Whitefield, a famous preacher in the period of the first "great awakening." He was often in Charleston on his widespread preaching journeys, and while he aroused hostility among some members of the Anglican church, especially the clergy, some Anglicans went to listen, and he attracted strong support from many Presbyterians and Baptists. It appears that his appeal lay in his emotional power and the focus of his message on sin and salvation. In the Grimkés' day many Presbyterian ministers were preaching the gospel with evangelical zeal, and Presbyterians in Charleston were numerous and influential.[37] Both Sarah and Angelina, in their first religious change, were moved by preachers of the Presbyterian faith.

In 1813 or perhaps 1814—Angelina was nearly nine—Sarah Grimké first responded to the evangelical appeal.[38] She went with a friend to the Presbyterian Church where the Reverend Henry Kolloch was a visiting preacher. When, twelve years later, she wrote of this time, she could recall the very text he preached from on that day and the fears that overcame her as she listened to what portended for those who refused to repent of their sins. Since sixteen, she had enjoyed Charleston's fashionable society—dances, teas, house parties, all the many pleasures—entering into it, she later claimed, with a feverish abandon. Evangelical religion deplored such frivolity, and Sarah's mental response to the preacher that day revealed the guilt that his message aroused in her: "What shall I do to be saved?" She turned away on this first occasion, but later she met this disturbing man again, this time when both were visitors in a plantation home. At dinner the first day the hostess inquired if Sarah had seen the latest play. Sarah replied, "I never attend the theater, my mother disapproves." Dr. Kolloch's gaze was suddenly riveted on Sarah: "I am glad to hear you say it." In the week that ensued the two were often together, until late in the week, the decisive moment came. "A serious solemn covering overspread our minds. . . . He was led to open some truths of the Christian religion to me." With quivering emotion she admitted her unreadiness to renounce the worldly life she led. At this he took her hand and said in solemn tones, "Can you dare to hesitate?" As she later told it, Sarah began to weep. "I trembled as he portrayed my doom," and she heard the urgent evangelical call, "Can you take up the Cross and follow Jesus Christ?" Sarah experienced what she believed was a "conversion," although this was not the end of her ambivalent feelings. For awhile she corresponded with Dr. Kolloch, but later she returned to her old pleasures again. Her father's illness and death brought the lasting transformation, for she had been his favorite daughter, and he, her mainstay. Confronted with his loss, she turned again to religion, as she groped her way through a long mental crisis. She was stirred momentarily by a rural Methodist revival that she attended while visiting relatives on a remote plantation and found herself so shaken by the "loud and threatening preaching" that she arose and declared her submission to God's will. Although she could not feel drawn to evangelistic sects, evangelical religion had done its work when it cut her adrift from her family church. When Sarah encountered Quakerism she adopted it as her faith and, at the same time, rejected human slavery, changes that set her apart from her people.

Mary Grimké's religious change was altogether different, although it may have happened in a time of revival. Angelina once told of a revival that occurred in Charleston in 1825, saying it had moved certain matrons of high estate to forsake "fashionable life" for "leadership on a moral and religious plane." She may have had her mother in mind when she wrote. But Mary Grimké never left the Episcopal church, nor did she ever alter her belief in slavery. What happened to her was the more usual change in those who were moved by evangelical religion to "repent of their sins" and find "salvation." She felt in herself a deepened religion, a strong secure faith that she had been "saved." She referred to this conviction in an 1825 letter addressed to Sarah in Philadelphia.[39] She was deploring the "fashionable amusements" of some friends, while admitting, "Unfortunately you and I thought as they do once," but she could add devoutly, "each must yield all" to attain "Salvation."

Mary Grimké's unswerving faith in her "salvation" was expressed repeatedly after Angelina and Sarah became abolitionists, since the daughters sought to bring their mother to the view that those who owned slaves were committing grievous "sin."[40] The mother's letters to them show her strong religious feeling, though she often spoke defensively under their attacks. In one letter Mary Grimké chided Angelina for being so uncharitable to those who did not think as she did about abolition, and she declared that her daughter should have become a missionary instead of taking up the cause of "your colored Brethren." She would then have been "obeying the command of Christ . . . for what is so praiseworthy as to be instrumental in saving souls." In a letter to Sarah her resentment was evident as she insisted on her right to think her own way. "I have never attempted to tell either of you [what to think]; for I thought you had as much right to hold to that which you were convinced of, as myself; notwithstanding I have been warned & threatened, with the displeasure of God, if I did not release my Slaves." Her conviction of God's approval remained unshaken. "I should not keep them in Bondage one moment, were I convinced that I was sinning against him, whom I love above all, but I am not convinced of this . . . for I do expect to die a Slave holder, & at present feel no compunction of conscience on that account." Whether she did or did not hold slaves was to her beside the point. True religion for her lay in belief in Christ and her confidence in the promise of eternal salvation. In one letter she spoke of entering her seventy-fifth year. "I feel this is not my resting place; for Christ is all in all; I have been Redeemed by his precious blood, and he will suffer no one to pluck me out of his hand for he has promised to keep those who love him to the end."

In 1826 Angelina came of age, and in that year she experienced "conversion." Thus her life felt the impact of the religious currents that had moved the South since the time of her birth, and perhaps she had been made more receptive by what had happened to Sarah and to her mother. Angelina's conversion was destined to be far-reaching in its eventual effect on the course she would take. If a woman possessed rare gifts as Angelina did, felt within herself the stirrings of ambition, yet lived in an age of woman's subordination, she would surely be confronted with profound frustration unless she found some force that could shatter the conventional fetters. Religion, for Angelina, seemed to be such a force, for when she came to flout the approval of men, she could still seek and find the blessing of her God. To do God's will on earth became her principal motivation. Yet it was linked with another, one more sensed than comprehended: a deep, compelling need to strip away those crippling bonds laid on her sex so that she could fully realize the powers that lay within her.

The Reverend William MacDowell became Angelina's mentor. A young Presbyterian minister, ardent and sincere, he left her moved and shaken by the fervor of his voice and its urgent call to "rise up and follow Christ." Thereupon Angelina forsook her people's faith and joined William MacDowell's Third Presbyterian Church.[41]

Angelina's conversion was the antithesis of Sarah's, whose every breath toward God had been drawn in fear. A few letters to Sarah and scraps from her diary reach back to that time. One diary entry dated October 1826 records: "3 months ago I for the first time openly avowed that I had enlisted under the banner of the Cross and 3 months before I obtained that Hope which maketh not ashamed . . . we must be about our Master's business." Life had taken a glorious turn for Angelina. Her days, which hitherto had held little meaning, now were saturated with a sense of high purpose. She had gladly left behind her old Episcopalianism, which she now viewed as "spiritually dead," "narrow," "bigoted" in its beliefs, and "exclusive" in its practice and in its preachment. In her new church, she found "principles of liberality" and exulted in the freedom that had been opened up before her. The church she had joined was a beehive of activity, so that Angelina's hunger for action was assuaged: church services, prayer meetings, religious societies, Sunday School, in which she became a leader, fervent efforts to find new converts, warm outgoing services rendered to the poor. She found herself caught up in its spirit of inclusiveness, something she had never experienced before. She herself organized a "female prayer meeting" where Baptists, Methodists, Congregationalists, and Presbyterians gathered monthly in warm fellowship. This "principle of inclusiveness" infused Angelina until it became for her a main moving force.[42]

Emotionally Angelina had been suppressed and starved; now as the months went by, all this was changed. William MacDowell was becoming more than her minister, the one who had enlisted her "under the banner of the Cross," more than the "mentor of her soul"—how much more became poignantly apparent in 1827 when her sister Sarah returned home, bringing personal crisis in her wake.

But MacDowell was not alone in bringing release to Angelina. She could now write of how she "loved" the church, "loved" all its members, "clung in fondness to them," finding in these people a warm comradeship of those committed to a sacred cause. Each meeting held in the church or a private home was to her suffused with common consecration. The communion table was a mystical experience, a "solemn feast" in which she rejoiced because it meant a "shared rededication," and it was all the richer because her church excluded none. Angelina flourished in this company of the elect where she could give without stint and find such great response. What she had found was more than religion, much as her new faith illumined and satisfied her. Angelina felt the wonder of something elusive, something she experienced yet could not articulate, an awareness that her frustrations and fears had abated and that she possessed powers hitherto unguessed. Her conversion had brought her a conviction of high purpose, a belief that she was called to fulfill some great mission, even though she had no notion of where her mission lay. She was finding life good in her native city, she could now tolerate her unfulfilled needs at home, and as yet she perceived no relation between her faith and her acceptance of human slavery.[43]

Her sister Sarah, meanwhile, had gone her separate way, and for some years Angelina felt out of touch with her. Sarah had settled in Philadelphia in 1822 and one year later had taken the fateful step of becoming a full member of the Orthodox Friends. During the first few years she wrote Angelina rarely, but gradually her letters grew more frequent, until her thoughts were turned again toward Angelina and she was once more "mother" to her "precious child." By the mid-1820s the two had drawn close, their correspondence a reflection of their renewed intimate bonds.

Sarah was now living in the home of Catherine Morris, sister of the Morris couple who had first befriended her. In her new life she was pursued by mental anguish,[44] convinced that God was calling her to become a Quaker minister, and Sarah was appalled at the very thought. "I could choose strangling rather than life . . . in the ministry." To add to her dilemma, a man began to woo her, a highly suitable individual, who may have been a Morris, although she wrote only "I.M." when referring to him. Her diary was filled with her conflicting feelings for him, for while she was drawn to him, she could not bring herself to marry. She told herself that God had the primary claim, and a husband might come between her and "entire dedication." In the midst of this man's wooing, Catherine Morris and other Friends began insisting that Sarah should return to Charleston because her primary duty was at her aging mother's side. By this time Sarah had no wish to return; to be a Quaker in Charleston would mean an isolated life, for after all she was changed from the person she used to be. Her journal in these months recorded her inner struggles and her growing suspicion, humiliating though it was, that Catherine Morris no longer wished her in her home. Sarah at last found an argument to counterbalance the

Friend's principle of a daughter's duty to her parent. When she had joined the Friends she had rejected chattel slavery, nor would she have been accepted had she countenanced the system. Now, while she agreed to make a visit to her home, she told her friends that to live there would be contrary to her principles.

The seat of Sarah's problem is amply shown in her diary. Since her father's death she had known a gnawing loneliness, and now her state was worsened since she had turned away from marriage. Her obvious longing was for a close companion to relieve the desolate emptiness that so continually beset her. All through these painful months, as Friends pressed her duty on her, Sarah sought heavenly guidance to tell her what was right. At last her thoughts "were led" to Angelina, who, Sarah told herself, was in a perilous state. Angelina by this time was an ardent Presbyterian. To Orthodox Friends, Presbyterianism was in error. Also, good Quakers abhorred human slavery, so in this regard, also, Angelina was sinning for she still accepted the enslavement of the Negro. In the weeks before the *Langdon Cheves* sailed for Charleston, Sarah wrestled with the Lord in behalf of her "dear Child."

Angelina had been yearning for Sarah's homecoming, this dearly loved sister who was still "mother" to her and who more than any other in the family had devoted herself to the religious life. Would not Sarah rejoice in all that religion had come to mean to Angelina? Would they not share their thoughts as never before and share their prayers and their sense of common purpose? Sarah's approbation was important to Angelina. When the *Langdon Cheves* docked on October 22, 1827, Angelina was full of joy, and Sarah was happy in her own devout way. "Landed this morning . . . welcomed on my return . . . by my dear mother with tears of pleasure and tenderness, as she folded me once more to her bosom. My dear sisters too greeted me with all the warmth of affection. . . . And my precious Angelina one of the Master's chosen vessels, what a mercy."[45]

Family prayers were held as usual the next morning—a mandatory observance for all the household. For some time Angelina had been conducting family prayers; her voice, that would one day hold thousands enthralled, no doubt had held this room in an uneasy quiet, since show of emotion would hardly be congenial to the reserved and conventional Episcopalian Grimkés. Angelina had been longing for Sarah's presence here, perhaps for reasons somewhat less than worthy. She may have seen herself, in her mind's eye, look up from the page of Scripture she was reading, to feel Sarah's warm, approving glance resting on her.

Family prayers were distinctly strained on the morning following Sarah's return. The drawing room was full, all family members seated and the household slaves standing near the doorways. When Angelina arrived her eyes were red and swollen, and she could scarcely force her voice to read or pray. Sarah had refused to attend family prayers. She was up in her chamber at her private devotions, "bearing testimony," she had told Angelina, against this thing Friends called "will-worship." "Been favored with strength to absent myself," she recorded in her journal late that same evening, "A trial to Angelina and myself . . . oh that I may be faithful to this, and to all other testimonies."

Sarah little realized what she was doing, then or subsequently in that strange winter. Sarah's aims, as she felt them, were simple and pure, and all too apt for the task at hand, to rescue this loved one from gross error and sin. True, Angelina believed herself "saved," but herein lay the challenge to Sarah's Quakerism; it was Sarah's belief that no mediator could bring man close to God. Who more than Angelina looked to mediation in her beliefs—and in the person of her cherished minister? Angelina was as yet far away from Sarah's kingdom.

But why Angelina, why not all the others—parent, sisters, brothers, kin? It was not that Sarah neglected these others. All through those months at home she admonished them and bore them in her prayers. She spoke more than once to the aging Mary Grimké, telling her sternly, "Get thine house in order for thou shalt die . . . prepare to meet thy God," until sometimes she felt she had pressed the theme too hard. Angelina, however, was the burden of her thought—Angelina, who, as Sarah now concluded, had become a chosen instrument in God's plans.[46] The inner light had revealed this truth to Sarah, and this, she felt, was what had really sent her home.

While Sarah seemed much changed to all members of her family, Angelina was the one who most acutely felt the difference: Sarah's sober Quaker dress, her suppressed demeanor, her frowns at display, her outspoken stern reminders, her withdrawals to her chamber to engage in private religious devotions, and finally her refusal to join her family in common worship either at home or in their churches. When Sunday came, dour and determined, Sarah set forth across the city to the tiny Friends Meeting.

Within a month of Sarah's arrival, Angelina had a dream. She was traveling and presently reached the bank of what seemed to be a wide but shallow stream, so she stepped in, assuming she could wade across. She found herself tossed by terrifying waves on a river that, in fact, was rapid and deep. She felt that every moment might be her last, though she told herself that if she had faith nothing was too difficult for her Father. And so it turned out, because at last she found herself safe on the opposite shore. Yet as she wrote of the dream she felt her hand tremble, little knowing, as she said, what each day would bring forth. "I am perfectly cold, I am in an awful state of lethargy. I have no evidence that I am a Christian. . . . My soul forebodes some heavy trial, some sea of temptation."[47]

A few days later Sarah became thirty-five and took this occasion to record how she felt her work was going. "I have passed through some feelings of anguish," she wrote, "under the awful conviction that one in whose welfare every feeling seems involved has only a name to religion without the spirit. . . . The awful language rushed into my mind, she is not of mine. . . . Oh," she exclaimed, "break the false rest, destroy the covering which is not of thy spirit."[48]

Three days later Sarah was "strengthened" again to write a letter to the "beloved individual" whose chamber, of course, was just down the hall. Angelina received the letter with tears and tenderness, she told Sarah, yearning to make her sister "less uncomfortable." Sarah was appalled at Angelina's words. "My sick heart desires a coming under the Cross for the sake of Him who bore it, not for me." But she felt reassured by the voice within, "Thou shalt see the inner travail of thy soul and be satisfied," even as it told her that she must be patient.[49]

Patience was not Sarah's paramount virtue, not when she felt so much was at stake. She now felt she knew the full scope of her task; William MacDowell seemed to her the main obstacle. Within a day or two she was dealing with this problem, and who can doubt the struggle between the sisters because, so Sarah recorded, Angelina was finding it hard to see her dire need to "crucify worldly lusts and desires." Who better than Sarah knew the "sacrifice" required, and why would she not share her knowledge with her sister when, as she believed, so much was at stake? Sarah shared her experiences without stint. Within two months of her homecoming Sarah had placed her diary in Angelina's hands, covering all the years that she had been away, including a special "account of her life" that she had written before leaving Philadelphia—an account that, she hinted, was put down especially for her sister to read.[50]

Angelina recalled vaguely some of the events that she found recorded in the journal, but much of what she read was a stark revelation, a glaring exposure of Sarah's tortured inner life. Angelina spent hours with this harrowing account, her pity and sympathies deeply aroused. The disclosures left her stricken and vulnerable as Sarah's long account drew to its close.

Angelina had read the part touching Sarah's love affair, the hard years of indecision, and how her sister at last had brought herself to "crucify" her heart's desire, lest the man who offered marriage should come between her and a complete union with the God she strained to serve. Then she came to Sarah's closing ill-disguised appeal. "What I have passed through will never be known but by sympathy and feeling . . . to any human being . . . I might convey it to the ear by language but experience only can adequately teach the isolated, forlorn and desolate feeling of one whose heart was susceptible to strong attachments, but who found that every tie was rent. . . . And no eye to pity. . . . It seemed sometimes as if there were no hand to save"—though Sarah swiftly added, lest her devoutness be doubted—"except as I regard it as a season of preparation, of treading down, of deep humiliation for that solemn service to which I shall be called."[51]

Thus one more stage was passed toward Sarah's unadmitted goal. Now her hope stood more clearly revealed, as she conspicuously continued to exclude Angelina. Sarah could debate the beliefs of the Friends with her sister, but she would not share her religious devotions, not so long as Angelina clung to erroneous doctrines. It deeply wounded Angelina to feel herself shut out, particularly on grounds that showed doubt of her sincerity. Soon she was finding family prayers a heavy burden because Sarah, "pious but a Quaker" instead of being "a helper to my joy, a partner of my trials," refused to countenance family worship by her presence. Nostalgically Angelina found herself remembering who good it was when, eighteen months before she, the youngest, had been asked by her mother to lead family worship. "Then I was standing upon the Mount . . . but O the awful darkness of my mind now." Why, she cried, was her family so divided. If only Sarah were anything but a Quaker![52]

Hardly three months had passed since Sarah's homecoming when she began to voice a fear that God was calling her to leave, to return to her life in Philadelphia. Angelina was truly shaken by the possibility, and Sarah herself was unready to go, for a special reason that she admitted only to herself. For although Angelina still clung to Presbyterianism, there were signs, as yet largely superficial, that momentous changes might be in the making. Up to January 1828, Angelina's journal entries were sporadic. Only scraps of her earlier diaries remain. On the tenth of January she began a new journal, one she kept faithfully for a good many years. The opening line signifies much. "Today I have torn up my Novels."[53] And Sarah, on her part, sedately reports, "My dear Angelina proposed destroying Scott's Novels which she had purchased before she was serious. Perhaps I strengthened her a little." So much did she strengthen that together the sisters immediately cut Scott's novels to bits. It would seem to be no accident that on that very day Sarah admitted Angelina to the fellowship of her prayers.

The mutilated novels were precursors of more to come. Not in vain had Sarah preached her Quaker doctrine that "we who are called with an high and holy calling [are] forbidden to adorn these bodies, but to wear the ornament of a meek and quiet spirit." Within the next few days Angelina was gathering up armsful of finery—handsome veils, laces, flounces, trimmings from her hats —and bringing all these, Sarah called them "superfluities of naughtiness,"—to deposit in Sarah's lap. Sarah forthwith stuffed a cushion with these beauties and jubilantly wrote an account of the occasion, evidently keeping a copy, since the original was sewn up in the cushion.

Affairs were now moving more swiftly toward their conclusion. Angelina began to use the Quaker form of dating, "Second Month 1, 1828," and soon the "thee" and "thou" of Quaker address. All of this was accompanied by a plainer apparel and by frequent sessions of prayer with Sarah.[54]

By mid-March, Angelina was made to confront the painful issue she had so much been dreading, that she might be called upon to leave the Presbyterian church. As spring advanced, she was torn by inner battles, pleading in her prayers that this cup might pass from her. Frequently she felt totally bewildered as to wherein she had "sinned" and been thrown into this state, where what once had meant so much—her church, its preaching, the fellowship of its worship, the prayer with its people, the teaching of the young, the active busy life so congenial to her nature—now could seem to bring only conflict of mind. It seemed strange, she felt, that she should be required to renounce a church in which she believed, in which she had been led to grow in knowledge and a sense of God's approval. For she could not concede that all this had been wrong and that she had been mistaken. What then had it meant unless it was one step, and perchance she was now called upon to take another. Sometimes Angelina would seem to accept the change, then conflict would return, and she would spend sleepless nights. How could she, she would plead, give up all her church had meant? But then she would hear a certain voice speaking, "Be still."[55]

A letter of Angelina's to a friend, Elizabeth Bascom of Camden, South Carolina, reflects the battle that was waged between the sisters and how inexorably Sarah had pressed her points.[56] Must she, Angelina wrote Elizabeth Bascom, give up her little church, "give up her Sabbath school" and her "colored Sunday school" only just then begun? Must she give up the "ordinances of Baptism," the "sacred feast of the Lord's supper," the fellowship of friends who were so dear, be shut out by them and be called "a fool"? Give up her minister? Yet what if it was wrong to look to man for mediation when only the voice within should guide? Did the minister's voice drown out the still small voice? And what if the ceremonies and doctrines that once had meant so much now seemed empty because "she had been shown" that what was needed was not symbolic water but the "baptism of the Holy Spirit and fire," not partaking of symbolic bread and wine but "sharing by faith in Christ's sacrifice"? No, she told Elizabeth Bascom, she could not find rest in any sect she saw around her; "inconsistency" was the character of them all. The Quakers, it now seemed, were the most spiritual of any sect, the most obedient, the "most crucified to the world." Then was not her proper place in their silent meeting?

Sarah surely believed in what she did. She believed that Friends had the one true way. She believed that Angelina was called to great things and that she was sent to save her younger sister. If, in saving Angelina, her own needs were served, who was she to renounce God's merciful goodness? Yet what could let Angelina so distrust her own convictions as to lend herself submissively to Sarah's obvious leading?

In the year that passed after Angelina's conversion, her convictions had deepened to the point where she believed that she was destined for a high calling and that God would presently open up a mission to her. Of course this was extraordinary for one in her station, particularly for a woman in her time and place. But Angelina Grimké was a unique individual who possessed a brilliant intellect, unusual talents, and a capacity for moral drive. It was as though she could not hold these gifts in check, even though the barriers seemed almost insurmountable. If she had been called, then her God would find a way. All the more she wished to make no mistakes now, and this increased her readiness to listen to Sarah. She felt that there was "much of self" in her commitment; she was aware of an unrelenting drive to achieve; she was sometimes disturbed by the force of her ambition, but she felt great exhilaration at those times when she had asserted leadership. While Sarah also believed in her sister's high calling, she fed Angelina's fear that fame might overcome her and could, if not controlled, possess her soul. With it all, Sarah asserted that her own way was right and that Angelina's way was replete with error—Sarah, who had suffered and sacrificed so much, all for the sake of doing God's will, who was convinced that what Angelina needed was to "be still" and let the inner spirit guide her. Angelina, while so sure, could still be plagued by uncertainty and, while morally brave, could be ridden by inner fears. As these forces buffeted her, she came to the decision that her "active labor" must cease for a time, while she "submitted to all the turning of His Holy hand."[57]

Sarah, not surprisingly, was now ready to leave Charleston and planned to take ship on April 18. She performed one more duty before she departed, reproaching Angelina for her estrangement from their mother. For Angelina all this did was open old wounds and humiliate her pride, for she could not feel to blame. In any case, her feelings were bruised by Sarah's leaving. This spelled desertion at a time when Angelina was confronting a major crisis. Sarah would be all she had left if she were forced to break the ties she had found in her church, the feeling of a home, for there, as she put it, were "father and mother, brothers and sisters." Old fears and submerged frustrations reasserted themselves, swamping Angelina's mind. She clung to the belief that God had a design, even though for the time she felt baffled and lost.

Two days before Sarah's ship was to sail, Angelina wrote, "Lord, I feel like clay in thy hands. Lead me just where and how thou pleasest." Small wonder she put it this way, for Sarah had taken matters into her own hands and had proposed to Angelina that the time had come when she should sever her connection with William MacDowell's church.[58]

On shipboard Sarah felt comfortably serene, sure that God had blessed the work of His handmaiden and had fulfilled His promise beyond her wildest dreams. Now that Angelina was "clay in the hand of the great Potter" and her zeal for doctrines and tenets dead, the spiritual eye was opened to the Truth, even to the point—Sarah had "hardly hoped for this"—of "full avowal of the Principles of Friends." While Sarah prayed each day that Angelina's strength would hold, it appears that she felt little real apprehension, as though she fully comprehended the human stuff with which she dealt, the tenacity that would hold Angelina to her course. So Sarah could write with great peace of mind, "The Lord has said she is mine —I will preserve her."[59]

Within a few days after Sarah sailed, Sunday, April 20, 1828, Angelina was taking her irrevocable step. "Is it possible, I ask myself, that today is the last time I expect to visit the Presbyterian Church?" Midweek she went to William MacDowell to tell him that she was leaving her beloved church. They wept together.[60]

Many letters ensued between Angelina and MacDowell, all of them lengthy, all poignantly revealing, with MacDowell in open battle for Angelina's heart and soul. Witness a letter that reached her in early May, delivered by messenger to her door: "While all is still around me, and many eyes are closed in sleep, I have retired to my study to relieve my aching and burdened heart. . . . And where is at this moment the friend for whom I have so often prayed— whose every step in the Christian course I have marked with the interest of a Father, or Brother. . . . Where is Angelina, and how does she feel? Is she happy? . . . Was there nothing real in those pangs that were felt when the heart was smitten by the power of truth? Nothing real in that joy that was felt?" The letter was long, it chided and pleaded, it traced the whole course they had trod together, united in a cause so glowing with high purpose. "Perhaps I have already said too much. I know you will forgive me. . . . Shall I call and see you, and when?"[61]

Angelina's reply sounded a recurring theme, "God is leading me by a way I know not." Her response was sent swiftly, by personal messenger, and was also long. Should he come to her? "O yes! . . . I almost wish to say come tomorrow, but perhaps I can scarcely bear to see you tomorrow for I now feel sick from the deep exercise of mind thro which I have recently passed . . . but come whenever you like for I shall always be at home."[62]

In succeeding weeks there were several meetings, and more long letters were exchanged, with MacDowell arguing, exhorting, pleading, and laying bare his heart as never before. Angelina, on her part, was shaken to the roots yet unable to reject the voice she heard within, while MacDowell repeatedly warned her that she must admit the possibility that she had been self-deceived.[63] All the while Angelina was in constant touch with Sarah, writing "dear Mother," "best beloved," the letters addressed to the Catherine Morris home, for Sarah was again living in Catherine's household.

Toward the end of May a decision was reached—one that Sarah said she "strengthened just a little"—that Angelina would journey to Philadelphia to spend the summer months with Sarah and her friends. MacDowell felt the threat implicit in this visit. When word reached him that Angelina would soon sail, he was prostrated by the knowledge that he had surely lost.

When at last MacDowell wrote, he spoke of shattered nerves, and in his desperation he resorted to attack.[64] He saw her, he said sternly, with almost no reflection, adopting a system that she knew little about—she herself had admitted as much. She had seemed to act on the principle that she was altogether infallible and could in no way be mistaken. He entreated; he warned her to pause, to think. Then he relented, begging forgiveness lest his words had been inexcusably harsh. "Yes, my beloved friend, wherever you go, and under whatever circumstances you may be placed, my warmest affections, my tenderest anxieties, my most fervent prayers will go with you. . . . I must ever continue to love you, though it should even turn out, that the more I love the less I am loved. The tie that binds me to you cannot easily be broken."

Angelina's hands had trembled as she opened the letter. She made herself reply the following day.

"O why didst thou write it? . . . Is it not enough that I have been called to surrender what was *dearest* to me, is it not enough that I have been required with my own hands to break the tenderest, the strongest, the most sacred ties? must I be reproached for it too? . . ." In turn, she melted and let her heart speak. "Beloved, know that thy expressions of love are softer than oil to my heart, yet are they drawn swords. I thought I had given thee up. . . . But my heart still vibrates at the touch of thy hand and out of the depths of sorrow my soul still exclaims, 'How can I give *thee* up.' Thou has been my best earthly friend, my counsellor, my guide, my *all* in this world, but the time has come when every idol must be abolished in *my heart.* . . . The voice of the spirit says, 'Go forward.' "

MacDowell had begged to see her before she sailed. It was her strong plea that he not come. "I feel it is best that we should not speak on this subject now. Let us wait patiently upon the Lord—in his own good time He will unfold to both of us why He has thus torn us from each other and scattered darkness and desolat'on in that path which was once strewed with the loveliest flowers. . . . Farewell my best beloved Brother."[65]

It was farewell, although Angelina would return to dwell a while longer in her native city, but by this time the gulf had so far widened that the estrangement of the two was almost complete.

Before she came home, Sarah surely had not guessed what William MacDowell meant in Angelina's life. But Sarah's perceptions had been sharpened by having been sought and having renounced her own love at the demand of her God. So Sarah was equipped for the task in hand, equipped by example as well as by belief to insinuate into Angelina's aspirations the need to sacrifice the heart's deep desires. "Every idol must be abolished in *my heart.*" Angelina's hand had underlined these words.[66]

So it was that Angelina found herself wrenched loose from the strong new life she had forged in Charleston, a life that had fed her deep personal needs and that might have compensated for the old deprivations that had plagued her in her childhood home, and that might have reconciled her to endure old fears when these arose to assail her. Now all constraining ties seemed severed, save the tie to the one to whom she was going, though even the bond with Sarah had been strained. There are hints in the record that Angelina perceived, faintly but with definite discomfort, that all was not right in what had passed between them. She comprehended fully that Sarah stood in need of her and, while it flattered and soothed, it disturbed as well. She had made herself believe that Sarah's mold should be her own, yet she could not feel at home within herself, a condition that became ever more intolerable to her.

4.

When Angelina reached Philadelphia in July 1828, she still accepted the existence of slavery. Sarah, while in Charleston, had rarely pressed the issue. There was so much else at home with which Sarah contended: her own religious struggles, Angelina's religious peril, and perhaps—there are hints of this from Sarah—temptations arising from the familiar life of ease in a slaveholding household staffed by many servants.[67] Sarah had let her people know that she felt slavery was a sin. On a few occasions she had reproached Angelina, although apparently Angelina was only made to feel uneasy. She reported one incident that reflected her discomfort, inserting it abruptly in the midst of other matters in her diary. The issue concerned a family servant named Kitty, and how Angelina became Kitty's owner. It seems that Kitty had been ill-treated and, to protect Kitty, Angelina had asked to own her. A fellow slave had then quarrelled with Kitty and given her a beating and, hoping to solve this problem, Angelina had hired out Kitty to a friend. Evidently Sarah had reproached Angelina for her participation in the ownership of slaves. The fact that Angelina felt defensive is seen in her comment, "I had determined never to own one."[68]

Angelina wrote little in her journal while in Philadelphia; for several months she wrote nothing at all. Only toward the end of her stay did she give hints of her inner turmoil, as she was pressed by Sarah's friends on the sin of slavery. Sarah was aware of how much was at issue, for Angelina never would be accepted as a Friend unless she squared herself on this Quaker principle.

Apparently the discussion went on for several months. Angelina stayed with Sarah in the Catherine Morris home and was frequently invited to the homes of other Friends. She would enter a home to which she had been invited, feeling warmly welcome, and bask in a sense of acceptance and approval. Then suddenly, so she told it, a gulf would yawn—the good Friends would begin their probing concerning slavery. Tears would fill her eyes, she would feel miserably cornered, longing to escape the role of one who stood condemned. She did not record precisely what these Friends said, only the feelings that so frequently assailed her.[69] Later there were clues as to what had gone on in the numerous and long conversations: the arguments against slavery based directly on Scripture, and these were learned people when it came to the Bible; arguments on grounds of humanitarianism and personal consistency in the light of one's beliefs; and arguments concerning the search to do God's will, for how could she respond to God's leading as long as she condoned this gross sin? Angelina was a challenge to these devout Friends, a woman who claimed she was drawn to Quaker principles but who as yet had not rejected the enslavement of men.

When Angelina's Quaker friends undertook to convince her that she should renounce Negro slavery because it was a sin, they had not the slightest notion of what they did or of the explosive matters with which they dealt. Antislavery had never brought disruption to their lives, no conflict of mind, no stirring of deep fears, no disturbance with their closest human ties, no requirement that they strip off the ways of their upbringing. Angelina was frequently in severe mental conflict as she contended with herself on the slavery issue. Just a few months before, while still at home, she could speak with ease of the "uncouth servant," and when, in her private chamber in quiet prayer, a slave had entered noisily, she could say it was "like a savage bear treading under foot the delicate flowers of spring."[70] Looking back, in later years, she could marvel at the outcome of her turmoil as she dealt with slavery: "Why I did not become totally hardened under the daily operation of this system, God only knows."[71] Angelina was sensitive and genuinely humane. She resented injustice, no matter who was the victim, and she now let intellect come to her aid, no longer blinking the familiar irrationalities. She was finally convinced that true religion was at issue and that she could not escape what was at stake: to make her life consistent with the truth as she saw it. It was not a new goal, but its meaning was new. In her inner struggle, she was aided by memories, images of slavery long buried which now could emerge and be seen for what they meant, the violence that was used to perpetuate the system.

Angelina spent five months in Philadelphia, returning to Charleston in November 1828. By the time of her return, slavery was an evil, not alone in God's eyes, but in her own. Hers was more than a vague feeling that slavery was sinful. She now saw it as an outrage against the mind and soul of the slave, depriving these human beings of their God-given rights. Even so, Angelina's was not a sweeping mission. She was not going home to seek the system's overthrow nor did her Quaker mentors envisage such a thing. Their parting injunction was simple and clear: that it was required of her, when she returned home, to do her duty toward her slaveholding people by convincing them that in God's eyes they sinned.

That Angelina comprehended some of what lay ahead can be seen in her thoughts on the high seas as she sailed toward home. As her frail ship rode out three terrifying storms and she lay in her berth fighting back fear, she told herself that these storms were as nothing compared to those that would soon rage at home when she spoke to her people of the sin of human slavery.[72]

II. When Can I Escape

"When can I escape from this land of slavery! . . . I do not expect to go there [north] and be exempt from trial . . . yet it is like a promised land . . . because it is a land of freedom."

ANGELINA GRIMKÉ, *Diary, August and September 1829.*

1.

What her family noticed when Angelina first came home was that they had another Quaker in their midst. Not that she had applied for membership as yet, but in all outward ways she was fully committed. Before she came home Angelina had dreaded being conspicuous as the Quaker garb would surely make her, and she called on all her pride to help her from shrinking. What a Quaker she must have seemed there in Charleston, sailing down King Street "among the gay & fashionable"—as she told it at the time—and not a whit different (she did not know this) from the former Angelina in carriage, step, high-held head, or striking appearance, encased though she was in prim Quaker garments.* Of course she fully realized all

*Formerly Angelina, whose family was wealthy, had dressed in an expensive and elegant manner. Her change to Quaker plainness made a sharp contrast. The pictures of Angelina and Sarah Grimké (frontispiece) suggest the type of clothing a Quaker woman wore in the 1820s to 1840s. The Quaker cap was probably the most distin-

eyes were upon her. "I am literally 'as a wonder unto many' . . . I am as a gazing stock (perhaps laughing stock)."[1]

But there was more than her odd dress and the swift change it marked from a few brief months before. If Angelina had been consistent with their notion of a Quaker—had been a passive, mild, humble female Friend, with downcast eyes and subdued pious voice—the grey monotones of her apparel would perhaps have seemed in keeping, and her strange views just one more, if extreme, peculiarity. Sarah, in some ways, had fulfilled this picture for them. As her people soon found out, Angelina was quite different from the Quaker that Sarah had exemplified at home. For one thing, she was twelve years younger, only twenty-three in 1828, and, unlike Sarah who tended to be devious, she was passionately direct and unsparingly outspoken, apparently undeterred by her youth. For the most part Angelina remained her old self, vivid, alive, eloquently articulate, and with new-found convictions that could cause acute discomfort.

Of course it was her lot that nothing had changed in Charleston since Angelina had gone away some five months before. The lovely homes still tugged at her heart as she saw them afresh after her return. After all, she was at home in these pleasant dwellings. She had no wish, of course, to stroll on the Battery among the fashionable, joining the rounds, nodding to acquaintances, chatting with friends, displaying newest gowns—the Battery was no place for a Quaker-clad Grimké.[2] But she had once enjoyed the intellectual elite; she knew her old circle still gathered, as in former times, to share music, books, and vivacious conversation. Angelina had been a brilliant and welcome member of this elite. It was deprivation to exclude herself.

Life in her home went on as before, especially in terms of what it meant to be waited on by slaves. Ready at hand were the terms of address and the accustomed modes of treatment so familiar to her: tones of command, kindly or peremptory, the obedience expected and reproof sometimes, the assumptions of each side as to the other's "place," with subservient slaves ever at the mistress's bid-

---

guishing feature. Angelina used the customary term "plain" to designate appropriate Quaker apparel (p. 64). By early 1828 she had discarded her laces and flounces (pp. 31-32). In 1829 when she was planning to leave home to live with Sarah in Philadelphia, she felt satisfied that her clothing was sufficiently "plain" to meet with the approval of Philadelphia Quakers. (p. 58).

ding. What other way was there than the customs embedded in her —and embedded in the slave when it came to that? When Angelina came home, the "normal" pressed upon her, and the old ingrained habits were all too ready to respond. These well-worn grooves of life were still part of her nature, despite her new beliefs with their bizarre demands.

The first days at home lulled Angelina's fears. "Perpetual bustle" surrounded her return; "anything but quiet," she exclaimed in her journal, thinking of the Quaker injunction, "Be *still*." She was soothed by the outpouring warmth of family welcome and found intense pleasure in many friends calling, especially the leaders and members of her old church. She had hardly landed when Mac-Dowell asked to call. With great relief she wrote Sarah fervently of how right it was to come and how sanguine she felt concerning the changes she could bring. She was sure her mother's change had already begun, an answer to their fervent joint prayers of the past months. She said her sister Eliza had noticed the mother's change, a wonderful transformation "in her treatment of the Servants and theirs of her." Angelina heaped glowing praise on her parent, and Mary Grimké warmed to it, admitting that she had tried and had been praying and reading Scripture to her slaves. "She seems willing to win by love instead of fear. So that on this account home is far pleasanter than it has ever been." Angelina could write of "surcease from mental conflict" and could tell of often sleeping at her mother's side.[3]

For a fortnight this sense of well-being continued until a chance happening shattered Angelina's illusory peace. Apparently a servant had been cruelly whipped, and there erupted in Angelina all her horror of violence, so that she became an accuser of her people who, in turn, felt ill-used. Oddly, she had had to force herself to speak, so that the incident was a bitterly disillusioning occasion. Far from its showing that she could bring change at home, it filled her with doubt of her own self-worth. She was plunged into misery by the inner revelation, pleading with her God "not to tempt me too far." "A few short days ago—my heart sang . . . how different are my feelings tonight." And then the inner plea that came to dominate her days, "I am ready to exclaim, when shall I be released from this land of slavery."[4] Thenceforth to "escape" was her consuming conscious need, though she could not yet know why she felt so driven.

There now began months of never-ceasing mental stress, an ambivalence forced upon her by twin drives within herself: on the one hand, "O to escape," on the other, "that I might live Religion" here at home. Since if she would "live Religion" she must condemn slavery, this was bound to bring interminable discord in its wake. Throughout those long months she argued with others and argued with herself as she sought her own salvation, straining to feel consistent in her raw new beliefs and to hold herself at home until her "mission" was completed. It is certain that she little realized the confusion this would bring and how it caused her to deal with others as she dealt with herself, at times with an almost ruthless hand, at times with defensive self-righteousness, often with a harsh, even callous, touch in her impatience with herself and her intolerance of others. She seemed almost to seek her own isolation, as though cutting herself off would somehow serve her goal.

If the Quakers of Charleston had been a viable group, zealously active in their peculiar faith, Angelina might have found a kind of home among them, and her need to escape might have been less acute. The one meeting she had known was Philadelphia's Arch Street Meeting, with its impressive elders, its devout testimony, and its air of pervading authority.[5] In this southern city there were not many Friends. The leaders of the sect were two older business men, the meeting house was small and bare and drab, and the benches almost empty on First Day. Frequently the meeting knew unbroken heavy silence throughout two long, oppressive hours. There would surely have intruded on Angelina's wayward thoughts memories from her joyous Presbyterian days: voices joining in fervent hymns, eloquent prayers of her beloved minister, a devout congregation moving to the Lord's table, the feeling of worship that hallowed the place, and the warm, friendly fellowship when service ended. Small wonder Angelina could write in her journal, "Went to meeting this morning—my soul is barren."[6]

Angelina soon sensed that something definite was amiss, and in time she learned the reason for the grim First Day meetings. The two older leaders had had a bitter quarrel, with hostility so extreme that they were not on speaking terms. "Feel exercised in meeting on account of the sad state of the Friends Society here . . . no Spring of Life in the midst of us—our little meeting . . . a well without water and ourselves trees without fruit." She knew but one way to battle disillusionment: she must try to bring peace in this unhappy situation, and her new doctrines gave her grounds for interfering. It was a Friend's duty to point out sin in others. Angelina knew the formula for such occasions, one she kept reverting to throughout that harsh winter. "When the Lord requireth us to remove sin in others, he inclined their hearts to receive our words, or He wonderfully prepared us to bear and forbear with them in the spirit of meekness and love." Meekness was not a strong point with Angelina.[7] Even so, she wrote these two older men—and she so young—remonstrating with them, and she "enjoyed a good conscience" until one of them replied. She recorded in her journal what "J K's" letter said, even though his letter was a sharp reprimand: She was a "busybody about other men's business"; moreover, she was not even a Friend and had no right to interfere in their society. "But can I be said," she argued with herself, "to have no concern in what has almost entirely destroyed the comfort of attending meeting, because I am not an outward member of the Friends?" The most shocking part was J K's accusation against the other Friend with whom he had quarreled. D L was a thief and a slave-holder, he had written her, and had cheated him out of a large sum of money. J K sent letters to prove his charges. Angelina could not bear to confront the damning proof and returned the documents to J K unread.[8] Even so, the fact remained—a Quaker here in Charleston was an owner of slaves. She continued to attend the meeting on First Day, though from this time on she felt shut out.

One continuing irritant, especially to her family, was Angelina's insistance on the superiority of Quaker virtues. In fact, she had to strain after some of them herself. She would write Sarah, "I fully accord with thy views on inward retirement," and she disciplined herself, as never before, to devote special times to meditation and prayer. She sought enlightenment in the writings of Quakers; "girding" her new faith was the way she put it. "I find Fox's Journal very interesting and an excellent . . . illustration of Friends' Principles." This was all very well in her private chamber. But Angelina was one who must act on her beliefs; she must strive to win others, lest she feel a sense of failure.[9]

Her people were not interested in Quaker writings; nonetheless she urged them on members of her family, in particular on her mother, who more than once was made to sit and listen as her daughter read aloud. She also sought out Thomas, her favorite older brother, now a well-established lawyer in the city. Thomas was a lecturer on peace and education; his broad, free-thinking mind could find interest in Angelina's, and he let her talk, responsive and kind, critical though he was of her new dogmatism. "Thomas and I had a long talk about Quakers. . . . I tried to convince him that they did not reject the Bible . . . got him to acknowledge that in several texts which I repeated that the Word was the Spirit . . . but he was immovable in his opinions." If all Quakers were Angelinas, Thomas had told her drily, he could like them because she was not the usual Quaker "but had carried into the Society much good from Presbyterianism," a comment not likely to cheer his sister.

Quaker principles required that she not join in family prayers, so, like Sarah, Angelina would not attend. It went hard to absent herself. "I thought it would be impossible for me to feel comfortable without attending."[10] Unlike Sarah, she tried to change family custom and besieged her mother to adopt silent worship. "Probably Mother has written on the subject," she wrote Sarah, as indeed the mother had, demanding Sarah's intervention. Sarah remained aloof, no doubt for her own reasons, and Mary Grimké had to find her own solution. And what a thing it must have been each evening before tea, Angelina and her mother seated in a darkened parlor, a grim Quaker "silence" pervading the room, while the clock ticked away the half-hour they had set. Nor did the dreary compromise see an end until mosquito season broke their stubborn wills.

For years Angelina had hated the discord in the home. Now she had become a focal point of it and, being unable to admit the part she played, blaming others soon became a refrain as she poured out her emotions on the pages of her journal. "Day after day and week after week I am tried in this way. There is such a spirit of finding fault, either the meal is given too late, or things are too cold, or they are badly cooked, or . . . they [family members] are rude to each other or to the servants. . . . So weary is my soul with this strife and contention." Her pent-up frustrations would erupt with sudden force, sometimes in outbursts of irrational, wounding anger, making her leave the table in abrupt, harsh displeasure and rush to her chamber in convulsive tears.

There had long been tensions between Angelina and Charles, the brother next to her in age. The record suggests that Charles was a weakling, and Angelina was unsparing in her criticisms of him: Charles had no profession, no purpose, no dignity, he was an idler and a wastrel, a dependent on her mother. And she reproached her mother for coddling this son. Angelina, and also Sarah since their inheritance, made a token weekly payment of five dollars for board, whereas Charles accepted bread and shelter from his mother, and in addition the elegant apparel he wore and the wine he imbibed. Charles not infrequently came home late at night drunk from one of his carousals with friends. Sometimes he had violent stomach cramps, and his moans and groans would arouse the whole household, with his mother hovering near to tend him in his pain. Angelina would fume "Inexcusable!" and she would punish Charles by attitude and word, excusing herself for her unkind behavior: "A man eating the bread of dependence!" "Drinking another's wine who works hard."

Henry, next to Thomas, was Angelina's favorite brother, and until now their relationship had been genial and close. Henry was a man who required respect. He was earning his place in the practice of law, and, as the oldest son at home, he was master in the house, a main bulwark for his mother. Even after Henry's marriage that winter, he brought his wife Salina to live in his mother's house, perhaps as a duty since a man should be there, and the younger son Charles could not be counted on. Now Angelina began to find fault with Henry for his violent temper and his punishment of the slaves. Henry was soon declaring that she had come home just to make her family miserable, and he took himself off to their country place, refusing to return if she continued her "complaining."[11]

She began to feel that slavery in itself caused dissension and that dependence on the slave was a corrupting family influence. "It appears to me there is a real want of natural affection among families in Carolina, and I have thought that one great cause of it is that members of families were not taught to do for themselves" but were brought up to be waited on by slaves and grew up "unamiable, proud, and selfish." She attempted to wait on her mother and reproached her parent for becoming irritated, accusing Mary Grimké of "preferring help from slaves." "It is their business" was the mother's sharp rejoinder.

Always her harshest behavior was exhibited toward her mother, a pattern made familiar by their long estrangement. Incident after incident is recorded in her diary. Her mother was unaccommodating, insisting she needed Stephen, the family butler, to serve tea, when Angelina wished to use him for an errand; her mother, loving luxury and "show," spending twenty-six dollars to repaper the drawing room; her mother, inconsiderate, not helping her widowed sister who was "in want of necessaries," although, as the mother pointed out, "Aunt Roger Smith had a daughter who dressed very well." "It was in great measure *her* fault that we have always lived in strife and contention. . . . I want her to see and feel the bitter fruits of her system of education."[12]

The conflicts with her mother soon focused on slavery, until even slight disputes in the end swung around to this overshadowing issue that now lay between them. Mary Grimké believed she had a right to hold slaves and refused to acknowledge that to do so was a sin. She was deeply religious, with a sense of God's approval. "I am ready to yield myself, & all I have to His blessed will" was her recurring assertion. She insisted that she knew black people as only an owner could, from a lifetime of experience, and that they were "fit for no other condition" than to be the slaves of a white master. As criticism mounted, the mother turned to attack. "There now, another cause of finding fault!" "I see no sin in these things. Let me alone!"[13]

The mother's sharpest weapon was Angelina's inconsistency. Was her daughter so righteous after all? Had she forgotten how recently she had changed and that now she condemned what for years she had condoned? Thus began one bitter quarrel, put down in full by Angelina's pen.[14]

"I acted accordingly to the light I then had!"

"Then you are not to expect everybody to think like Quakers."

"True believers had but one Leader who would, if they followed Him, guide them into all truth———"

"Yes, last winter . . . nobody who wore a bow on their hats could go to heaven!"

"I remember saying no such thing."

"Of course, you never do wrong."

"Mother"—Angelina now in tears—"I should be sorry to think so, for I know I do sin, and if ever I said what thou accuses me of, I do condemn myself, I am very sorry . . . I freely own my fault."

Mary Grimké was now on the offensive. Angelina herself had thought slavery was right. The whole trouble lay with Quakerism. It was turning Quaker that had made her daughter so contrary, disapproving of things that nobody else saw harm in. Angelina's pride rose up in rebellion. "None but the power of God could ever have made me change!"

Mary Grimké then launched into a painful accusation. In her diary Angelina would not record precisely what it was, but clearly it had the power to make her cringe. It had to do with Kitty, Angelina's erstwhile slave. The mother "taunted" her, Angelina wrote, for having hired out Kitty and for some ill treatment that then befell the woman. She accused her daughter of making a remark about Kitty that so shocked Angelina she would not quote it in her diary. "I was greatly excited," she wrote that night. For days she wrote of feeling "great heaviness of spirit," "so acute have been my sufferings on account of Slavery," denying having said the ugly thing yet haunted by it. In her guilt and misery, she cried out against her mother and her "wretched upbringing."

Angelina was deeply shaken by her mother's new hostility. "I am bound to bear testimony!" she would exclaim to her mother, and the next moment she would weep, head on her mother's shoulder, pleading "that she did not love her mother less, and if she sometimes spoke in a spirit that alienated . . . "[15]—but then as though compelled, she would return to the attack.

Soon the slavery issue reached beyond the family circle. Angelina was aggressor, but not without her mother's aid. Mary Grimké, for her own reasons, lent herself to the exchange, grimly insistent on discussions of slavery when friends, in all innocence, came at teatime or later in the evening. Angelina told in her diary of these abrasive arguments.

"Would'st thou be willing to be a slave thyself?" This became Angelina's constant theme. The answer no was all she needed. Then they had no right to enslave the Negro, for Christ expressly said, "Do unto others as thou would'st have them do unto you." "Suppose thou wast obliged to free thy slaves, or take their places, which would'st thou do?" If the answer was free them, "But why," if they really believed what they contended, that the slave's situation was as good as their own? She was told of how "depraved" slaves were and unfitted for any other place in society. "What made them so depraved? Was it not because of their degraded situation, and were *they* not to blame for it? Was it not that the minds of slaves were totally uncultivated, and their souls no more cared for by their owners than if they had none? Was it not true that, in order to restrain them from vice, coercion was employed instead of the moral restraint which, if proper instruction had been given them, would have guarded them against evil?"

She hammered away at the effects on the owner. "A Carolina mistress," she argued with one friend, "was literally a slavedriver" —a slave foreman was called a "driver" in the field—"and I thought it degrading to the female character, making the mistress as great a slave to her servants in some respects as they to her." Look, she exclaimed, at "the constant stream of orders given . . . orders that might easily be avoided . . . and the domineering spirit [they developed]. They are such fine ladies that if a shutter is to be hooked, or a chair moved, or their work handed to them, a servant must be summoned."[16]

As time moved on, her arguments grew bolder. "Should not a slave be whipped for a terrible crime?" a friend demanded. Angelina said, yes, he ought to be punished. "But the root of the evil in Slavery is in the fact that the owners seldom thought of giving moral instruction. They even denied the Bible to their slaves by their refusal to let them learn to read." Her friends began to warn her of how imprudently she spoke. Indeed her answer was odd for a champion of the slave: "I was not speaking before servants. I was speaking only to owners," as if she still shared the slaveholder's fear lest the slave be aroused to thoughts of rebellion. True, her further words seemed to sound a different note: "This wrong has long enough been covered up, and I am not afraid or ashamed for anyone to know my sentiments."

On rare occasions, Angelina met some response, invariably from women and profoundly fatalistic. "Slavery has embittered my whole life." "Something in my heart has told me it was wrong." "It is the greatest curse of women," one friend exclaimed, and of course she referred to the mistress, not the slave. "I sympathize with what you say," said a friend, "yet I can see no slightest hope."[17]

A day came when friends, their patience exhausted, demanded that Angelina cease to speak to them on slavery. By this time the chasm was too wide for her to bridge, and in any case, she felt she had no choice except to speak. "But why! And it an institution so contrary to the spirit of the Gospel . . . a system which nourishes the worst passions of the human heart; a system which sanctioned the daily trampling under foot of our fellow creatures." Their ears were now closed, they began to avoid her, and she found no new friends who would listen.

If Angelina felt a mission toward family and friends, how profoundly she would feel it toward the leaders of the church, the religion that had been the "cradle of her soul." And could she not believe that there were grounds for hope in this church that she had forsaken and to which her heart still clung, the church she had once believed would withstand all tests, even to the crucial test of Christian consistency?

The slave had never been an issue in her church, the Third Presbyterian Church of Charleston. Angelina had left her church in 1828, at a time when she herself still accepted slavery. It was many months later, after returning from Philadelphia, that she challenged the church's leaders on the sin of owning slaves, with consequences to herself that she little anticipated.

While Angelina recorded little about her hours with these church leaders, a document exists that shows clearly how they argued. In December 1833, just four years after these conversations, the Presbyterian Synod of the States of South Carolina and Georgia met in Columbia, and there an extensive report was made on the "religious instruction" of slaves within the synod.[18] If she later read this report, as she may well have done, there surely echoed in her mind her tense, long debates with Elders McIntire and Napier in early 1829.

Angelina says she pressed them, as she had pressed her mother. Did they not admit that to hold slaves was a "sin"?[19]

In effect, it was this question that the Presbyterian Synod strained to deal with in its report of 1833. "We are not accountable for our birth in the slave states; we are not responsible for the fact of being masters. We are not responsible for the creation of this relation." "Under the law [these Negroes] are our *property*; their persons and privileges are at our disposal . . . they are absolutely dependent; nor can any person step in between us and them, or touch them in any particular whatever, without our permission."

They admitted that Negro slaves had "immortal souls"; they admitted that the church had a duty toward them, a duty to "instruct," a duty to "save." They admitted further that "the Church had failed." "Throughout the slave-holding states [we admit], either custom or law prohibits them [slaves] the acquisition of letters."

Yet the matter, said the synod, must be dealt with "judiciously."

"The same sermons and instruction are not suitable for whites and negroes. . . . The two classes are *distinct* in their education, station, associations, duties, trials, and should have a distinct Ministry . . . they should be instructed and preached to for the most part *separately*." "Ministers of their own color had little to commend them. . . . Such a Ministry is looked upon with distrust. . . . Masters fear doctrines subversive to our interests . . . and that religious instruction will lead to insubordination." It is Christian teaching to instruct the slave, "Be *obedient* to the Master . . . with fear and trembling . . . as unto Christ. . . . Be industrious and saving, less addicted to crime. . . . Work more faithfully and cheerfully. . . . Render obedience to whom obedience is due." The master must be persuaded to permit such instruction. A white ministry could tell him that his "pecuniary interests" would be served thereby, that religious teaching would "contribute to his safety," because the Gospel would "soften down and curb [the slave's] passions" and thus secure the country against "subversive dangers."

The synod confronted the question of slaveowners' morals. "We cannot go into any special detail," but then the synod, as if driven, poured forth its painful guilt. "We know we are chained to a putrid carcase; it sickens and destroys. We have a millstone around the neck of our society, to sink us deep in the sea of vice; our children are corrupted from infancy; nor can we prevent it."

Yet the synod, at all cost, dared not denounce slavery. "And sow the seed of discontent and revolt? It is impossible." No, the church's duty was plain and sure. "Slaves were heathen in this Christian country"; it was the church's obligation to "evangelize these heathen. . . . Salvation of souls . . . this the great object . . . that [the slave's] soul may be saved." Many masters "feared to let their [slaves'] souls be saved" lest "the certain end of it will be emancipation." So the master must be given clear reassurance that slavery is directly "sanctioned by the Bible, and nothing but the Bible," and if the slave "is taught the Bible, the whole Bible, and nothing but the Bible," slave masters had nothing in the least to fear. Moreover, in attending to their slaves' eternal interests, masters had performed "this charge upon their souls," and they need not "tremble when they went to meet their Maker."

Doubtless it was with some such arguments that the elders stood their ground. Their final words to Angelina she remembered long years after and told them to Weld. "Wait. Riper years will one day set you straight."

The elders were slaveowners, the minister was not. In turning to the minister, Angelina clung to hope. William MacDowell received her gravely. Not many months before they had been so close, so at one in high purpose, so atuned in mind and heart. On that January day in 1829, she confronted him with slavery and with his elders' complacence, with the fact that they had remained unchanged. Did the minister deny that slavery was a sin?

"It is a sin," MacDowell replied. "It is a great evil. In itself, the system is wrong. . . . And yet," he continued, "what could men do? Attempt to uproot it and deluge the country with the evils of a servile war—evils far beyond anything slavery itself entailed?"

MacDowell knew Angelina as no one else did; he had once known her inner thoughts and sensed her deepest fears, though perhaps he little guessed precisely what he did in raising the awful specter of a "servile war." She had yet to come to terms with this old dread.

Did this mean then that MacDowell would do nothing?

What could he do, MacDowell answered sadly, save pray and wait.

"Pray and *work*!" Angelina cried in passion. "Speak in your sermons as you have spoken to me."[20]

This was not the end of Angelina's confrontation. Young though she was, her influence was dangerous, nor could she be permitted to malign her former church. On February 7, 1829, Angelina received two visitors from the church, MacDowell and Elder Thomas Napier. She sensed before they spoke that they had come officially. They were sent, they said, as a committee from the Session of the Third Church to ask her: did she not know she had broken the vows she had made when she had entered the Presbyterian church, and did she not remember she had promised to submit to the church's discipline?

Angelina felt no threat as she listened to the two men, answering them apparently with serenity and good will. She thanked them for coming while rejecting their contention, since for nearly a year she had not been a church member.

The matter might have ended here if the decision had been MacDowell's. He won a postponement of several months from the session, and during this time, he labored with Angelina to persuade her to recant her serious doctrinal errors and return to the fold of God's elect. For it should be noted that the complaints of the church leaders were religious: slavery was never mentioned in their accusations; what they had to say stands fully recorded in letters that were exchanged in succeeding months. The minister's concern was with Angelina's soul, with the ordinances of God, and with the unsoundness of her new faith. He was the authority on this high and holy ground, he the accuser, she the one who had sinned. Not that Angelina was a helpless neophyte; for several years she had schooled herself in doctrinal matters. Her letters were as lengthy and as learned as his. The correspondence continued for several months; then abruptly it was brought to a close.

On an evening in mid-May, Elder Napier called, alone this time, to deliver a document that cited her to appear on the evening of May 19 before the members of the session to stand trial for broken vows.

"Very little passed between us. . . . I was composed whilst he was here." She gave Napier her reply: she would comply with the summons. But as soon as he left she rushed to her room, there giving way to a flood of tears. Angelina often said her "pride was her bane," "so proud," she exclaimed, "she was proud of her pride." Pride alone upheld her throughout this time. She felt desolate and alone. "No friend, no human counsellor, no sympathizing heart." She was often in tears in the privacy of her chamber but refused to show her distress when among her people. "It has often been the case after passing through much exercise that I could then go amongst my family with cheerfulness."[21]

Pride made her walk alone to her trial and take her stand before these men who had once so much admired her. She believed they had no right to summon her before them; she had written them as much and repeated it that evening. She had "reperused," she said, the Profession and Covenant and insisted she had broken none of her vows. At the time of her admission she had indeed promised "to submit to the government and discipline" of the church. But having "voluntarily withdrawn from the Church," did she not stand on very different ground from those who, whilst continuing within its ranks, did things to incur its censure? The Confession of Faith, she insisted, simply had no provision that covered her case, hence the session had no right to proceed against one who, like herself, had withdrawn from membership. The elders insisted she had not withdrawn. It was true, she replied, she wrote no "formal resignation," but she had told the minister she was severing her connection, and she had ceased attending the church.

The session had an answer for Angelina's contention. She could not withdraw, she could only be expelled.

As it turned out, in the final decision, the men stopped short of so drastic a step. Perhaps it was the minister who in the end swayed them. Perhaps her high station held these men in check: it was no slight thing to be a Grimké of Charleston. Or perhaps, who knows, they had satisfied their need to find sin in this young woman who had made them feel guilt. "After mature deliberation, and careful examination of all the circumstances of the case of Miss Angelina Grimké, it was unanimously resolved that the Session deem it expedient for the present to make trial of the effect of solemn admonition. They do therefore direct their Moderator or pastor, in the name of the Session solemnly, and affectionately, to admonish Miss Grimké of her errors, and endeavor to bring her to repentance, and until the effect of this is seen, the Session will proceed no further."[22]

Immediately, the minister wrote Angelina. "I promised you last night to let you know as speedily as possible the decision of the Session . . . and now discharge a duty enforced on me." He pleaded that he had made it a subject of special prayer, and he believed God would approve

> this sincere and humble effort to bring back to his fold, one who, we cannot but think, has wandered from the good way. . . . It is, my beloved friend, a serious thing to offend, or grieve God's dear children. You do believe, I think, there are some of his dear children in that Church, with which you once felt it a privilege to be connected. . . . How they [the members] have been grieved when they have seen her turn her back on these ordinances, but seem to view them even with horror, as though they were rites of a Heathen Temple. Angelina, can this be from the Spirit of God? Can it be . . . all these are wrong, mistaken. . . . In the name of the Church then, my dear friend, I do most solemnly admonish you of your danger. . . . Examine not with a view to see whether Quakerism or any other "ism" is right, but to ascertain what God has revealed . . . examine with the spirit of humility. . . .

With these words, MacDowell's pen had faltered. The very script shows his agitation. "I have written this while the City is buried in sleep, and am greatly exhausted. I wish to say much more to you, but have not the strength."[23]

The letter was delivered by messenger next morning. Angelina was dismayed by the session's decision. "Why do they not cut off the withered branch at once, instead of leaving it to die by inches. . . . What more can be said or done to me or done for me than what has been said and done already!"[24] A few more letters passed between them, with Angelina pleading for "dismission" forthwith, since they had asked "the impossible" of her.

How grim was this, her final isolation. "Lord," she exclaimed, "Thou knowest how hard it is for flesh to bear my situation here. . . . Once so much beloved and bearing so high a character for zeal and piety—now regarded as a poor deluded creature."[25] It hardly mattered now if the session expelled her. Already the church had played its part. It had condoned slavery, it had dealt with her unjustly, and thereby unwittingly it had cut clean through the last frayed threads that had bound her to it.

When Angelina had returned to Charleston, it was in the clear belief that at some distant day her "work" here would be done and she would be "released" to return to the North. Let her people but acknowledge that holding slaves was a "sin," and would she not then be free to leave this place? At best she only sensed what most strongly held her here and that her profound need lay within herself, so much so that she had been compelled to come back home to confront and comprehend the full evil of human slavery. "For two or three months after my return it seemed to me that all the cruelty and unkindness which I had from infancy seen practised towards them [the slaves] came back to my mind as though it was only yesterday. . . . The house of correction"—the dreaded work house—"it seemed as though its doors were unbarred to me. Night and day they were before me, and yet my hands were bound as with chains of iron. I could do nothing but weep over the scenes of horror which passed in review."

Nor were her feelings spared from fresh disturbing scenes. One Sabbath, after many months at home, as she was returning alone from Friends meeting, she met two white youths guarding a slave woman who pleaded with the boys in tones of great distress. One boy threatened loudly, "I will have you tied up!" "Dreadful apprehension" swept over Angelina: she knew this woman was being led to the work house. "My knees smote . . . my heart sank within me." It had ever been so since the long ago, and, as in former times, she could only think of flight. Then came the unexpected, for as Angelina passed, the woman cried for help, "Missis! Missis!" Angelina recorded, "My lips were sealed." She exclaimed in her journal, "How long, O Lord!" harrowed by her guilt and her helplessness.[26]

Her most painful confrontation was with her brother Henry; it may have been the decisive turning point. Henry, next to Thomas, was Angelina's favorite brother—this despite her dread of his volcanic temper. Henry had a body servant named John, and John was an issue throughout that winter, one Angelina could not leave alone even as she feared the inner voice demanding that she speak. When his master's wrath threatened, John would run away and hide, though eventually hunger would drive him back again. Angelina had come to dread the time of John's return, knowing she would be awakened in the night by fearful sounds—the swish and thud of the lash, her brother's angry curses, John's screams of pain. She had been at home some months when John ran away again, and she felt herself "directed" to remonstrate with Henry, to plead with him not to thrash John. For two days and nights she wrestled with her fears: she could not bear to raise the barrier between them, yet she would feel stultified if she turned away. The approach of another night spurred her on, since once dark fell the slave might return. Perhaps her dread of what would follow blotted out other dreads.

Angelina could never feel easy with the memory of that hour when at last she entered Henry's chamber. Her arm went round his shoulder as he was seated at his desk, and she pressed her face against his face, in a self-conscious, almost forced affection, as she began to plead that he not thrash John. Henry was blunt and callous in his rebuff: he intended "to give him [John] such a whipping it would cure him of doing this same thing again." Angelina's anger rose, she accused him of "treating John worse than he would treat his horse"; and Henry, defiant, excitedly exclaimed, he "considered his *horse* in *comparsion better* than *John*." Her accusations became more strident—he had no feelings of humanity; he loudly accused her of meddling in his business; she wept and told of how she "suffered" at home. He began to taunt her for her inconsistencies, declaring that she had come back home just to make her family miserable; why not, he demanded, go back to the North, leave them alone. She would go, she cried, when at last God released her, but while she was at home, she must speak against slavery. He turned on her harshly: "She was meddling with his private feelings, something she had no right to do." As if a light broke, her tone changed, and she feelingly appealed "to the witness in his own bosom to the truth" of what she said. Angelina would not forget Henry's sudden agitation, as though confusion and despair had flooded his mind, or ever cease to hear his despondent bitter voice. Did she not understand how she harrowed his feelings, that he felt something within himself that fully met all she said, that this was the reason she made him so miserable?[27] Never would this moment's clear perception leave her, as though the mind of her brother the slaveholder stood revealed, and he knew himself doomed in the way of life he cherished, a life from which he found no means and no will to escape.

During the spring and summer of 1829, Angelina, like a pendulum, swung back and forth. One day she could write, "Now no prospect of my return to the North" and a few weeks later, "escape not yet in sight," yet she had the "impression" that she might go in late summer. For years she had been plagued by a rash on her hands that persistently returned when she was tense and troubled. The rash had reappeared now in virulent form, and her physician seemed unable to check or even soothe it.[28]

Sarah, in these months, had kept up a constant pressure. She knew her sister's conscience and her stubborn will should Angelina decide that her duty lay in Charleston. As the months went by, Sarah's state of mind worsened. Her Quaker ministry had proved a feeble gift, and her attempts to exercise it were rebuffed in her own meeting. "Oh the fiery trial, how can I endure it." She wrote Angelina of her "disconsolate spirit." Chiefly, Sarah was bitterly lonely, which made her more fearful at Angelina's long delay. In these very months she had finally lost her suitor, by whose decision is not made clear, though Sarah had seemed to cling to what she termed their "heavenly union." Now they had decided to "withdraw *altogether*" and each to get along in the "solitary path." In fact, she was appalled by her solitariness, and if she would not marry there was only Angelina. Sarah told Angelina how she had prayed for her coming, yet reminded herself constantly, "Wait patiently on the Lord." Sarah's letters became frantic by midsummer. While Angelina was distressed by her sister's lonely state, she still did not yet feel "released" to leave home, not even when Sarah wrote her bluntly that the "Most High" had told her, "I will give her to thee . . . & I will bless you together," adding that he gave her this message for Angelina, "All the days of thy appointed time are fulfilled in that land."[29] In September, Sarah wrote directly to her mother asking that Angelina join her in Philadelphia. Mary Grimké showed the letter to Angelina, who recorded that her mother "did not oppose though she regretted it."

Angelina had begun to examine her wardrobe. "There is not a single thing I've worn in Carolina, that I cannot go to Philadelphia and wear among Friends with their approbation."[30] While she longed to go, she yet felt the ties of home, with all their subtle pulls so deeply rooted in her. Even her belief in her mother's cold indifference was momentarily shattered as her departure became apparent, and her mother, coming suddenly into Angelina's room, caught her daughter in her arms, her tight reserve broken as she burst into tears.[31] Against her mother's pain, Angelina weighed Sarah's need—all she felt she "owed to Sarah"—and also her own need to "escape the land of Slavery."

This need to escape kept sounding in her journal: "shut in a prison," "bound by fetters," "now nine months [in] this perpetual turmoil," "When can I escape this land of Slavery." "Sometimes," she wrote, "I think the children of Israel could not have looked toward the land of Canaan with keener longing than I do to the North. I do not expect to go there and be exempt from trial, yet it is like a promised land . . . because it is a land of freedom." It was the end of September before she felt "release" had come, and in mid-October she took ship from Charleston, leaving her home with all it held, assuming she would one day return.[32]

2.

Conceivably Angelina might always have remained merely an obscure southern Quaker lady, making her home among Philadelphia Friends, on the whole faithful to her adopted beliefs, including the belief in the sin of slavery. This was the life Sarah had been living and expected to live to the end of her days. For a brief few years Angelina seemed to live it. There were sufficient reasons, some in the Friends Society, that saved Angelina from bondage to orthodoxy. Even within herself, behind her outward trappings and the Quaker manners she had assumed, she was increasingly restive to the point of rebellion at her enforced inactivity and the harsh, narrow discipline.

She entered the society at a critical time. The Quaker-Hicksite schism was just a year old when she reached Philadelphia in 1829. Angelina made her way straight to Arch Street Meeting, as she was bound to do—it was Sarah's meeting house. She lived with Sarah in Catherine Morris's household, and Catherine's brother, Israel Morris, was an Arch Street leader. Arch Street elders, strictly Orthodox men, were at the forefront of the struggle against Elias Hicks.

Angelina knew little except the Orthodox side, and this hemmed her in for a few crucial years. Yet having known the Quaker faith for so short a time, she lacked the strong tradition that would tend to make her cling; and how could her trust grow in the leaders of her new faith who, while asserting their belief in "the conquering force of love," yet were involved in unseemly quarrels. She might and did at first espouse one side as right. As it chanced, it was the side on which she would feel least at home. The Hicksites were insisting on liberty of thought. The Orthodox took refuge in the other extreme, some leaders even viewing the final disunion as a "winnowing away" of those of unsound doctrine, with themselves the remnant that was "pure in faith." One effect of the split was to weaken the society in the total impact of its authoritative voice. Moreover, many Hicksites were active abolitionists; the Orthodox were more passive, their tones restrained.[33]

When Angelina had left her home to live in Philadelphia, she believed that she was moving toward a definite career, so she had been driven to leave by more than the need to escape slavery and the fears it held for her. Her new-found beliefs were a positive force. It was always so with her, to try to bring change in others where convictions were at stake: she had turned to Quakerism as the purest of religions and away from slavery as the grossest of sins. But Angelina had come to sense through the turmoil of past months that demands on her nature were involved in her struggle. She might not understand the fierce pressures she felt within, as her submerged great gifts struggled to break through, talents that pushed and tugged at all restraints, brilliant gifts that within a few years would bring Angelina striking public recognition. The new faith she had adopted offered a career. Indeed, this may have been one of its appeals. Angelina, in past months, had had her sense of mission strengthened by the conviction that at least she knew what "God's call" meant: that He intended her, like Sarah, to become a Quaker minister. And Angelina "was not murmuring against the appointment." Unlike Sarah, she longed to begin. "My restless ambitious temper, so different from dear Sister's, craves high duties and high attainments, and I have at times thought this ambition was a motive to me to do my duty and submit my will. . . . The hope has often prompted me to give up small things, to bend to existing circumstances, to be willing for the time to be trampled upon. These are my temptations."[34]

Almost at once her new freedom was threatened and by the very Friends who she thought had set her free. While still on trial for admission to the society, the examining overseer, Jane Bettle, confronted Angelina with a disquieting demand. "One of the testimonies the Society always supported was the duties of children to [their] parents." It was less than a year since her "escape," and now they were insisting that she go back home. There followed sleepless nights and miserable days, with only her sister to share her woe, and Sarah was stubbornly opposing the demand, so disturbing was her fear that she would lose Angelina.

These Friends were not subtle in the pressures they exerted— Catherine Morris, in whose home the sisters lived, the overseers, and other Arch Street members—and finally Angelina, ever plagued by her "duty," gained her own consent and capitulated. "Last evening when sitting in silence with Sister . . . 'a horror of great darkness fell upon me.' . . . *Thy* will be done," she forced herself to say, "but O! my soul sank." Without a word to Sarah, she sought out Jane Bettle, the overseer in whose hands her fate rested, to say she was ready to accept her duty. She would return to Charleston to be with her aging mother.[35]

Jane Bettle's sternness melted when Angelina told her, and at meeting next First Day all was warm approval. Indeed, Samuel Bettle fell on his knees and offered fervent prayer "for one in their midst being tried." Angelina recorded this surprising recognition, puzzled yet flattered, and related how, after meeting, Jane Bettle came to greet her, tears of approbation in her eyes. And "R. C." a leading member, "almost for the first time" came and pressed her hand. Catherine Morris stood beside her, glowing with pride.

Did some suspicion flit through Angelina's mind that the Bettles were not without a personal stake? Samuel and Jane Bettle had a beloved son who in recent months had called on Angelina, infrequently as yet—his behavior most correct; even so, the word had spread that the Bettle son was "interested." Socially, of course, who could be more suitable than a daughter of Judge John Faucheraud Grimké of Charleston. But the Bettles were birthright Quakers, pious, inflexible, complacent in the uniqueness of their cherished Quaker heritage. Could they fail to look askance at this glamorous southern woman who had yet to be admitted to the Society of Friends?

In the end, it was Sarah who rescued Angelina—Sarah, ever resourceful when deep needs were at stake. One week later Angelina could write, "I have been passing through too much to commit to paper since 2nd day. The tempest has spent its fury, but the roaring of the billows and tossing of the vessel still indicates what I have been exposed to." For Sarah had argued bitterly, giving no ground: if their parent required a daughter, then Sarah would go; as the elder child, it was her obligation. She carried her argument to the overseers, to Catherine Morris, to all who would listen. To Angelina, Sarah pressed a further point, put it bluntly and without equivocation: if Angelina went away, she might lose the Bettles' son, and Angelina admitted that she felt "some interest."[36]

It so happened that Sarah was absent in Charleston when, in late 1830, at the age of twenty-six, Angelina was admitted to the Society of Friends. By the following spring young Bettle was calling regularly. But now Angelina began to show ambivalence, at times reaching out then conspicuously withdrawing from this young man in whom she felt "some interest." Her reaction was similar throughout that year towards all that might enchain her. There was her sudden departure from the Catherine Morris household—Sarah had hardly sailed before Angelina left. She moved to her sister's, the home of the widowed Anna Frost who had been running a small school since she came north in 1821. Angelina said she moved because Anna "needed" her, nor could Friends gainsay this "family obligation." Yet there is more than a hint of an urge to escape the close supervision and inflexible discipline of Catherine Morris's strict Quaker home.[37]

Training for the Quaker ministry was not a formal program, and Angelina found her road made long and rugged. The Orthodox of Philadelphia were a formidable people and in no haste to induct this young convert. And temperamentally Angelina was out of tune with their demands—an odd Quaker minister who found northern winters frigid and sewed fur inside her cap to keep her ears warm— time and again she offended in small ways. Nor could she seem to curb her stubborn drive toward overt action. She would plunge into activities, momentarily elated, and find it galling and bewildering when told she must withdraw because she had failed to gain permission of the Friends Society.

Fortuitous circumstance brought Catherine Beecher to Philadelphia. Catherine was the daughter of Lyman Beecher, an older sister of Harriet Beecher Stowe, and a prominent woman educator in the 1830s who, in her Hartford school for girls, had dared to assert the appropriateness of female academic studies. Angelina met Miss Beecher socially, was thrilled with her mind, and then and there pressed her as to the possibility of becoming a teacher. Where now was her call to the Quaker ministry? In any event, Miss Beecher responded by inviting Angelina to visit her at Hartford, and dates were set.[38]

Sarah had remained in Charleston for a year, so there was no Sarah saying, "Child, be *still*," the repeated admonition of the devout Quaker. Nor was Catherine Morris near to admonish or restrain, since Angelina was now staying at Anna Frost's home. Her sister was a conventional Episcopalian, and while Anna might demur, she would not stand in the way of this decision. As for young Bettle, momentarily, it appears, his image had receded. With her small inherited income, Angelina's funds sufficed, and a Quaker friend, referred to as "S" in Angelina's diary, was eager to join in the expedition. Impulsively Angelina struck a quick blow for freedom, and without a word of consultation with her Arch Street Meeting mentors, she set off with her friend on this remarkable journey. Was she blind to the risks her actions entailed—in her failure to consult leading Friends about her visit, on her plan that envisaged a professional career, in the desertion of her suitor when he was most attentive? Angelina would later take stock of her behavior, but by the time this happened it was far too late.

Angelina left a long, detailed record of this journey, infused with the excitement of so sudden a release. The revelation in these pages of the woman she really was, once she had discarded what she thought she ought to be, was extraordinary in the completeness of her transformation. She was a striking young woman, the record says, "tall, graceful, shapely head covered with chestnut ringlets, delicate complexion and features, clear blue eyes, which could dance with merriment or flash with indignation, dignified, gentle, courteous bearing."[39] Nor could demure Quaker garb, much like a nun's habit, conceal her arresting qualities. She commented dryly on their nun-like appearance and the protection it afforded the two young women travelers.

They left on July 4, 1831, traveling by stagecoach and briefly by water. It took them four days to reach their destination, Catherine Beecher's seminary in Hartford, Connecticut. They found themselves guests in Miss Beecher's home and were caught up at once in the purpose of the visit. At nine the next morning Angelina was at the school, remaining until one, then back again at two. Small wonder she remarked on her extreme fatigue. Study and observation became the routine, and her friend "S" sometimes joined her. Miss Beecher, she found, had "very sociable manners, been in our room several times today . . . converses freely and agreeably." Teatime and evenings were spent in conversation, usually in Catherine Beecher's inviting study. Numerous times the comment is found, "Spent evening pleasantly with C. Beecher," or "took a walk with CB after dinner." Angelina discussed her future with Catherine Beecher and was elated when Miss Beecher said that six months would prepare her, provided she concentrated all her powers on her studies.

Twelve scholars boarded in Miss Beecher's school; others came in from the surrounding countryside. As pupils they impressed Angelina: "Very genteel in manners and appearance, under excellent management, house quiet." Angelina wrote approvingly of Miss Beecher's philosophy, how she stressed basic studies that were rarely offered girls, though Miss Beecher thought it folly to require more Latin than was needed as a background for English. She especially emphasized the scholars' duty to be useful; these young women had no right to spend their time in idleness, fashion, and folly; as individuals, they must serve society; especially she encouraged them to go into teaching. Four of her graduates had opened a school in Huntsville, Alabama. Miss Beecher saw teaching as a boon to single women: "As teachers, single women would be more useful in this, than in any other way."

At first Angelina felt self-conscious about her religious difference, aware of the customs that set her apart yet straining to be loyal to the Quaker faith. People showed some curiosity concerning her distinctive dress and the "thee" and "thou" of her special speech, as though they had never seen Friends before. Even in the school she felt conspicuous. The school day was opened with Scripture reading and vocal prayer. It "tried" Angelina to be obliged to remain seated. Catherine Beecher, a Presbyterian, showed some interest in the Quaker beliefs of her guests, but she did not question their custom of remaining seated. Indeed, Angelina felt somewhat deflated: "They have not yet found out why we sit at prayers and grace, no doubt will want us to explain our views." On Sunday, she drove three miles to Friends Meeting, and a sore let-down it was in these exhilarating days. "Two men and one woman plain [Quaker clad] . . . and a few young persons, it was poor indeed."[40]

Angelina soon forgot her distinguishing marks or remembered them only upon occasion, often with wry amusement. For with each passing day, she felt her sense of freedom grow. She no longer strained to seem to like what she disliked and felt free to leave alone the things that bored her. She was mentally alert, intellectually searching, eager for new experiences and seeking them out, nor was she asking herself whether it was wrong for a Quaker or a woman to do these things. She was absorbing not only all the school could offer but every new experience that offered itself.

She asked to visit various institutions—the Hartford Deaf and Dumb Asylum and the Asylum for the Insane. She was driven in an open carriage to Weathersfield State Prison and reported in detail the conditions of the 180 male and 80 female convicts. She saw the prison cells and learned the plan of prison discipline, observed the work rooms where prisoners were employed, and noted how prisoners were controlled in case of threatened insurrection—the keeper was to shoot if the men moved from their work benches. She compared this prison with the Pennsylvania system and with Auburn Prison in New York State, clearly familiar with these two pioneer systems and the dispute that then was raging over their respective merits. She was absorbed for hours in a visit to a factory, a "Wool and Cotton Card manufacturing" concern where ingenious machines employed dog-power, and she was so "surprised and gratified" by her inspection of the place that she put down pages of detail, describing precisely the novel method of manufacture. She inquired and was told that the inventor was a Bostonian named Wittmore and that, although invented thirty years earlier, only recently had the purchasers of the patent learned how to manage the machines properly and make a profit. All this she wrote down with absorbed fascination.

She met new and stimulating people on her journey, a Dr. Comstock of Hartford who knew her brother Thomas—she had brought a letter of introduction to him—and Lydia Sigourney,* with whom they had tea. On the journey home she met old Charleston friends in Northampton, the Napiers, and climbed Mount Holyoke with them; and she discovered the beauty of the Catskills with Robert Habersham, his daughter, and a Dr. Phillips, also friends from Charleston.

On the journey, Angelina poured out her love of nature, something she had rarely done before. Many pages were devoted to delightful expeditions. One was in Hartford, nine miles from the school, to a place called "the Tower" where she enjoyed the charming scenery, the lovely distant views, and the high spirits of the youthful party with her. They left Hartford on July 20; Catherine Beecher was accompanying them as far as New York. Their stage took them through West Springfield and South Hadley Falls, with a first stop in Northampton. It was here she looked out on the Mount Holyoke range at sunset and described it with joy. From western Massachusetts they moved on to the Catskills—the beauty of these mountains filled almost a page. Here she walked to an impressive falls, a drop of nearly two hundred feet. "I was left alone and could enjoy in perfect silence the sublimity of the scene; silence save the rushing noise of the tumbling foaming cataract . . . here I could have sat for a long, long time. . . . I rose and began the toilsome journey up the steep and rugged hill; it is narrow, thought I, just like the way of life, too narrow to admit of help from any human arm. Here is a trial of my individual strength, and I must stand or fall alone."[41]

There were these sober moments. Yet she was still relaxed, savoring every hour of the remaining lovely days. She was greatly amused by a charming young male stranger who attempted by various ruses to make her acquaintance, one of which was to bow and ask for a Quaker cap, explaining solemnly that he had promised one to his sister. "We had many jokes and conjectures about

---

*Lydia Huntley Sigourney (1791-1865) was a poet and author of books for young people. For a while, before her marriage in 1819, she had conducted a girls' school in Norwich and Hartford, Connecticut.

the strange request," "he sent us off in a full laugh"; when the young man persisted, "C & S joined me in a fit of laughter which lasted full five minutes. I dared not look up at all, but shook all over." She enjoyed this cap incident, "trumped up" though it was, as she put it, "to conceal his sauciness."

At last the three women reached New York, "crossed in the steamboat and rode through Brooklyn," and took leave of Catherine Beecher, who was setting out for Boston and carrying with her Angelina's warm assurance that she would soon return to Hartford to prepare for becoming a teacher. After tea, Angelina and her friend strolled to the Battery, "a delightful promenade," Angelina remarked wistfully, knowing that next morning they must take the stage for the long and dreary ride to Philadelphia.

3.

For one glorious month she had shut from her mind the spurious freedom her willful journey gave her. Now she was reentering her former prison house, "My mind is under some exercise," and the conflict that had so plagued her once more filled her days. Should she return to Hartford to prepare for teaching? There was the alternative "of equal importance and solemnity that had previously engaged my serious consideration . . . and does still." To marry young Bettle or to set off on her life's work—"These two concerns seemed to be directly opposite to each other." Why was it so, she kept asking herself, "for it seems as if both could not be right and yet they have successively come before my mind." She could not fail to feel the disapproval all around her. There had been a solemn First Day at Arch Street Meeting when again Samuel Bettle spoke the common mind, this time "to those in a state of insensibility." Angelina knew well of whom he spoke although she had not yet revealed the full extent of her disaffection. Finally she made herself seek out Jane Bettle, the overseer, and told her of her wish to be a teacher. Jane Bettle was cold, she "could not see it at all," it spelled danger to Angelina to be thrown entirely with Presbyterians. In late September Sarah returned to Philadelphia to find Angelina under a cloud.[42]

The tone of her critics appalled Angelina. Meanwhile, young Bettle had not even called, an embarrassing blow that wounded her pride. "It seems that they were all tried at my going away instead of staying at home to receive his visits." Many were saying that she was "fickle." "I am not fickle—my feelings towards him have re-

mained unchanged, even when I thought he treated me with neglect." Caught up as she was in a web of disapproval and in need of
somehow winning back respect, Angelina began to doubt her plan
and to see it through other eyes than her own. She could write, "I
was persuaded by the enemy"; the "enemy" had told her she was
"required to sacrifice him in order to become more useful as a
Teacher." Finally she told herself, "I acknowledge my error." The
problem now arose of how to let the Friends know. She decided
first to tell "dear Jane Bettle" directly that she had abandoned all
prospects of studying to be a teacher. Yet to do this seemed so
"humbling," "equivalent to saying, I am now ready to receive E's
[the son's] visits." Sarah urged her on: "Do it in all simplicity." Instead, Angelina decided she would write, though next morning she
arose at daybreak and destroyed the letter, for it had been "written
under too much natural excitement." In the end, she left it to Sarah
to let them know—Sarah would explain when next she saw Jane
Bettle.[43]

Ostensbily Angelina had abandoned her plan, yet her conduct
was curious if this were so. Throughout that winter she pursued her
studies, rising by lamplight, breakfasting at seven, and settling
down to work assiduously on her books. She was living at Catherine Morris's again, and "dear Catherine" had offered to put a
stove in her chamber, even provide coal, but Angelina refused because she was more "inured to the climate now." Instead, she used
the parlor where a fire always burned: one hour devoted to geome-
try and arithmetic, one to chemistry, one to anatomy, and a period
for the Bible, using heavy commentaries—this was her regimen
every day. After a time history was added, and ever after it remained her favorite. She found herself saying, "Time flies rapidly
instead of hanging heavily as it used to do."[44]

Time flew while her mind was engrossed in her studies, but let
evening approach and she found herself waiting. She had returned
from Hartford in midsummer, and it was late November before
Bettle began to call again. Nor were his visits frequent for several
months: not until April did he come with regularity. Angelina
found this "long dispensation most humbling."[45]

She was not let alone to dwell with her books. Her friends—even
Sarah—looked askance at her studies, fearing they meant she still
clung to her plan. They repeatedly attempted to redirect her energies, searching out activities that Friends could approve. Angelina

became a visitor to Arch Street Prison, a Quaker benevolence all could admire, and she continued to go even when her interest waned. Before she went to Hartford, she had helped establish a new center of private poor relief. Now she returned to her visits to the poor, dealing out tickets that the indigent in turn would present at a depository in exchange for free clothing. Some Quakers feared the plan would pauperize, and she herself thought it might, unless the visitors were careful and wise. Friends tried to involve her in a kindergarten. She was plaintive and candid in her effort to resist: young children, she insisted, held no interest for her. She knew what she longed for—that all her powers should be called forth. Nothing she was doing made real demands on her.[46]

During that winter, a second suitor began to call, "I C" in her journal. While his coming meant a "delicate situation"—he and young Bettle sometimes ran into each other—she let "I C" call regardless of complications, apparently because he was an interesting conversationalist. "I have always loved the society of intelligent men . . . for I often think no one was ever so weak as I am on this point." The problem was compounded, for it now developed that young Bettle was inarticulate or, perhaps, just dull. "I do not understand how we ever are to understand each other fully," she wrote. She tried to believe she was becoming attached to him then would write of her dejection after one of Bettle's visits; "there is never that unreserved spiritual intercourse which I so much desire." Later young Bettle appeared to try. At times she felt he was showing more "candor," even "designedly" expressing his opinions so that she might see the man he really was. As the spring came on and Bettle's visits were more frequent, the greater Angelina's ambivalence grew. Once she went so far as to test out her feelings against what she had known in her first love, shutting herself away with William MacDowell's moving letters, lost in the emotions of that former time.[47]

Angelina's ambivalence was not a superficial conflict. Much lay in the balance, as she herself sensed. Her integrity was involved and her hope of fulfillment. She sought blindly to avoid an avowal by Bettle, sometimes leaving the house when she thought he might come and remaining absent for two or three hours. One dreaded complication she finally faced. Bettle had spells of an acute illness. "A new fear has come over my mind . . . that I have prevented an open avowal . . . before I find out whether his health will be restored or not. O how my soul shrinks from such selfish calculation." She could not accept this image of herself and swept toward the danger with impulsive abandon: "Lord, give him unto me, even if I have to be his nurse all his life."[48]

Angelina was not destined for this grim eventuality. Young Bettle died in late 1832. She was saved from far worse than an invalid husband, as she herself came to know when, after seven months, she sat down with her journal and took stock of herself, unsparing in the bluntness of her self-appraisal.[49]

Samuel and Jane Bettle had rejected Angelina, to the point of refusing to have her call when their son died and other friends came to console. The message they sent to her included these words, "The less the world intermeddled." But the world already had done its intermeddling. When young Bettle died, friends had come to Angelina to bring consolation, assuming her engagement to him, and Angelina had accepted their sympathy. And then his parents had openly rejected this assumption by the overt act of refusing to see her. Angelina, in her pride, met their terms. "How wise," she told the world, "was the path they had chosen."

Oddly and suddenly, she saw it as wisdom. The Bettle son had hardly been placed in his tomb when Angelina was aware of profound relief. She felt some grief but no despair; on the contrary, "a heavy load rolled off my heart, a dark cloud rolled back from my soul." "If," she mused, "I had been received as a daughter, I should have given up everything to be with them." A prisoner of the strict and rigid Bettle clan—this was the fate the Bettles had saved her from.

Perceiving this much let her acknowledge old "temptations." In the months that followed, she probed her thoughts—a ruthless, honest effort to know her whole self. She admitted to her ambivalence when young Bettle had come wooing. "In this connection," she told herself, "I should have found piety, talents, influence, amiability and wealth." "The cup of prosperity" was almost in her grasp, and she said she had found it "an intoxicating draught." Angelina had felt required to reject her own high station, resting as it did on the mudsill of slavery. And in adopting Quakerism, she had supposed that she was turning her back on luxury and wealth, so much so that she had condemned her love of these to her mother. She had arrived in Philadelphia to find she was mistaken: austerity of a kind, but wealth and comfort too, and an undisguised acceptance of position and power—all these in the family of the man who sought her hand. Here indeed she had experienced a subtle undermining: she might retain her Quaker principles while enjoying means and status. For the first time, Angelina revealed an old conflict that must often have assailed her when she felt she must leave home. It had not been simple then, as she had made herself think, to relinquish the ease, the luxuries, the position of a daughter of the wealthy slaveholding Grimké family. And now she had almost been entrapped again. She could not see the ludicrous in her bizarre experience, but she did perceive the irony in the means of her release: an unwitting gift from Jane and Samuel Bettle, who had not the slightest notion of setting Angelina free.

The Bettles little guessed what they had accomplished, nor did Sarah dream of the part she had played when she lent herself to what the Bettles had required. Since her first encounter with it, Angelina had been nagged by the passive nature of Orthodox Quakerism. Time and again she had voiced her rebellion at Sarah's stern injunction to "be still," to "wait." She exclaimed in her diary, "The activity of nature finds it very hard to wait"; "I am tired beyond what I am able to bear with patience and resignation . . . the struggles of my rebellious soul." Patience and resignation were behind her now, an exhilarating thought in the days that lay ahead.

4.

There were signs that Angelina sensed the antislavery ferment even in those months of her personal upheaval. All the more would this be true in the early 1830s and in the Philadelphia of those stirring years, one focal center of rising abolitionism. She might note few events as they came to pass, but a day would come when she realized how they had moved her, how the rising violence in them increasingly disturbed her and insistently battered against her conscious mind.

No man was more attacked than William Lloyd Garrison, even at this time when his career had just begun. In 1829 when Angelina settled in Philadelphia, Garrison, just her age, lived in nearby Baltimore, an "incendiary" young man in the eyes of that slave city, who, in public print, was proclaiming his demand for "immediate and complete emancipation." He was frequently threatened and in the end jailed, a flagrant injustice, abolitionists said. When he left Baltimore, he spoke in Philadelphia.[50] Angelina did not hear him, though she may have read of him; the *Inquirer* gave a graphic account. Garrison founded the *Liberator* in 1831. Angelina did not become a reader for another three years, nor would she know Garrison until 1835; yet she would soon know those who in turn knew him, and he was not overlooked by an alarmed public press, so that what was happening to him drew ever closer until she became aware of his disturbing presence.

Some events more than others had the power to stir her. The Nat Turner revolt occurred in 1831. Only ten years before, Denmark Vesey and his fellows had threatened bloody rebellion in her own city. Now Sarah was in Charleston, still visiting their mother. Angelina's agitation was clearly apparent, as suddenly her letters showed the urgency she felt and she pleaded with Sarah to hasten her return.[51]

Hardly were Nat Turner and his fellow slaves hanged—a few months at most—than the Virginia legislators were plunged into debates concerning gradual emancipation. Angelina was reassured by these debates and by the fact that some Virginia newspapers could, out of new-felt fears, call slavery a "curse," a "heaviest calamity," an "unmitigated evil."[52] She wrote her brother Thomas in wistful tones, asking whether he thought emancipation could come by peaceful means, with enlightened slaveholders beginning to take steps to end this dreadful evil.[53]

The Prudence Crandall case left no room for illusions. For Angelina, it came at a critical time—the months of 1833-34, when she was consciously groping toward abolitionism.[54] Prudence Crandall, herself a Quaker, had become a teacher and had established a school for girls in a pleasant Connecticut town. Leading local citizens had urged her to come and had helped her buy a property in which to house her school. But then a Negro farmer's daughter asked to be admitted. The girl was fully qualified, so Miss Crandall would not refuse, despite the bitter opposition of her white mentors. When white pupils were withdrawn by her angry patrons, she opened her boarding school to Negro girls; sixteen soon arrived from all around New England. Violence was heaped immediately on Prudence Crandall, the attacks instigated by prominent local white men. Abolitionist leaders began to take her part, though they were at a distance and her attackers were at hand. Miss Crandall and her pupils were insulted on village streets, the well they used for water was filled with filth, refuse was heaped on the school's front porch, and local merchants refused to sell the school supplies. A court case was brought against her and dragged on for months. Meanwhile, the abolitionist Samuel May had come to aid her. When finally the house was set on fire, May and his friends managed to save it, but then a mob came in the night armed with clubs and iron bars, smashing doors and windows while the pupils quailed inside. With this, it was decided, they could stand no more. The pupils were sent home, and Miss Crandall closed the school. Here then was a lesson Angelina could not miss: even women were not spared violence if they spoke out for the oppressed, not even in the North, so nowhere was safe.

Angelina was now reading abolitionist papers; they were in her hands by early 1834. Antislavery publications were rapidly increasing in number. The American Anti-Slavery Society had just been formed at a convention in Philadelphia in December 1833, an historic meeting for the nation and the slave, and for Angelina, though at the time she took no note.[55] She could not have dreamed, though she did dream of the future, that within four years she herself would be a woman leader in this movement, more notorious than any other woman abolitionist. It is certain that she was reading abolitionist papers in 1834, because in that late summer, her brother Thomas Grimké came north to lecture and stopped to see his sisters in Philadelphia. Angelina later told of their long, serious talks, as they debated slavery back and forth, and how Thomas, though a slaveholder, had showed deep concern, asking Angelina to send him all the writings she could assemble that presented fact and argument against human slavery.[56] The request was one she was never to fulfill, for Thomas contracted cholera while lecturing in Ohio and died within a week. Angelina, by then, was reading the *Liberator* regularly and perhaps the *Emancipator*, the new offical organ of the Anti-Slavery Society, and books and tracts that opposed the system and argued the case for "immediate emancipation." More and more what she read told of mob attacks and urged abolitionists to respond by peaceful means.

In 1834 she first heard the name Weld: Theodore Weld, the "most mobbed man" in the movement, as he would be termed within a year or two when he had begun his great western crusade.[57] In 1834 he burst suddenly into view, welcomed by abolitionists, anathema to opponents. This was the year of the Lane Seminary "rebellion" and the students' "great debate" that was led by Weld:

how to banish slavery—by "colonization" (the gradualist plan to send freed slaves to Africa), or by "immediate emancipation"? In the end, "immediate emancipation" won, a student antislavery society was formed, Weld at the forefront; it was Weld's tenet, which his followers accepted, first to discuss, then to "act"; and these students of the ministry announced their intention to launch a fervent effort for the abolition of slavery. A confrontation followed the students' action against the Lane authorities; president, trustees, and even some of the faculty took sides against them. The trustees seized the helm, issuing peremptory "Rules" and "Orders," banning an antislavery society at Lane, with dismissal the punishment for any student who joined.[58] All this was publicized in Ohio papers; and the antislavery papers spread the story on their pages. In late 1834 a mass of students withdrew from Lane, insisting on continuing their abolitionist labors. Some entered Oberlin College to continue their studies. Many, led by Weld, became full-time crusaders and, in time, notable figures in the abolitionist movement. But in 1834 most were still little known except for Weld who was then in his early thirties. His incomparable powers as a reform leader were increasingly remarked in the West and East, as he began his sweep through the mid-western states—the crowds he drew, the mobs that attacked him, the multiplying numbers pouring into the movement—until his name became a by-word in antislavery circles. At a later time, Angelina told Weld of how his words and deeds had so greatly thrilled her that just to hear his name was to feel herself moved.[59]

Violence was increasing throughout 1834, with abolitionists and free Negroes the butt of attacks. Reports reached Philadelphia of rioting in New York, although New York City papers claimed there were no "real" riots, because the victims of the rioters did not counterattack. Philadelphia papers quoted the New York press: "The objects of the mob were, it was said (but of course on such occasions there is much rumor and exaggeration), the African churches and schools, some other churches, and the houses of Arthur Tappan and others [white abolitionists]." Further reports told of Negroes being injured, Negro stores looted, Negro families set upon. The situtation was made more critical by falsified handbills designed to inflame the public against antislavery men and women.[60] The *Liberator's* pages noted widespread attacks in New England, New York State, and in the West. Angelina no longer blinked who the sufferers were and why they were victimized by ugly mobs.[61]

In late 1834 George Thompson arrived from England, a fiery abolitionist, an "incendiary" foreigner. Thompson came to Philadelphia March 3, 1835. Angelina was not uncertain as to what she would do, so it was not for this reason that she felt mental stress. Her decision was made when the notice reached her hands, as though it was the moment she had known would come. She had guessed that Catherine Morris would coldly disapprove, and it truly hurt her pride to remain in Catherine's household, but Sarah's harsh rejection was a painful surprise—Sarah did not wish her to attend the Thompson meeting.[62]

Angelina knew the violence George Thompson had aroused, the mobs that had met him since his arrival—in Maine and New Hampshire, in Massachusetts, in New York—threatening crowds that gathered outside his halls, missiles hurled, even into female meetings, and disturbers upon occasion forcing him to leave town. Sarah knew some of this and so did Catherine Morris, though not from the pages of Angelina's *Liberator*—neither of them would touch the sheet of the odious Garrison. They believed what they read in the "pro-slavery" papers—Angelina was now using abolitionist terms—papers that dubbed Thompson "incendiary British 'missionary,' " "apostle of fanaticism," "Foreign Fanatic," "hired by the immediate abolitionists" to preach "social equality and physical amalgamation," a man who deliberately "courted mob action."[63] What so moved Angelina was Thompson's nonviolence, which he held to on principle, regardless of abuse, and his refusal to compromise or temper his doctrine of full and immediate emancipation of slaves. And no doubt descriptions of the man drew her strongly: brilliant and young (only thirty, just her age), tall, graceful, of a "fine attractive countenance," an orator, Garrison wrote, whose appeals "electrified."[64]

No announcement had appeared in the local papers, a deliberate omission as Angelina came to learn, lest mobs be incited to molest the peaceful gathering. The male antislavery society had passed the word, by pen and verbal notice, that George Thompson of England, noted abolitionist, on the evening of March 3, would lecture in the Reformed Presbyterian Church on Cherry Street. Arnold Buffum, who arranged it, was amazed at the outpouring—no less than a thousand people filled the place.[65] There were Quakers and non-Quakers, Negro and white, and, surprising to some, many women were in the audience. Angelina was present, as she knew she must be.

If Sarah had been fearful of the Thompson meeting, she was reassured when no violence occurred and could write without distress of Angelina's experience, though in the same letter she spoke favorably of colonization.[66] Angelina had become an avid reader of the *Liberator* and had begun to mingle with local women abolitionists. That spring of 1835 Sarah could write of Angelina to Sarah Douglass, a prominent Negro educator in Philadelphia, who by this time had become a warm friend of both sisters: "Her mind is deeply engaged in the cause of immediate unconditional emancipation. I believe she does often pray for it."[67]

That Angelina was wrestling with a difficult decision is seen in a strange letter she wrote that spring, although mention of this letter cannot be found in any of her papers that remain. The letter is known only because the answer has been preserved and can be read as Angelina read it then. Among the small company of Friends in Charleston, there was one who had remained her friend, and it was to this man that she addressed her letter.[68] The reply was unsigned, deliberately so. Her request was filled with danger for the man to whom she had written. As he himself said, "Should [this letter] by accident fall into the hands of a Carolinian, it might produce strong prejudice against me. It is my misfortune to be obliged to reside here." Angelina was inconsiderate only when her need was urgent.

"Respected Friend," the man's letter began. "[I was unable] to attend thy humane request till this morning. I visited the Work House (or as it is more generally called Sugar House) this morning.

"I arrived just in season to hear the stripes that were applied to the last of the number who were whipped. I shall hardly be able to answer *all* thy questions, but hope to most of them. . . ."

She read on,

". . . As it was thy wish that I should be particular in describing the mode and instruments of punishment. . . ."

And further,

"I examined the room for whipping, and could have seen the punishment inflicted but my feelings revolted. . . ."

On the second page,

"Thou wished to be informed for what faults they may be punished either by whipping, Treadmill or otherwise, and whether they are naked when whipped. The offense is anything whatever that the master or owner may choose to have them punished for, whether imaginary or real, for if a man bring a slave to be punished, I never could learn that the question is asked whether they deserve what they are to suffer or not, so that it makes the power of the owner entirely absolute."

No evidence can be found that Angelina mentioned this letter in her writings, in her speeches, or that she quoted even obliquely from its stark contents, although in her work for the antislavery cause, her most telling weapon was her firsthand knowledge, and she spoke of the work house many times. She may have been mindful of protecting the writer, yet she was ingenious and could have found a way. It seems almost certain that in seeking this knowledge, once she had set herself free to seek it, she was doing so for herself alone, not so much to know facts, as to confront a shadowy dread that had long stood between her and her peace of mind.

She had let five months pass without writing in her journal, until on May 12, 1835, her entry began, "I have become deeply interested in the subject of Abolition." Only now did she reveal what she had been through—the doubts, the questioning, the uneasiness of her days, and that there had been a mental struggle, subtle and prolonged, as she had listened to abolitionists, and read what they wrote, and yet had remained skeptical or afraid of their doctrine, so that freedom for the slave at times seemed "hopeless." All the while she had been torn by a deep personal guilt at the continuing "horrible traffic in human beings," "those degraded, oppressed & suffering fellow creatures," and she sitting still, lifting not a hand. She even put down a certain fear she had felt, that prison, even death, might be her portion if and when she cast her lot with the despised abolitionists. She was afraid that God might "require" her to go back to Carolina and preach abolition there; and suppose, when danger threatened, she were to be like Peter, "who was frightened into a triple denial of his Master"? In the end, the "Power of Truth" had conquered all her fears—by May she was able to record it in her journal—and the principles of abolition, as she had come to know them, had taken strong root in her own beliefs.[69]

So at last she was ready for her crucial decision. Philadelphia had a Female Anti-Slavery Society. To join this group would mean a virtual break, for not alone would Angelina be joining with non-

Friends, but, perhaps even worse, with Hicksite Quakers, some of whom were prominent abolitionists in Philadelphia. Chief among the latter was Lucretia Mott, a Hicksite minister and a leader among the women. Angelina refused to consult Arch Street Friends as she made her decision. When Sarah sternly reproached her for flouting her clear duty, Angelina had but one answer: it would be sheer deceit to seek their permission, since she had made her decision and could not change.[70] By late spring she was an avowed abolitionist, openly committed to "immediate emancipation."

III. Let It Come

"If persecution is the means which God has ordained for the accomplishment of this great end, EMANCIPATION; then . . . I feel as if I could say, LET IT COME; for it is my deep, solemn, deliberate conviction, that *this is a cause worth dying for*."

ANGELINA GRIMKÉ *to William Lloyd Garrison, in her historic letter of August 30, 1835.*

1.

Throughout that summer Angelina's tensions mounted, as she moved towards a turning dimly seen ahead. She could still be shaken when her "wisest and best friends" insisted it was damaging for her to join those of other faiths, no matter how worthy the cause might appear. It forced her to deal directly with their charge, and she admitted they were right; her ties to the Society of Friends had been weakened by her new associations. But if the Orthodox Friends she knew took no part in abolitionism, the "great moral Reformation of the day," would it not be right for her to leave the Friends and do her duty where God called her? Small wonder she was finding Friends Meeting "dull and lifeless." She could not repress her impulse for vehement debate—slavery was "so exciting a subject." She deplored her turbulence and impatience with her op-

78

ponents, reproaching herself for her "unsubdued will," her "violent opposition because they could not think as she did." "I never felt my temper harder to control." She could say she ought to shun "everything like argument," only to find herself caught up in it again.[1]

July was filled with disturbing events. Right at hand in Philadelphia, in mid-month, a ferocious anti-Negro riot had raged. She could almost hear the sounds and see the flames. Allegedly a Negro worker had struck his white employer, and for two solid days whites rioted against blacks, to the terror and despair of the large black community.[2] By this time Angelina numbered Negroes among her friends, not only Sarah Douglass and her mother and sister, but the prominent Forten family and other Negro men and women who were active abolitionists. Anxiety for these friends brought a greater shame and horror at the white mob's actions.

The *Liberator* was unsparing in its tales of persecution. Week by week the sense of pressure grew, until Angelina's thoughts were focused on this crisis and on slavery, the pervasive and corrupting force. She was appalled by the callousness of many northern Christian leaders in their shunning of the abolitionists. The *Liberator* was scathing in its denunciations: a Presbyterian General Assembly, meeting in Pittsburgh, effectively shutting out many antislavery petitions by sending them to a committee composed largely of southern men; the Baptist General Tract Society of Philadelphia instructing its agents to avoid the slavery issue; New Hampshire Methodist bishops, in a pastoral letter, insisting that Methodist pulpits be denied to abolitionists, whether or not they were ministers in the church. Some clergymen proclaimed that the laws must be obeyed "even if God's commandments [against slavery] were violated"—these words were attributed to a Boston minister. In Boston that May an antislavery convention, when refused Faneuil Hall, had been shut out of seven churches. In Philadelphia antislavery meeting places were so few that a movement was begun to build an antislavery hall, forever dedicated to freedom of speech. Pennsylvania Hall it was called when it opened, an historic hall for Angelina Grimké.[3]

Theodore Weld was at the height of his crusade in Ohio and Pennsylvania, as were also the mob attacks. He knew a mob would gather in nearly every town he entered, as it would for almost any outspoken abolitionist. Thus, when, with Henry Stanton who was another "Lane rebel," he set out to recruit and train other men as agents, he not only trained them in how to argue, persuade, and win new adherents to abolitionism, but he also taught them how to deal with mobs. Perhaps few of these men had the audacity of Weld, the spirit that simply felt no fear, the drive, the sense of high mission, and the unusual gifts. Some of all this Angelina surely sensed as she read the sparse accounts of Weld's triumphs in the West, for even then Weld refused to permit his deeds to be exploited, despite importunings by the antislavery press. One phrase of Weld's that Angelina had seen in print stood her in good stead in the coming weeks—"this is a cause worth dying for." Who better than Weld knew what it meant—a man whose life was threatened frequently by mobs.

Persecution failed to dampen antislavery ardor; on the contrary, it seemed to stimulate the movement. This was the summer when a fund was raised to spread tracts and broadsides throughout the land—thirty thousand dollars, a substantial sum. The *Emancipator* was published regularly now, and three new monthlies began to appear.

Southerners in the North began to take drastic action. Abolitionists, among themselves, expressed great alarm. New York City became a focal point of virulent southern sentiment. In August a large public meeting was planned, with seven thousand southern white men converging on the city—this was the word passed among abolitionists— a meeting called to protest the "alarming agitation" with its doctrine of "immediate and unconditional emancipation of slaves." "Northerners interfering in the South" was the cry. Lydia Maria Child, a prominent abolitionist, wrote a friend that she would not venture out on New York streets because of the great antiabolitonist furore. Known abolitionists even stayed away from church. "Five thousand dollars was offered on the Exchange . . . for the head of Arthur Tappan." Elizur Wright, of the American Anti-Slavery Society national office, was "barricaded in his house with shutters, bars and bolts." It was rumored that assassins had been imported from New Orleans, and large sums of money were being offered for the kidnapping and transporting of George Thompson to the South. Thompson had been hidden away, "a close prisoner in his chamber," until he could be spirited out of town to Boston. The journey to Boston was then filled with alarms: he was hurried through New Haven because it was filled with southerners attending the Yale commencement and also through Hartford, where colored churches had been burned and where threats against Garrison and the Tappans were rife. Thompson reached Boston safely but was hidden away again until he could leave the country—nowhere here was safe. When a ship sailed for England, Thompson was aboard. Garrison, who had been in Canada on family business, returned in early August to find the North ablaze. He and Samuel May, both well-known by sight, were kept off the streets at night by their anxious friends, and even in the daylight hours they were not considered safe.

On August 15 the *Liberator* appeared, a Garrison headline splashed across the page: "REIGN OF TERROR" against abolitionists. "All Pandemonium is let loose. . . . Rapine and Murder have overcome Liberty and Law, and are rioting in violent and bloody excess —all is consternation and perplexity, for perilous times have come." He poured out the meaning of the alarming events, the attacks on abolitionists, and their continuing peril. "And what has brought our country to the verge of ruin, and substituted anarchy for order, rebellion for obedience, jacobinism for religion, and blood-guiltiness for innocence? THE ACCURSED SYSTEM OF SLAVERY!" He denied flatly the guilt of abolitionists: "These allegations are diabolically false." They had never sent a pamphlet or paper to any slave; they had never in any document advocated the right of the oppressed to rebel; they had never said that Congress was empowered to legislate on the subject of slavery in slaveholding states; nor had they ever returned evil for evil. All they had ever done was say that slavery was contrary to the Declaration of Independence, a sin against God, and should be "immediately repented of and forsaken." "Finally . . . we tell the South that we regard its threats and warnings with supreme contempt and utter scorn; that our course is still onward, right onward."[4]

Southern papers called on the North to "suppress the abolitionists," and in Boston the *Morning Post* and *Boston Atlas* were demanding public meetings to "put down the abolitionists." Leading citizens were swift to respond to the call. On August 21, Faneuil Hall was the scene of a strident mass meeting against abolitionism. The mayor of Boston was the presiding dignitary, influential Abbot Lawrence a vice-chairman of the gathering. Particular abolitionists were scathingly denounced: George Thompson, "a professed agitator" who hailed from the "dark and corrupt institutions of Europe"; Garrison, the prime agitator of them all. A ringing indictment went out from the meeting to arouse the countryside against all abolitionists. Garrison deemed it wise to go into seclusion to a small rural cottage outside of Boston. Not that his work suffered real interruption; articles for the *Liberator* kept pouring from his pen.[5]

Angelina was alone when she confronted her decision, alone in that Sarah was away on a mission. Sarah was disturbed by conditions among the Friends, for the Society was torn by internal dissensions. She felt that as a minister she should try to mediate and was at this time visiting various meetings in Pennsylvania and New Jersey with depressing results. "There will be great trials yet," she wrote mournfully, "they are not at an end . . . siftings and resistings, rendings and rerendings, until it [the society] is purged and purified."[6] Absorbed as she was, Sarah's perceptions were so blunted that she was virtually unaware of Angelina's state of mind.

For some weeks Angelina had known she must act. Finally a day came when she decided to put aside all material that bore on abolition, whatever it might be; when the *Liberator* came, she shut it out of sight; and she remained aloof from abolitionist friends.[7] This was not to close her eyes to the dangers of the times but to confront them directly and in full comprehension; to do this she believed that she must gain calm of mind and quietness of spirit. She wished to feel assured that she was not ruled by mere feeling. It was the third week in August when she felt herself ready. The *Liberator* of August 21 had just arrived, with Garrison's "Appeal" prominently displayed, with the headline "Forbearance of Abolitionists."[8] "Utterly deprived of that protection and of those immunities which belong to them as citizens, and given up to be the prey of ruffians and assassins. . . . How have the abolitionists behaved under all these provocations? . . . Have they, in a single instance, returned evil for evil? . . . given blow for blow? . . . " She came to the part so crucial to herself: "We appeal to the world. . . . What other body of men, whether political or religious, besides abolitionists, would suffer themselves to be insulted and outraged, and their meetings forcibly suppressed or systematically interrupted by their opponents, without making a prompt and violent appeal to the *lex talionis*? Thanks be to God that the abolitionists are generally men of peace. The spirit of non-resistance and of forgiveness is omnipotent." Then what she had feared had not come to pass, and abolitionists stood firm against any form of violence.

Immediately Angelina knew what she must do: she must voice her commitment, unequivocally and at once, and address it to the man who had written the "Appeal."[9] It is true she put aside her pen several times and spent sleepless nights counting all it might cost, and when the letter was completed, she held it from the post, imploring her God to tell her that she was doing right. For though she might not comprehend the full price she would pay, she was not unaware of a good measure of the cost: the cost as a daughter of her slaveowning mother, whom she knew she would wound beyond her power to heal; the cost as a sincere and respected Friend, who would be ostracized, perhaps disowned, because she was refusing to abide by the Friends' discipline; the cost as a woman, for deep in her heart she knew that the glaring restrictions that were placed on her sex stood between her and the work she felt called to; the cost as a sister, for on this occasion Angelina knew she was deliberately excluding Sarah from this most crucial and far-reaching act and, by doing so, was severing those bonds that had held her back from finding her own course.

When Angelina began to write, she told herself she did it to "relieve her mind," and perhaps her God would not require her to send it. Yet no spirit of uncertainty pervaded her thoughts in the hour in which the letter finally poured from her pen. She dated it "8th month, 30th, 1835." And she knew she would send it when she reread the lines that declared her full commitment—and that there would be no turning back. For she was now convinced that freedom could be accomplished without the dreadful violence of a bloody slave rebellion, provided abolitionists themselves remained nonviolent, even accepting persecution as the means to their great end.

> My mind has been especially turned toward those, who are standing in the forefront of the battle; and the prayer has gone up for *their* preservation—not the preservation of their lives, but the preservation of their minds in humility and patience, faith, hope, and *charity*. . . . If persecution is the means which God has ordained for the accomplishment of this great end, EMANCIPATION: then, in dependence *upon Him* for strength to bear it, I feel as if I could say, LET IT COME: for it is my deep, solemn, deliberate conviction, that *this is a cause worth dying for*. I say so, from what I have seen, and heard, and known, in a land of slavery. . . . Yes! LET IT COME—let *us* suffer, rather than that insurrection should arise.

The days went by and Angelina heard nothing. She wondered if

SLAVERY

AND

THE BOSTON RIOT.

The following letter was written, shortly after the Pro-Slavery Riot in Boston, by ANGELINA E. GRIMKE to WILLIAM LLOYD GARRISON. The writer is a native of Charleston, South Carolina, where she was educated, and has resided, till recently. This fact gives importance to her opinions on the subject of Slavery, as she has had an opportunity to be acquainted with it in all its bearings. The truly Christian spirit, which breathes in every line of the letter, cannot fail to commend it to the favorable notice, especially, of all Christian professors.

PHILADELPHIA, 8th month, 30th, 1835.

Respected Friend :

It seems as if I was compelled at this time to address thee, notwithstanding all my reasonings against intruding on thy valuable time, and the uselessness of so insignificant a person as myself offering thee the sentiments of sympathy at this alarming crisis.

I can hardly express to thee the deep and solemn interest with which I have viewed the violent proceedings of the last few weeks. Although I expected opposition, yet I was not prepared for it so soon—it took me by surprise, and I greatly feared Abolitionists would be driven back in the first onset, and thrown into confusion. So fearful was I, that though I clung with unflinching firmness to our *principles,* yet I was afraid of even opening one of thy papers, lest I should see some indications of compromise, some surrender, some palliation. Under these feelings, I was urged to read thy Appeal to the citizens of Boston. Judge, then, what were my feelings, on finding that my fears were utterly groundless, and that thou stoodest firm in the midst of the storm, determined to suffer and to die, rather than yield one inch. My heart was filled with thanksgiving and praise to the Preserver of men ; I thanked God, and took courage, earnestly desiring that thousands may adopt thy language, and be *prepared* to meet the Martyr's doom, rather than give up the principles you (i. e. Abolitionists) have adopted. The ground upon which you stand is holy ground : never—never surrender it. If you surrender it, the hope of the slave is extinguished, and the chains of his servitude will be strengthened a hundred fold. But let no man take your crown, and success is as certain as the rising of to-morrow's sun. But remember you must be willing to suffer the loss of all things—willing to be the scorn and reproach of *professor* and profane. You must obey our great Master's injunction : " Fear *not* them that kill the body, and after that, have nothing more that they can do." You must, like Apostles, " count *not* your lives dear unto yourselves, so that you may finish your course with joy."

Religious persecution always begins with *mobs :* it is always unprecedented in the age or country in which it *commences,* and therefore there are *no laws,* by which Reformers can be punished ; consequently, a lawless band of unprincipled men determine to take the matter into their hands, and act out in *mobs,* what they know are the *principles* of a large majority of those who are too high in *Church* and State to *condescend* to mingle with them, though they *secretly* approve and rejoice over their violent measures. The first martyr who ever died, was stoned by a *lawless mob ;* and if we look at the rise of various sects— Methodists, Friends, &c.—we shall find that *mobs began* the persecution against them, and that it was not until *after* the people had thus spoken out their wishes, that laws were framed to fine, imprison, or destroy them. Let us, then, be prepared for the enactment of laws even in our *Free* States, against Abolitionists. And how ardently has the prayer been breathed, that God would prepare us for *all* he is preparing for us; that he would strengthen us in the hour of conflict, and cover our heads (if consistent with his holy will) in the day of battle ! But O ! how earnestly have I desired, *not* that we may escape suffering, but that we may be willing to endure unto the end. If we call upon the slave-holder to suffer the loss of what he calls property, then let us show him we make this demand from a deep sense of duty, by being ourselves willing to suffer the loss of character, property—yea, and life itself, in what we believe to be the cause of bleeding humanity.

My mind has been especially turned towards those, who are standing in the fore front of the battle ; and the prayer has gone up for *their* preservation—not the preservation of their lives, but the preservation of their minds in humility and patience, faith, hope, and *charity*—that charity which is the bond of perfectness. If persecution is the means which God has ordained for the accomplishment of this great end, EMANCIPATION ; then, in dependence *upon Him* for strength to bear it, I feel as if I could say, LET IT COME ; for it is my deep, solemn, deliberate conviction, that *this is a cause worth dying for.* I say so, from what I have seen, and heard, and known, in a land of slavery, where rests the darkness of Egypt, and where is found the sin of Sodom. Yes ! LET IT COME—let *us* suffer, rather than insurrections should arise.

At one time, I thought this system would be overthrown in blood, with the confused noise of the warrior ; but a hope gleams across my mind, that *our* blood will be spilt, instead of the slaveholders' ; *our* lives will be taken, and theirs spared—I say a *hope,* for all things I desire to be spared the anguish of seeing our beloved country desolated with the horrors of a servile war. If persecution can abolish slavery, it will also purify the Church ; and who that stands between the porch and altar, weeping over the sins of the people, will not be willing to suffer, if such immense good will be accomplished. Let us endeavor, then, to put on the *whole* armor of God, and, having done all, to stand ready for whatever is before us.

I have just heard of Dresser's being flogged : it is no surprise at all ; but the language of our Lord has been sweetly revived— " Blessed are ye when men shall revile you, and persecute you, and say all manner of evil against you *falsely,* for my sake. Rejoice, and be exceeding glad, for great is your reward in heaven." O ! for a willingness and strength to suffer ! But we shall have false brethren now, just as the Apostles had, and this will be one of our greatest griefs.

A. E. GRIMKE.

her letter had been cast aside—and felt some shame at her growing relief. Thus three weeks had passed when Catherine Morris came to tell her that James Bettle was in the parlor, a surprising circumstance, for since the time of young Bettle's death, Angelina had continued to maintain her distance. Sarah again was absent from the city, so Angelina confronted Friend Bettle alone.

She saw a copy of the *Liberator* in Bettle's hand, an odd thing in itself, in view of how he scorned it. Angelina's own copy had not yet arrived. Bettle's face became livid, and he was trembling in his rage as he placed the open paper in Angelina's hands. There, spread across its columns, was her letter to Garrison, every single word, she could see it at a glance, and her name was signed to it. It was headed with lines of fulsome praise for "Miss Grimké," and it linked her with her brother the "distinguished Thomas Grimké."[10] Angelina felt hot blood suffuse her face.

If William Lloyd Garrison had been a different type of man, Angelina's letter might never have appeared or, if it had, with a pseudonym appended, a common practice in her day. But Garrison was an astute propagandist always, and when he saw the rare prize that had fallen from the blue, his excitement could hardly be contained. It is true, he had consulted various friends—Angelina learned this at a later time—in the way a Garrison would consult.[11] "Miss Grimké did not *say* I could publish the letter"—this was the gist of what he said—"but is it not my bounden duty to the cause?" Angelina later admitted that she had thought it might be published and felt she had no right to forbid it, but "I had no idea, if it was, that my name would be attached to it." Yet could a Garrison renounce the impact of a Grimké-signed letter when the writer was the daughter of a slaveholding Charleston family? Thus, without a by-your-leave, he published the letter, writing the introduction that Bettle now pointed to.

When Bettle found words, he was bitter and harsh. He upbraided Angelina for Garrison's words: the bare mention of her brother's name was a disgrace when coupled with hers in the odious Garrison's paper; he pronounced Garrison's lines the "ravings of a fanatic." He called on Angelina to denounce the letter; if she would not denounce it, then change portions of it; write Garrison at once, in effect, recant.

She maintained her composure during the confrontation with Bettle, heard him to the end, and the end was long in coming. When her turn came, she refused his demand, and her tones, though quiet, were distant and cold. She declined to write to William Lloyd Garrison or to change any part of what she had said. She felt willing to bear any suffering, she told him, if only it was made an instrument of good. She felt her great unworthiness in being used in such a work (the high-held head belied her words), but she remembered that God chose the weak of this world wherewith to confound the wise. She would continue, she told him, on her present course; her principles required it, so she had no choice.[12]

Her pride hid her shock while Bettle stood before her. Once he was gone, her world fell apart. She was utterly miserable. She believed her character was altogether gone "among her dearest, most valued friends." "I was indeed brought to the brink of despair." And she felt humiliated. "Oh! the extreme pain of extravagant praise!" And to be "held up as a saint in a public newspaper, before thousands of people. . . . Blushing and confusion of face were mine, and I thought the walls of a prison would have been preferable to such an exposure." Bettle had known intuitively how to strike a vital blow when he condemned her for Garrison's mention of her beloved brother's name. "To have my name, not so much my name, as the name of Grimké, associated with that of the despised Garrison, seemed like bringing disgrace upon my *family*, not myself alone. I felt as though the name had been tarnished in the eyes of thousands who had before loved and revered it. I cannot describe the anguish of my soul."[13]

Was it strange anguish for a convinced abolitionist to be irrationally disturbed by "disgrace" to the family name? And it would spell disgrace to all her kinspeople, even to Sarah, as Angelina quickly learned. Sarah was no longer called "mother" by Angelina, for their Quaker mentors had forbidden the term; but Sarah remained the closest and dearest person to her, and Sarah had turned on Angelina with every weapon she possessed. "She thinks I have been given over to blindness of mind . . . that I do not know light from darkness, right from wrong . . . that I cannot see it was wrong ever to have written the letter at all . . . she seems to think I deserve all the suffering I have brought on myself."[14] As yet Sarah had not given any ground, as her journal showed—"how dangerous . . . to slight the clear convictions of truth," "she listened to the voice of the tempter."[15]

It was as though a year were lost in Angelina's reckoning, as the months went by and she could see no light ahead, no opening since her letter to William Lloyd Garrison, no sign to show what more she could do. At first there was the coldness, the complete isolation, except for Jane Smith, a friend in Philadelphia. She had known Jane Smith, also a Quaker, most of the years since she had come to the city. After she had begun her public activity in 1836, it was to Jane she wrote, letters filled with thoughts and experiences in her anti-slavery work. At this critical time during 1835-36, only Jane, among her friends, was supporting Angelina.[16] Angelina had no home, no place to live, except with Catherine Morris or with her sister, Anna Frost, and frigid disapproval was her daily bread with either. Once she wrote Jane Smith, pointing out her homeless state and pleading to be a boarder in the Smith home, but Jane's mother was an invalid and Jane served as her nurse, though Angelina, on occasion, stayed with Jane. Now through Sarah's efforts Angelina left the city and remained away many months of that year, first with friends of Sarah's in Burlington, New Jersey, then with other friends, Margaret and James Parker in Shrewsbury, New Jersey. Sarah appeared anxious to have Angelina away.

In some sense the year was a contest with Sarah. Angelina soon sensed one of Sarah's aims—that Sarah still hoped her sister would recant—and Angelina proceeded to deal with this issue directly. Within a month of her letter to William Lloyd Garrison, Angelina was writing to Sarah,[17] "My Beloved Sister." She wrote, she declared, "in all the tenderness of a sister's love," though her words were blunt as they had never been before. She told Sarah she felt "utterly condemned by the standard" her sister had set up by which to judge her, "namely, the opinion of her friends," which her sister seemed to feel was "an infallible criterion." She was willing, she said, to be condemned by others "without a hearing," but she expected more of her sister. Even so she felt she owed "a duty of vindication," although she felt no hope that her sister would acquit her. "Thou has been with me in heights and in depths, in joy and in sorrow. . . . Thou knowest what I have passed through on the subject of slavery; thou knowest I am an exile from the home of my birth because of slavery, therefore, to thee I speak." Angelina then related at considerable length how she had come to write to Garrison and how for days she had struggled and prayed to know if it was right. Once the letter was published, her sister knew what had followed and knew her anguished misery at the storm she had raised. But recently, she told Sarah, "a light arose." She remembered how often she had told her God of her willingness to suffer anything that came, if only she could aid in the cause of emancipation. And "the query arose whether *this* suffering was not the peculiar kind required of *me*." Since then, she said, she had "found some peace." Sarah had not counted on Angelina's finding peace.

Sarah had then enlisted Catherine Morris to aid her and had called on other Arch Street Meeting Friends. For awhile they laid siege to change Angelina—their plan, if they could, to deflect her course by involving her in acceptable interests. Now they were pressing her to become a teacher, urging her to pursue her studies further, pointing out the dreadful state of the prisons that so badly needed her work for their reform. They even urged on her to become an author—there were well-known female authors in that day—and Angelina even started on one or two "books," all on weighty subjects and Biblical in nature, not so much to please them as to give herself direction in her groping and floundering.[18]

But as the months went by and Angelina did not change, Sarah herself began to give ground. She had grown more miserable in the Friends Society, feeling the hostility of certain leading Friends, in particular of her old enemy, Elder Jonathan Evans, who only recently had silenced her, a minister, in a First Day meeting when she had risen to speak. Her diary was filled with her loneliness. Her letters were displaying a more placating spirit, almost an acceptance on Angelina's stand. Once she voiced her willingness to "give up" Angelina, if "such a sacrifice should be required of me," though later she was "hoping that the Lord would cast our lot somewhere together." When she had arranged for Angelina to stay awhile with the Parkers in Shrewsbury, Sarah had already come far. Some slight evidence was her insistence on making the hard journey by stagecoach merely to accompany Angelina.[19] By this time it was the summer of 1836, a full ten months since the letter to Garrison.

As chance would have it, Margaret and James Parker, though Orthodox Friends, were of a liberal turn of mind and were both tolerant and concerned about the plight of abolitionists. However, they were ignorant of Angelina's situation, for Sarah had not informed them, and they saw no abolitionist papers. Margaret Parker told the story in later years.[20]

At the outset Angelina did not mention slavery; for months she had kept her thoughts locked within herself, wary, distrustful, reluctant to speak. Margaret Parker was curious, knowing the Grimké background, and when a chance opening came, she broached the subject. Angelina answered, Mrs. Parker pressed for more, and in a way to make Angelina know that here was interest. The floodgates opened, and from that day onward, whatever the two were doing, sitting, walking, riding, or engaged in household tasks, slavery and abolition absorbed their conversation. Margaret Parker felt little hope that abolition could be accomplished. Angelina insisted that it *must* come, there was no alternative, and the free states must bring it; if they did not, "all would go down in blood." They spoke more that once of Nat Turner's insurrection and what had happened in Virginia only three years before. Time and again, Angelina would exclaim, "Is there nothing I can do?" What could a woman do, how strike an effective blow?

On one particular evening, as Margaret Parker told it, Angelina seemed depressed as though her mind was greatly burdened. For a time they sat in silence. When Angelina rose and kissed her friend goodnight, Mrs. Parker felt tears fall on her face, surely the tears of a profound frustration. Margaret Parker's chamber adjoined Angelina's; unable to sleep, she kept hearing faint sounds. The sobbing continued, so she went to the room. Moonlight streamed through the open window. Angelina, on the floor, head buried in a pillow, was weeping as perhaps she had never wept before. Embarrassed at being seen in her great straits, she promised she would go to her bed at once.

Apparently the crisis brought its resolution. The idea must have surfaced as she slept, for Angelina appeared at breakfast next morning, face radiant and filled with high excitement. "It has all come to me, I see it now! I will write an 'Appeal to the Christian Women of the South.'" At last, here was something a woman could do. She began to write that day and wrote for two weeks, with hardly a letup. When the work was completed, she read it to the Parkers, not because of doubts, for she had said what she believed and required no reassurance.

It appears that Angelina had not known how widely her letter to Garrison had been publicized—in abolitionist papers, in some church journals, and in a broadside printed by tens of thousands and circulated throughout the North. It is certain she had not guessed how well her name was known wherever abolitionists and their sympathizers gathered. So the letter she now received came as a surprise. It came while she was still at work on the "Appeal" and almost too absorbed to comprehend what it meant: the long dreamed of opportunity was opening before her.

The letter that came was from Elizur Wright of the Office of the American Anti-Slavery Society, inviting Angelina Grimké to come to New York to lecture on abolition to women's groups "in parlor meetings." The very notion of lecturing came as a shock to Angelina; at the same time she was stirred, even thrilled at the thought. She told herself sternly she must finish the "Appeal." She wrote Elizur Wright that she would consider his proposal, then told him of her "Appeal to the Christian Women of the South," asking if the society might be interested in it.[21]

Angelina and Sarah were now exchanging letters frequently, and much of the old warmth seemed to have returned, except that Angelina no longer consulted Sarah. The "Appeal" was almost finished before she even told Sarah of it, and she announced that she had decided to attach her name to the "Appeal," "for I well know *my name* is worth more than *myself*, and will add weight to it." She had come this far since her letter to Garrison. Sarah was not asked to read the "Appeal," though Angelina half-apologized for the omission, explaining that a friend was just leaving for New York and would deliver the manuscript to the Anti-Slavery Office. Angelina told Sarah of Elizur Wright's invitation and how "it was truly alarming" to think of giving public lectures, but then she commented serenely, "it might be required of me." Sarah's response reflected her alarm. She said she was now willing for Angelina to do the work God called her to and she would help her sister in all ways she could.[22] Sarah was now close to her own full acceptance.

Meanwhile Elizur Wright's reply had come. "I have just finished reading your Appeal, and not with a dry eye. I do not feel the slightest doubt that the Committee [of the American Anti-Slavery Society] will publish it. Oh that it could be rained down into every parlor in our land."[23]

It appears that Sarah made one more try. It was no doubt she who suggested to Angelina that perhaps her sister's duty lay first with Quakers. They had well-to-do friends in Uxbridge, Massachusetts, E. and L. Capron. Angelina wrote to them: could she come to Massachusetts to work among Friends, labor with them to join the growing movement to boycott the products of slave labor? She had not expected Capron's extreme agitation. He was so alarmed that he traveled to New Jersey to persuade Angelina not to come to Massachusetts. So great was the opposition to abolitionism among Friends, he declared, that her "character would be destroyed." Catherine Morris swept away any remaining hesitation. Angelina could not work among Friends, Catherine said; to do it, she would require a certificate of permission and a companion from her own meeting, and these would not be granted. Angelina was caustic in a letter to Jane Smith,[24] now her main confidante in spite of Sarah's change. "Dids't thou ever hear anything so absurd? I cannot feel bound by such unreasonable restrictions, if my Heavenly Father opens a door for me, and I do not mean to submit to them." Her break with the Friends was almost complete. "As a servant of Jesus Christ, I have no right to bow down thus to the authority of man, and I do not expect ever again to suffer myself to be trammelled as I have been. It is sinful in any human being to resign his or her conscience and free agency to any society or individual, if such usurpation can be resisted by moral power." She seemed now to fully realize how far matters had gone. "I feel as if I were about to sacrifice every friend I thought I had. But I still believe with T. D. Weld"—she had not yet seen Weld, but what she knew had deeply stirred her—"that this is 'a cause worth dying for.'"

Angelina's "Appeal" was rushed into print. Within a few weeks notices had appeared in antislavery papers and in other reform journals that were willing to show sympathy with the antislavery cause. All spoke in glowing words of this unique "Appeal," written by a woman who was a slaveholder's daughter. The "Appeal" was selling briskly in local antislavery meetings.

Angelina now decided it was her duty to go to Charleston. Six years had passed since she had seen her mother. Also, without a doubt, she felt she was "required" to declare among her people that she stood for abolition. The "Appeal" reached Charleston on the heels of her letter telling her mother of the intended visit. A bundle of the tracts had arrived by ship and were seized from the U.S. mails by local searchers. A letter from her people told Angelina what had happened. The mayor of the city had heard of her intention and had called on Mrs. Grimké. Miss Angelina Grimké should be informed, the mayor said, that she would not be permitted to land in Charleston; the police had been instructed to guard the boat; and if she should elude their vigilance and go ashore, she would be arrested and held in jail until a vessel arrived that could return her to Philadelphia. Friends in Charleston wrote her urgent letters: the people of Charleston, they said, were so incensed that she could expect personal violence at the hands of a mob. Angelina did not doubt that violence could occur. She remembered what had happened to her brother, Thomas Grimké, when a few years before he had opposed nullification and found himself confronting an angry mob at his door, which he defied so courageously that the mob had finally dispersed. And the issue she had raised was far more explosive—nothing short of "immediate" emancipation of all slaves. It seems certain that Angelina would not have given way to personal fear. Were it not for her family, she wrote her Charleston friends, and that her coming would distress, or worse, place them in peril, something she had "neither heart nor right to do," she would certainly have exercised her constitutional right and proceeded to Charleston to visit her relatives. She added as she seized the chance to state her view, "If for that, the authorities inflicted pain and penalties, I was ready to bear them, assured that such an outrage would help to reveal to the free States the fact that slavery defies and tramples alike upon constitutions and laws, and thus outlaws itself."[25]

It was not that Angelina thought she might escape mobs; they were rampant in the North as in the slave states, and the mobs were no respecters of the female abolitionists. She was fully informed on what had happened in Boston soon after her letter to Garrison had been published. Boston's militant Female Anti-Slavery Society had told the whole story in "Right and Wrong in Boston," a tract widely read among abolitionists. The women had held a meeting, despite all threats, in an upstairs room in the antislavery hall, expecting Garrison to arrive and speak. A howling mob had gathered, "respectable gentlemen," many of whom were known to the ladies present, a mob that had invaded the stairs and pushed in while the women were continuing with their meeting. The mayor had appeared, urging the women to disperse, asserting that he was unable to afford them protection. Then the news reached them that Garrison was in the streets, as they had feared, at the mercy of the angry crowd. Finally they had concluded they would meet in a home—in any event they could not hear each other speak above the noise of the mob—and had proceeded down the stairs, walking quietly two and two, and the mob had given way to let them pass.[26]

The "Appeal" had been published in early September. A few

weeks later Angelina wrote Sarah that she was going to New York to see Elizur Wright concerning his proposal that she lecture to women's groups. It was clear that Angelina had determined to accept, even though she could feel shaken at the thought of "public lecturing." Sarah was dismayed and left at once for Shrewsbury, declaring she would accompany Angelina to New York.[27] Sarah's diary revealed how great was her turmoil, as she made her last attempt to hold Angelina back. She herself related the debate that ensued, recording its substance not long thereafter.[28]

Angelina said directly, "I believe this to be God's call. I cannot decline it." Sarah urged, wait, don't decide suddenly, consider it well. Angelina replied, that she had nothing to decide, it was decided for her. "This is all like a dream now; but I can't undream it, and I can't resist it. I *must* go." Sarah reminded her, that she had never spoken in public, never even to an audience in a parlor; moreover, for four years, she had been a Friend; in Friend's meeting all were free to speak as the Spirit moved them, and Angelina "had *never uttered a word in the meeting.*" Angelina agreed but said serenely she had never felt she *must* speak; if she had, she would most certainly have spoken. Sarah then turned to Angelina's nature, saying that she was constitutionally "very retiring, self-distrustful, easily embarrassed . . . and had a morbid shrinking from whatever would make her conspicuous." Angelina admitted it; she knew she was diffident concerning responsibilities, "but when I feel that anything is *mine to do,* no matter what, then I have no fear. Just so I feel now." Sarah tried another tack: she would be going among strangers, wearing strange Quaker garments; and, in any case, those who came to listen would be prejudiced against her abolitionism and because she was a woman; this opposition might prove too much, and she might fail. Angelina conceded that it seemed presumptuous, preposterous, yet she could not refuse, so strong was her conviction that she must go. Sarah by this time knew the battle was lost; even so, she made one last plea: if Angelina went without the sanction of the Friends, the Friends Society would view it as disorderly and would probably feel compelled to disown her. Angelina replied, as she had once before, that her mind was made up, so she would not ask their leave; and while it would be unpleasant to be disowned, it would be misery to be *"self*-disowned." At this point Sarah conceded her defeat and announced what she intended to do. "While we have been talking, I too have made my decision. It is this: Where thou goest, I will go; what thou doest, I will do my utmost to help thee in doing."

The outcome, it appears, was no surprise to Sarah, and perhaps she felt a profound relief, so miserable had she been in the Friends Society. With no sister as companion, the outlook was grim. For Sarah was a failure as a Quaker minister, tortured in speech, disapproved by Quaker leaders, even publicly rebuked, because in meetings she forced herself to speak, something Friends did not do until moved by the Spirit, and they could not believe this woman was so moved. Sarah had written in her diary just a few weeks before, "Amidst much to try and exercise me on account of my precious sister and myself . . . [yet] enabled at this eventful crisis to leave our concerns in His hands, believing that He will not permit us to do wrong, but will enable her to see whether the proposal for her to enter into active service in the Anti-Slavery cause is in accordance with His holy will—and for myself whether or not I must still continue in this city of bonds—Oh I am ready to say 'spare me Oh Lord' . . . Oh my God deliver me from the oppression of men." The Lord spared Sarah, as she prayed He would. Thenceforth, it was literally "whither thou goest, I will go." Angelina's people soon became Sarah's people, and rightfully so. For while Sarah was not the stuff of which crusaders are made, she believed in emancipation of slaves, believed in full equality for men and women of all races, even though she had yet to become an abolitionist.[29]

Angelina said little of her thoughts concerning Sarah. It is certain she was ambivalent and felt guilt for it, although to have Sarah with her would greatly smooth her way. In 1836 Sarah was forty-three, a sedate older woman in her sober Quaker dress, an ideal female companion in the coming years, when her brilliant younger sister would become a public figure. One thing stands clear: their relationship was changed, and Sarah's was no longer a restraining, guiding hand, even though by indirection she would sometimes have her way. It was not that Angelina sought to be the dominant one but that she had found a cause that would demand all her powers, and she felt she must be free to set her own course.

2.

For many abolitionists the year 1836 began an unforgettable time in the antislavery movement. It was not the accomplishments for the society was still young, and abolitionists were still a persecuted handful in the many localities where bands were being formed. But in 1836 antislavery men and women were still ardent and unrent by open schism. There was a sense of growing power among leaders of the movement, fed by high fervor, single-minded aim, a reliance on the efficacy of nonviolence, and a conviction that the tide was turning in their favor, despite attacks on meetings, unruly mobs, and the increasing boldness of proslavery men. Even the numbers of adherents were increasing: in 1835 over 300 new societies; by 1838 the national organization reported a total of 1,350 societies, with a membership of 250,000.[30]

In 1836 one fresh strategy that was planned directly affected Angelina Grimké: a widespread campaign to win new adherents by training and sending forth into communities throughout the free states a band of "Anti-Slavery Apostles" to carry the gospel of "immediate emancipation." These men would go as agents from the national society to speak and organize until the free states were won. In biblical spirit, they would be called the "Seventy," for they too would be going as lambs among wolves. The man who was to train them, Theodore Weld, knew all there was to know about the ways of mobs and how to deal with these curiously excitable northern men who could not bear to hear that black slaves should be set free. Weld and Henry Stanton were to select the Seventy, and when finally they gathered in the City of New York on November 8, 1836, for the training convention, there was hardly a man among them who would not one day be known as one of the men who had led the movement.

There was another innovation, startling at the time. This was the inclusion of a woman among the Seventy, Angelina Grimké, her name now known, though very few had seen her face. Elizur Wright had met her in the Anti-Slavery Office, as had Mrs. Abby Cox with whom she had stayed on that brief visit when she and Sarah had come to New York to talk of "parlor meetings."[31] It is not directly stated why Angelina was singled out, she alone among the numerous able women who were active in the cause. Lucretia Mott, for one, why was she not present, as she had been present when the society was formed at that first convention in 1833, and she had even been permitted to say a word on the floor? And there were other Massachusetts female leaders: Lydia Maria Child, writer and journalist, who later was an editor of the *Anti-Slavery Standard*; and Maria W. Chapman, leader in Boston, who had proposed the appointment of "Female Agents" and was eagerly organizing, on a national scale, a separate women's antislavery convention. These women and others had been active for several years; those in Massachusetts had confronted ugly mobs; they knew what it meant to organize for abolition. It is true that Angelina was now widely admired for her "Letter to Garrison" and her "Appeal to Christian Women"; Elizur Wright had talked with her, she had certainly entranced him, and it may be that he had sensed her unique gifts. But more than all else, she was a slaveholder's daughter with a distinguished name and lineage and she had turned against slavery. Where else would they find a combination like this for the "female agent" who would speak to women's groups? Moreover, Angelina was free to go, whereas other women were married and had home duties; also Angelina had a small income and would accept no compensation.

In fact, two women attended the convention. At Angelina's side was her sister Sarah, who was present at every session of the three absorbing weeks. Certainly Sarah's presence made Angelina seem less conspicuous. At the same time, it won Sarah to the cause of abolition. Angelina could write in great relief to Jane Smith that Sarah was now united to the "abolitionist brethren in spirit & in love." For the first time in years, Sarah was aglow.[32]

In itself this convention of reformers was remarkable, an "intellectual feast" it seemed to those present, as one after another of these extraordinary men lectured to the chosen on the full meaning of abolition: Theodore Weld; Henry B. Stanton; Beriah Green; James G. Birney; William Lloyd Garrison; John Greenleaf Whittier; Charles Stuart, who was Weld's close friend and mentor; the Burleigh brothers; Gould McKim; Theodore S. Wright and Samuel Cornish, two Negro leaders who impressed Angelina; and others who would become well known. These men became Angelina's friends and "brethren" in the months that followed the Convention of the Seventy. First and foremost among them was Theodore Weld, organizer and principal leader of the convention. Certainly he was foremost in Angelina's thoughts; her letters to Jane Smith showed how deeply he moved her, as she felt the sheer power of his stimulating mind[33]—she had "always loved the company of intellectual men."

The meetings continued for twenty-one days. "We sit from 9 to 1, 3 to 5, & 7 to 9, from day to day, & never feel weary." Weld, for one, scarcely took time to sleep, since he must prepare lectures, converse with the agents, and deal with the many decisions demanding his attention. And it was much the same for all the leaders and for those who would be "agents"—"brethren" in the cause, this their term, this their feeling. Angelina Grimké became their "dear Sister," and of course Sarah with her—she was now an abolitionist. Perhaps never again in the annals of antislavery was a gathering so imbued with selfless commitment.

The meeting was remarkable in its meaning for Angelina. For years she had sensed potential powers within herself and was convinced that she was called to some great purpose. Her inner frustrations were melting away as she felt herself involved in mind and emotion. Woman though she was, she was accepted here, equal among equals, an astounding thing. For unwittingly these men had let the barriers fall, though some would live to regret this day.

She was fully aware of her heightening emotions; she supposed it meant that at last she felt released and that herein lay the source of her enhanced joy. Perhaps she scarcely realized how the name of Theodore Weld began repeatedly to appear in her letters to Jane Smith. As it chanced William Lloyd Garrison introduced them; she wrote Jane of it and how Weld took her hand: " 'My dear Sister,' & I felt as tho' he was a brother indeed in the holy cause"; and in succeeding letters: "Today . . . able speeches . . . from T. D. Weld"; "Theodore D. Weld . . . to begin the Bible argument"; [34] "A most noble speech from T. D. Weld . . . on the question of What Is Slavery. I never heard so grand & beautiful an exposition of the dignity & nobility of men"; then more than a page setting forth what he said. She did not neglect other men in her letters: "We have been introduced to a number of abolitionists—Thurston, Phelps, Green, the Burleighs, Wright, Pritchard, Thome . . . and Amos Dresser, as lovely a specimen of meekness and lowliness of the Great Master as I ever saw." She told of other lectures, Beriah Green's for instance, his speech "tho' *good* was not grand"; and added, "it was excellent but lame in comparison to that of TDW." [35] She was greatly moved by Amos Dresser's story, going particularly to hear him speak to a large Negro school. She admired Henry Stanton, who spoke one day on the "safety of immediate emancipation." Then she expressed hope that T. D. Weld would speak at a meeting of the Female Anti-Slavery Society. Thus Weld became "the Lion of the tribe of Abolition." "At first sight," she wrote Jane, "there was

nothing remarkable to me in his appearance & I wondered whether
he really was as great as I had heard, but as soon as his countenace
became animated by speaking I found it was one which portrayed
the noblest quality of the heart & head."[36]

The Convention of the Seventy ended in late November, and the
moment had arrived when Angelina should begin. She felt much
trepidation at the thought of "public speaking," even quailed before
it, at moments longed to flee, but the prospect held a powerful
attraction. Theodore Weld now came to her aid. He had much to
share on the art of public speaking and how to make most effective
the arguments against slavery, so that soon he had imbued her with
confidence in her powers.[37] By mid-December her first meeting had
been set.

The meeting was called, not for a private parlor, though this had
been the plan in the Anti-Slavery Office, but for the session room of
a large Baptist church. The minister, Mr. Dunbar, made the offer,
and the Female Anti-Slavery Society accepted, of course with the
consent of the "Misses Grimké." At some point which is lost in ob-
scurity, it had been decided that Sarah would share the platform
with Angelina, though it was not yet clear whether she would
speak. On Sunday four churches made announcement of the
meeting, except that, as planned, the Grimkés' name went unmen-
tioned—it was merely the quarterly meeting of the female society.
With the moment close at hand, hitherto suppressed doubts began
to be voiced by the Grimkés' friends. Even Sarah expressed a fear,
which she had held in check, that Angelina's lecturing would be
called "Quaker preaching" and would arouse latent prejudice
against a woman's public speaking, thereby injuring their cause.

The sisters were guests in the Henry Ludlow home. Two days
before their meeting, Gerrit Smith arrived. A wealthy man from
upstate New York, he had been won to abolition from a colonization stand; and soon the Grimkés would know him as one of their
warmest friends. It was breakfast time when he appeared, the hour
for morning family prayers. He was asked to lead them. Gerrit
Smith prayed ardently for the Misses Grimké, begging the Lord, in
almost anxious tones, to lead them aright in the times ahead. Was
Gerrit Smith feeling doubt of the wisdom of what they did? As all
rose from their knees, the doorknocker sounded. A printed notice
of the meeting was handed in the door. This notice bore the names
of the Misses Grimké, South Carolina abolitionists, who would

address the female meeting. The mention of their names was altogether unexpected. Angelina felt a momentary shiver of dismay,
unaccustomed as she was to see her name in public print, and she
began to voice some distress to her friends but quickly fell silent.
Gerrit Smith broke in, his tones agitated, pleading with Angelina to
beware, to lecture only in private parlors or their gatherings might
be called "Fanny Wright meetings"—Fanny Wright, the bold and,
to some, strident lecturer on the rights of woman as well as other
topics. At this crucial moment, T. D. Weld arrived. Already he had
expressed full support for Angelina and had grieved with her over
"that factitious state of society which bound up the energies of
woman instead of allowing her to exercise them to the glory of God
and the good of her fellow creatures," words that were wonderful to
Angelina's ears. When Weld was told of Gerrit Smith's comment,
he brushed it aside—"Do not fear, trust in God."

The meeting was called for three o'clock. Three hundred women
were gathered in the session room. Henry Ludlow opened the
meeting with prayer, then he and Mr. Dunbar left the room, for had
they remained, they would have breached the sacred custom that a
female should not speak to "promiscuous" audiences.

Angelina was elated after this her first "lecture," though she
spoke of it quietly in retrospect. She felt "perfectly unembarrassed,"
she wrote to Jane Smith, "dear Sister" spoke also, and many came
up to talk with them at the end. Another meeting was planned by
vote of those present.[38]

The Grimkés went home with Julia Tappan for tea, and there was
T. D. Weld, all anxiety to hear what had happened. Only now was
revealed the shocking incident at the meeting. A "warm hearted"
abolitionist male had slipped in, though he was promptly escorted
out by the indignant Henry Ludlow, who had been watching outside as a protector of the ladies. Weld spoke directly and in strong
terms. "His noble countenance lighted up & he exclaimed how su-
premely ridiculous to think of a man's being shouldered out of a
meeting for fear he would hear a woman speak." Angelina reported
that she and Sarah smiled, and she commented—they had come
far—that though others might think they should not lecture before
men, this idea seemed "very strange" to them.

3.
The first weeks of public life passed on a muted note. Angelina's

appearances were secluded and sedate. New York abolitionists were conventional men—Elizur Wright, Arthur Leavitt, the Tappans, Gerrit Smith—and were concerned that no hint of ugly notoriety should mar the public image of their unique female "agent." Soon Sarah was speaking regularly at Angelina's side, very probably with full support from these men, who would feel less uneasy with the older Sarah present—a woman of middle age, sober Quaker mien, and a flat, uninspiring mode of speech.[39]

The meetings began in December 1836 and continued around New York City until early spring of 1837. They served as a kind of apprenticeship, perhaps, although no one conceived of the matter in this way. Angelina and Sarah were "agents" in a sense since their lectures had some official sanction, but at their own insistence they received no pay and financed themselves in all their travels. How "officially" they were "agents" would become a moot point when later they came into conflict with the men.

They launched a series at Henry Ludlow's church, at three o'clock on Thursday afternoons, at first in the session room, but the audiences grew so large that they were forced to move to the church itself. "6th meeting yesterday . . . crowded hall . . . people coming in a way far beyond expectations." Angelina was delighted when the number reached three hundred, all females of course, as no men were allowed. They tried various topics, not all of them with success: "the testimony of southerners . . . to the enormity of slavery"; and three weeks devoted to the "laws of the slave states" with illustrations, which might have lightened the heavy topic. Angelina lectured on "slavery as cruel to the body, heart, mind and soul of the slave," but the subject proved too large for one meeting, so "mind and soul" carried into the next week—she still had much to master in the lecturer's art. There was a memorable moment after one early lecture. Angelina stood greeting those who came up to meet her—the room was dim and faces blurred—when a woman took her hand exclaiming, "I am from Charleston. . . . Don't you know me? I am Prudence." The almost forgotten voice was now familiar. "Prudence!" and Angelina held the hand still faster. Prudence had been the white nurse of one of her brother's small children and had lived with his family for four years. "O!" said Prudence, "I never expected to see such a day as this."

Angelina told how others were calling their talks "lectures"; they hardly merited the term, she felt. "I don't know in fact what to call such novel proceedings. How little! how *very little* I supposed when I used so often to say, 'I wish I was a *man* that I might go out & lecture'—that *I* ever would do such a thing—the idea never crossed my mind that *as a woman* such work could possibly be assigned to me." In anticipation, Angelina found it hard to lecture. "The day I have to speak is always a day of suffering," and it continued to be so as the years went by. She ignored the feeling, however, and when she walked on the platform she was in full command. So despite this difficulty, she could say with a full heart, "Dear Jane, I love the work."[40]

The sisters had moved to the home of David Sands. Sarah spoke happily of the change, "a comfortable home, a nice little parlor to ourselves." Angelina had a special reason to welcome the parlor. Theodore Weld had become a frequent caller: "Brother Weld was here"; "Brother Weld happened by." In January, Weld spent two entire afternoons in the Grimkes' "little parlor" reading aloud his "Bible Argument against Slavery" before it went to press. Angelina commented, "it was quite a treat," but she was not uncritical of Weld's mode of writing. "I do not admire the style, so don't expect too much from it, but the plan and arguments are admirable and conclusive." Angelina more and more consulted Weld, and not only for herself. That spring she was writing Jane Smith that Weld "advises strongly against it [a plan of Jane's to write a certain tract]. And if you knew Brother Weld as well as I do, I expect his judgment would have quite as much weight with you as it has with me."

As spring drew near, invitations poured in. They had lectured several times across the river in New Jersey and began to make plans for upper New York State to meet the many calls urging them to come. They wished to go early because plans were afoot for a national female antislavery convention in New York City, and already they were involved in arrangements for it. The sisters departed New York before the ice had left the Hudson, their principal destination Gerrit Smith's country home, a large estate near Peterboro. It was planned that they would lecture in surrounding rural towns, and they hoped to be in Albany for the state antislavery convention. Gerrit Smith was with them as they set out from New York. A meeting had been arranged in the city of Poughkeepsie, and they got no further; next day the ice forced them to turn back. The meeting in Poughkeepsie held surprises for them. While they knew it had been called by the Negro community, they

had not expected so large a crowd: three hundred people sat awaiting their arrival, men as well as women, nor did Gerrit Smith feel he
could ask the men to leave. "For the first time in my life," Angelina
exclaimed, "I spoke to a promiscuous assembly . . . and found the
men were no more to me than the women."[41]

When Angelina had come north, she had expected more freedom, in particular that black people would have a kind of equal
treatment. Her disillusionment was great when she encountered
blatant prejudice and saw discriminatory practices taken for
granted everywhere. More than from others, she had learned from
James Forten, a prominent Negro businessman, of the conditions of
colored people. It was Forten who, in the early 1830s, had gathered
pertinent facts on Philadelphia's black community to show how its
people sought to advance themselves. He cited good schools, their
several churches, benevolent associations for mutual aid, an active
lending library, a debating society, a temperance society, Bible societies, a literary group, and also a considerable range of occupations; except, said Forten, "owing to prejudice," many were prevented from improving their lot. So except for the few, his people
were poor, the conditions of their lives ugly and drab.[42] The most
shocking knowledge was of the mob attacks, periodic outbursts of
senseless hostility, physical assault, and property loss wreaked on
Philadelphia's colored community. Angelina knew of these—at a
distance, of course—and knew the helpless fears of her Negro
friends, their impotent despair as they confronted white assaults.
The most recent had been in late 1836; word reached her in New
York of the three-day mob attack in Philadelphia, and she heard
that Forten had been wounded.[43] And what could she do, except
inquire of his condition, voice her shame at these white deeds, and
try as she could to accept her new perception that prejudice and
violence were inextricably linked.

An even harsher disillusionment lay in wait. It would be hard to
find more devoted men and women than those who espoused the
abolition cause. Yet they were not immune to the prejudices among
whites, and though often accused of "amalgamationism," many of
them feared it and deplored any taint of "social equality." Angelina
had not known until she reached New York of these feelings and
fears among abolitionists. There had been the controversy between
Lewis Tappan and the revivalist Charles Finney over mixing of
white and colored on public occasions, with Finney protesting
when, in May 1835, both white and Negro choirs sang together at a

convention of the American Anti-Slavery Society. Some claimed that the July anti-Negro riots in New York had been caused by this "mixing." Lewis Tappan flatly rejected the accusation—"the choirs sat separately in the orchestra, the whites on one side and the colored on the other!" and did so by order of a committee. Arthur Tappan, his brother, also made his stand clear when he was similarly accused of fostering racial mixing: no, he said, he made a clear distinction between association in *public* and social intercourse, and from the latter practice he carefully refrained.[44] Theodore Weld practiced a kind of "social equality," yet even he had been making certain distinctions, asserting that he mixed with colored people socially only when the parties were their own—their weddings, their funerals, gatherings in their homes, his canon of judgement to avoid intercourse that might harm the colored people.[45] Perhaps Weld was not so rigid when Angelina came to know him, for she found nothing to complain of in his behavior. In New York she had been teaching a Sabbath school for Negro children when a young girl, "quite poor," asked the sisters to tea. Weld, who was present, said he would call for them, as he did around eight on a Sunday evening. "I have seen him shine in the Convention (of the Seventy) & in the refined circles, but never did I admire him so much, his perfect ease at this fireside of poverty showed that he was accustomed to be the friend & companion of the poor of this world."[46]

Male abolitionists in Philadelphia were at this time torn by the issue of equality. One local men's society, in 1836, engaged in a prolonged debate for five meetings over the question, "Is it expedient for colored persons to join our Anti-Slavery Societies?" The meeting voted "Yes" by a two-vote majority.[47] But for the second question, "Is it expedient for Abolitionists to encourage social intercourse between white and colored families?" While the meeting admitted to the need "to remove public prejudice," even so, it declared, it was not "our object, or duty, to encourage social intercourse between colored and white families," a viewpoint that Angelina was terming "sinful Prejudice."

It was in New York, as she was launched into public life, that Angelina was confronted with the fact of flagrant prejudice. She discovered "the canker" when she spoke to New York women in meetings that were sponsored by the female abolitionists. She was astonished to find no colored women present. In Philadelphia, Negro women played an active part—the Fortens, Mrs. Purvis, Sarah and Grace Douglass—these were names she was apt to mention.

She was not long in learning where the trouble lay: "colored members were unwelcome" in the New York society; the few who had joined were allowed no participation. When she wrote Jane Smith, Angelina was aroused. "No colored sister has ever been on the Board & they have hardly any colored members even & will not admit any such to the working Sy." And she was blunt in describing how she felt: "Until our sisters here are willing to give up sinful prejudice, it is a canker worm among them & paralyzes every effort—they are doing *literally nothing* as a Sy for the colored people." Angelina and Sarah took the matter in hand, as they felt obliged to do in view of their beliefs. They asked to attend the monthly meeting of the managers, "& believed it right to throw before them our views on the state of things among them, particularly on Prejudice." She and Sarah spoke, she said, "in love and tears," and some tears were shed by those whom they addressed. One woman of the board moved to tender the Grimkés thanks, and another said, "I second it with all my heart," but by and large "the work was hard," and the New York women continued in their former ways. In response Angelina proposed to organize a New York antislavery society of colored women and then invite white females to join the new group; thereby she hoped to isolate those who were prejudiced, but this was one project she had no chance to carry out.[48]

Thus matters stood when the time approached for the national Female Anti-Slavery Convention to be held in New York in April 1837. Angelina was greatly agitated for fear the New York women would wield a baleful influence. "We had better have no National Society until we can have one of the *right stamp* & I do not think one can flourish in this city while Prejudice banishes our colored sisters from an equal & full participation in its deliberations & labors."[49] Angelina began herself to recruit colored delegates to outweigh the New York influence. She had warned the New York women of what they should expect, "that the Philadelphia Society had colored managers & would most probably send colored Delegates." She knew Grace and Sarah Douglass were hoping to come. The problem of housing was acute. She did not trust the local women, and she searched for housing. She had been urging Mrs. Forten and her daughter to come. "If I had a house here nothing would afford me more pleasure that to offer them a home." She knew two colored delegates were expected from Boston. She wrote

Providence and Fall River, urging colored delegates, expressing to Jane Smith her hope "that something may be done to break down this adamantine wall in this proud city." When Sarah and Grace Douglass began to waver in their decision to come, she wrote urgently. "You my dear Sisters have a work to do in rooting out this wicked feeling as well as we. You *must be willing* to come in among us tho' it *may be* your feelings *may* be wounded by 'the putting forth of the finger,' the avoidance of a seat by you, or the glancing of the eye. . . . I earnestly desire that you may be willing to bear these mortifications. . . . They will tend to your growth in grace, & will help your paler sisters *more* than anything else to overcome their own sinful feelings. Come then I would say for we need your help."[50] Angelina was not asking for these women to sit silent. On the contrary, what she wished was to have them speak their minds and mince no words about the indignities they had suffered, that bitter fruit of prejudice that they were forced to eat. She wrote to Jane, "If only one of these dear Sisters would only rise in our Convention & tell us in simplicity & godly sincerity the direful influence of this feeling on their hearts & minds & prospects in life, we believe it would produce a deep & thrilling effect." In fact, she added, "if [they] do not come up strongly to our support I do not know what we shall do. . . . I feel as if I could say to them with regard to this Meeting, If you will go with me, then I will go, but if you will not go with me then I will not go."[51] She wished these women present on another account. She planned to move that the convention issue a "Letter to Free People of Color" that would be drawn up there. "It will be absolutely necessary that some of them [colored delegates] should be on the Committee to examine it before it is printed," so that it would bear no taint of the prejudiced mind.

Yet another prejudice had been confronting Angelina, one she had been sensing with pervasive ill-ease. In the Convention of the Seventy, nearly six months before, she had enjoyed the meetings; she was especially pleased that they had made no intellectual distinction. If some of them had showed how greatly they were drawn to this appealing, brilliant, and articulate southern woman, such male attentions were nothing new for her, though surely they must have added zest to the occasion. Now, since the convention, she had become a "female lecturer." The New York men who were the more conservative abolitionists began laying down restrictions touching Angelina, in particular the rule against men attending her meetings. Her meetings meanwhile were growing in size, and these antislavery leaders became even more rigid, fearing that at any time the barriers might burst and men come pouring into the Grimké meetings. Some male objectors spoke of St. Paul's injunctions, others voiced fear of the taint of "Fanny Wrightism," and all indicated that the "sacred cause" might be injured if unwomanly notoriety resulted. To Angelina the men's treatment seemed more and more absurd. It offended her sense of right, struck at her pride, and made her feel restricted from doing all she might. Thus the matter stood at the female convention.

This first national Female Anti-Slavery Convention met in New York in April 1837. Seventy-one delegates attended the gathering, and a hundred more women were present at most meetings. Negro delegates had come, and there were good discussions, more than any of them had dared to hope for, "& this contributed very much to the animation & interest . . . threw open our hearts & minds to each other's views, and produced a degree of confidence in ourselves . . . very essential & delightful." To Angelina's joy, a woman fugitive slave was present, and she was "perfectly amazed, hardly knew how to express herself, such were the emotions of her heart."[52] Angelina and Sarah did not register as delegates from Philadelphia but put themselves down as "representatives from South Carolina," and when they pledged money to the cause, they declared it to be "for our sinful State." The business of the convention went smoothly and well, principally because of the experienced women delegates from Boston. Angelina was soon a close co-worker with these women. She delighted in their minds that were so harmonious with her own and in their courageous history in Massachusetts. From them she gained knowledge of a practical kind—how to organize and conduct a national gathering like this one; she was stimulated by the experience and lent herself fully to it. Perhaps these Boston women, more than any other influence, opened up to Angelina the cause of woman's "rights."

In the period before she entered on her public career, Angelina had been unmindful of a "woman's rights" issue. She could say at this time, "I verily believed in *female subordination until* very recently."[53] She was consciously concerned with her own opportunities and her conviction that God had called her to a mission. When she felt pulsing through her what she often termed "ambition," she believed it could be right when it was guided by God's will; for why would God have given her the talents she possessed if she was not meant to use them? As the days of the New York female convention moved along, Angelina spent many hours with her experienced Boston friends—Lydia Maria Child, Mary S. Parker, Maria Chapman, and Anna Weston. These women had long upheld the rights of females to equal opportunity in the causes they espoused.[54] Hardly conscious of any change, Angelina found herself an advocate of woman's "human rights," and she could say of her Boston co-workers that she was finding them "sound" on all basic issues, "their sentiments on Prejudice, the province of woman, and other important topics" were so similar to her own. Thus she and they worked unitedly on these issues. They aided her in writing a resolution against color prejudice; she joined them in preparing a declaration on woman's rights. She could exclaim, when their resolutions passed resoundingly, "Some of our Resolutions will certainly frighten the weak & startle the slumbering, particularly those on Southern intermarriages and the province of woman."[55]

In late spring of 1837 the Grimkés left New York for a brief stay in Philadelphia. By this time they no longer had a home. They had lived at Catherine Morris's, but their tenure there was ended, and at best Sarah visited Catherine only on occasion—something that Angelina avoided if she could. Their widowed sister, Anna Frost, had a house in Philadelphia which served as her school, her means of livelihood. But Mrs. Frost was opposed to abolitionism, and for a while was completely estranged from her sisters. Angelina had Jane Smith and her sympathetic family, so occasionally the Smith home served her as a haven. Both had other friends from the Arch Street Meeting days, and although some voiced fondness, they were puzzled and disturbed by the sisters' activities. Their few possessions—clothing, books, pieces of furniture—were in storage here and yonder with their friends.

Before leaving New York they had confronted the question of where they would campaign next. They could live in Philadelphia, using it as a center; at one point Angelina favored this course, a dreaded outlook where Sarah was concerned. There was upper New York State; this was Sarah's choice; the Gerrit Smiths would welcome them to their handsome country home, and here they could make headquarters. It was even suggested—they did not say by whom—that Angelina and Sarah might go separate ways, thus covering more ground. Angelina was willing, though doubted its wisdom. Sarah refused; she would have none of it.[56] The most pressing invitation came from Massachusetts, from male as well as female abolitionists. Angelina decided they would go to New England. It may be that Weld's influence helped to sway her choice, for Sarah could write lugubriously to a friend, "Massachusetts is the place that Brother Weld recommends our laboring in, and altho' a disappointment to me, having a great inclination to the western part of this State at the Gerrit Smiths, yet this cause of abolition, not my gratification, is what I am anxious to promote."[57]

In Philadelphia clothes must be made ready for several seasons, since they would be gone a year or more. It was while in Philadelphia—this appears to have been the time—that Angelina and Sarah took a step that they had long contemplated.[58] Arch Street Meeting House had a separate "Negro pew," as did other Friends meeting houses and many churches in the North. On First Day, when they entered, Angelina and Sarah pushed past the two white Friends stationed at either end of the long seat to serve as "guards," lest the unwary enter, and took their seats beside the dark Quakers in the "Negro pew." It little mattered, they had done so much already to flout the rules and ways of their Orthodox friends.

In May, Angelina and Sarah left Philadelphia for their long, tedious journey to their New England field of labor. They were met in Boston by their antislavery friends, given a few days' rest, and began their crusade.

4.

A thrilling sense of freedom now infused Angelina, as though the old strictures had been wiped from her mind. She was in Garrison country; it was indeed a freer air, freer within the ranks of antislavery crusaders. Most Massachusetts abolitionists accepted notoriety, tolerated strong language—this was the result of the *Liberator's* work—and assumed forthright activity on the part of the women, a policy that the men and women leaders had hammered out together. Opposition was rampant, vituperative, and unyielding, as Angelina soon learned when she faced it in person. There was also strong opposition within the antislavery ranks, a vocal minority that opposed the Garrison group. But the Grimkés were surrounded by the militant abolitionists, whom Angelina Grimké joined as a brilliant pioneer. It was an almost perfect climate for the release of Angelina's full powers in the emancipation cause.

She began June 6, 1837.[59] Within fourteen days she had lectured seven times—Dorchester, Boston, Brookline, North Weymouth, Roxbury, South Weymouth, and Boston again. Her first Boston meeting was in Washington Hall with four hundred women present, an historic moment for her since this was the hall where the women had been mobbed by "respectable citizens" only two years before. A parlor meeting was held in Samuel Philbrick's home, a country estate in what was then rural Brookline, and it was this upper-class town's first antislavery gathering. "Very hard to speak to such stony hearts." More than once that first fortnight, she spoke of "great apathy"—she was sure many came out of sheer curiosity. When a few men began slipping into her meetings, they caused no shock, nor were they asked to leave. In the second Boston meeting with six hundred persons present, some fifty men were scattered through the crowded hall. It was the largest meeting Angelina had yet confronted. "Very easy to speak . . . great openness here."

On June 21 they arrived in Lynn, by the 1830s a busy, thriving place. Sarah was lecturing also, although not each time her sister spoke. Angelina was the voice that drew the throngs. And throngs came to hear her in the city of Lynn, though it was only two weeks since her tour had begun. In the afternoon Angelina lectured to a female audience—a crowded hall with five hundred present. For the evening the abolitionists had engaged the largest hall, and it was crowded to the doors—a thousand men and women—her "first large mixed audience," she exclaimed. Never had she faced so large a crowd before. She might quail before the hour, but once she had started speaking, she knew no fear: "great openness to hear & ease in speaking." On the following day a third meeting was planned. Clearly the planners were men of little faith; they could not believe so many would come again, so the hall they secured was smaller in size. Seven hundred crowded in, with a hundred more standing, and on the outside of each window stood several men, heads seen above the lowered sash, while hundreds more were turned away. "Very easy speaking indeed," she could say. Angelina was lecturing for as long as two hours, and it was said her voice carried to the farthest ear, and she herself marveled at this undreamed of gift.[60]

The sisters stopped in Danvers to hold one meeting, then a day of rest, and on to Salem. Salem was Lynn all over again: six hundred, a thousand, eight hundred for their three meetings: and then a fourth meeting of three hundred colored people, members of the

Seaman's and Moral Reform Societies, and afterward she had tea with some of the Negro leaders, always a stimulating time for Angelina. They returned to Danvers for a second promised meeting. Angelina had "scolded" abolitionists there for their apathy and poor planning, so she expected few to come, but eight hundred poured out to hear her. On July 2 they were back in Salem to speak at a colored Sabbath school, where the four hundred present were largely from the Negro community.

Henry C. Wright was a Massachusetts agent who had assumed the task of managing the Grimké tour. He often accompanied them and always made arrangements, from their standpoint an excellent system: they felt well cared for and untroubled by details. Wright, by self-appointment, had undertaken to send reports to the *Liberator*, sometimes describing in fulsome terms the Misses Grimkés' exciting and triumphant lecture tour. Henry C. Wright was already a controversial figure and for the most part frowned upon by the New York abolitionists. Like Garrison, he was anti-constitution, he advocated an extreme, nonviolent approach and opposed civil government, he was an ardent "peace man," and while first and foremost working for abolition, he never hesitated to press his other causes. The New York office was all the more troubled when the word began to reach them of what Wright was doing. They feared the notoriety the Grimké sisters were receiving, feared that Wright was exploiting these unique women, using them, they felt, to the detriment of the cause. A month had hardly passed when criticism began to drift back to Boston and to the Grimkés' ears. But they liked Henry C. Wright—Angelina said, "one of the best men I ever met with," so they virtually ignored the rumors that reached them. On July 3 they arrived in Newburyport to make the Wright home their headquarters while they filled engagements in the surrounding towns. Angelina voiced pleasure in this excellent arrangement. Mrs. Wright and her daughter were charming to the sisters, insisting on their resting, helping them sew, waiting on them often. This home was a boon to these weary travelers.

On the fourth they were taken to hear John Quincy Adams. Abolitionists were critical of Adams's views, so Angelina listened closely and was guardedly pleased at his comments on "free discussion and against slavery." Once the holiday was passed, their own meetings began. Three were scheduled for Newburyport, a poor arrangement, Angelina felt, because each followed on the heels of the other. Both sisters spoke on the first evening, but when Sarah felt a cold coming on, Angelina later held the platform alone. The first audience was large, around eight hundred, and Angelina particularly noted that she "found great ease in speaking," but she observed something further for almost the first time: "Great prejudice here against women's speaking in public, very hard soil."[61]

They were scheduled for Amesbury on July 10, to remain overnight, then back to Newburyport, and on to other towns. John Greenleaf Whittier's mother lived in Amesbury with an aunt and a sister, and they took the Grimkés in. Angelina and Whittier had become warm friends in those memorable weeks of the training of the Seventy. Whittier, they found, was absent in New York "serving the good cause," but his womenfolk, she felt, were as "thorough going as their dear J.G.W., whom they seem to know how to value."[62]

As it turned out, Amesbury was momentous. The meeting was held in a church, and it was well-attended with some six hundred present. The Grimkés were hardly seated on the platform when a letter was handed to them stating that two young gentlemen were present who knew the South and had formed opinions different from those of the speakers; they asked to state their views at the meeting. Sarah arose and read the letter to the audience, then asked the two young men to proceed. The men spoke, Angelina answered them, and the discussion continued for perhaps an hour, the audience all the while listening intently. Angelina later commented. "They were inconsistent and ardently betrayed that they had had a pretty close affinity to Slavery." But now she had a task to perform and spoke at length on the "Dangers of Slavery & the Safety of Immediate Emancipation."[63]

The sisters assumed that the matter was ended. Far from it, for the young men persisted in their demands. Since the hour was late, they requested another meeting, a further opportunity to argue the issues. Had the Grimkés' Boston mentors been at hand, perhaps something different would have eventuated, but that night the sisters had to make their own decision, and they promised another meeting when their engagements permitted. It was set for one week later, July 17.

They proceeded on to Ipswich, where two meetings were held, five hundred in the afternoon, eight hundred in the evening. At Essex they had a meeting in the Christian Church, to which men came straight from the fields and workshops in their work clothes, nearly four hundred men and women present here; at Byfield, five hundred. Then they drove the eight miles to Newburyport, arriving late at night, "sick with fatigue." Yet Angelina could exclaim that she was amazed at her endurance and how swiftly she recovered with just a little rest.

The "debate" at Amesbury—it was now called "debate"—was set for the evening of July 17. A "jam" was expected for this extraordinary event when "two Massachusetts men [would] defend Slavery against the accusations of two Southern women." A "trying and uncommon predicament" it might be, but Angelina showed no reluctance as the evening approached. In fact, the debate went on for two evenings, with a thousand or more people present at each meeting. It was not until the first meeting was well under way that Angelina comprehended how mistaken their decision had been. These young men were proslavery, and the Grimkés, so to speak, had presented them with an audience of a size and kind they never could have commanded by themselves. Their arguments were those of the slaveowner himself, so familiar to the Grimkés from times gone by. "Our very souls were sick," Angelina said. And by now she surely sensed the furore that would follow, how the papers would be full of this strange affair of two respectable southern ladies debating two young men before large mixed audiences, audiences made up not only of abolitionists but also the curious and hostile.

At this uneasy moment there appeared a "Pastoral Letter" that recently had been adopted by the Congregational ministers of Massachusetts, a document so portentous in abolitionists' eyes that from that time on it was "*the* Pastoral Letter." The "Letter" did not cite the Misses Grimké by name, there was no need; it was clear who was meant and crystal clear what the "Letter" sought to do. In the villages, towns, and cities of Massachusetts, Congregational churches were usually large halls, sometimes the largest in the community. One aim of the "Letter" was to close these churches to all antislavery speakers, doing so, of course, on high moral grounds, because "the perplexed and agitating subjects now common amongst us" might divide the members, bringing "alienation and division." Moreover the "rights" of the ministry were invaded when someone other than a minister presumed to deal with moral issues, particularly with the rights and wrongs of slavery. "Your minister is ordained of God to be your teacher"; even if he had failed to preach on certain topics as frequently as his congregation might desire, it was a "violation of sacred and important rights to encourage a stranger to present them." "Deference and subordination" should be the relation of a people to their pastor.

The second aim of the "Letter" was even more specific. It called urgent attention to the "dangers which at present seem to threaten the Female Character with widespread and permanent injury." New Testament authority clearly defined "the appropriate duties and influence of women. . . . The power of woman is in her dependence. . . . When she assumes the place and tone of man as a public reformer . . . her character becomes unnatural." Woe to any who encouraged females "to bear an obtrusive and ostentatious part in measures of reform," thereby countenancing those of the female sex who have so far forgotten themselves "as to itinerate in the character of public lecturers and teachers."[64] Thus the "Letter" sought to discredit the Grimkés and to discourage attendance at their antislavery meetings.

By mid-July, the Grimkés were notorious. The "Pastoral Letter" had been widely read. The Amesbury debate was used to lash out at them. Angelina found herself thoroughly exhilarated. "But our *womanhood*, it is as great an offense to some as our Abolitionism . . . the whole land seems roused to discussion of the province of Woman, & I am glad of it."[65] The public press had taken up the issue. Most papers attacked them. The *Lynn Record*, on the contrary, ridiculed the furore. "It is curious to notice the fearful apprehensions entertained by some wise heads that they shall really be trodden down by female usurpations. . . . Some newspaper editors . . . affected ridicule and fearful dreams. Others are seized with fits of 'delicacy' and 'delicate subjects.' Why? Who are the persons? What have they done? The female 'incendiaries' who have set the universe on fire, turned our little world upside down, are Miss Martineau* and the two Misses Grimké."[66]

The "Pastoral Letter" proved effective in some towns, where Congregational meeting houses and also other churches began to close their doors on the antislavery message, especially when it was

*Only three years before, in 1834, Harriet Martineau, the distinguished British author and lecturer, had come from England to travel and lecture widely in the United States. She was well known for her opposition to slavery. Her book, *Society in America*, was published in 1837, the year Angelina began her New England crusade against slavery.

carried by female advocates. More and more church people, it was claimed, were becoming hostile to the cause of abolition. But then the "Letter" had certain contrary consequences. Local Congregational ministers were forced to take a stand: would they admit the Misses Grimké to the pulpits of their churches? And not a few examined the Scriptures for themselves, to find their own authority as to whether they should allow the sisters to speak. When the churches were closed to them, other halls were found; hence from this time on many Grimké meetings were held in public halls—any place from a barn to a city hall to a large theater—whatever could be hired. Far from any lessening of the size of their audiences, even in the more rural areas people crowded to hear them.

The sisters were now reaching smaller towns following Amesbury, yet even in places like "the Bradfords" and Haverill, crowds of from four to six hundred attended. At Andover, despite a heavy thunderstorm, the meeting house was full—eight hundred present, with many faculty and students scattered through the hall. "I never felt as if I was speaking before such a formidable array of talent & learning & prejudice against my womanhood." Even so, she could report, "all went well." Methuen followed Andover; again it was raining, though the clouds lifted when meeting time came, and Angelina faced a thousand people in the hall, the "largest audience that had ever collected here." In the week after Amesbury, she lectured seven times, to audiences totaling four thousand persons, and between lectures there were journeys from town to town by stagecoach or carriage.

On July 30 they arrived in Lowell and found themselves guests of the son of Quaker friends. The son and his wife were warm abolitionists, which made the stay with them pleasurable and relaxing. Sarah was complaining of a cough she had developed, so it fell to Angelina to confront the Lowell meeting alone. She had not expected a large attendance at Lowell, supposing it was "only a manufacturing place," but the local people had engaged the city hall, the largest hall to be secured in the city. "I was fairly frightened, and when I found myself in a city audience of 1,500, surrounded with a blaze of light from chandeliers & lamps, I hardly knew what would become of me." There can be no doubt that it was a glorious evening, for Angelina used a phrase she reserved for her best meetings: "The Lord stood at my right hand . . . and carried me through." Again on the second evening 1,500 came, and Angelina held them enthralled for nearly two hours.

Sarah, during these weeks, had been lecturing less and less, even when she had appeared on the platform with her sister—first it was a bad cold, then a persistent cough, then she was fatigued and obliged to rest. The lectures continued to be scheduled close together, often as frequently as every other day. In late summer Angelina wrote Jane Smith that several weeks had passed since Sarah had lectured.[67] When Jane Smith reported that friends were disturbed lest Sarah's health was being undermined, Sarah herself dealt with the matter. Her friends, she wrote, need not be alarmed; she had a slight cough, but this was no ground for uneasiness. Moreover, she added—saying it for the first time—"it furnishes a reason for me to be silent and leave dear AEG to do the work which I believe God has specially appointed her. I almost always feel as if I were in the way of the work being better done. . . . I feel peaceful in my silence." By this time Sarah was fearing what she would later come to know.[68]

Meanwhile attack had come from another quarter. Catherine Beecher, Angelina's one-time mentor and friend, was so aroused by Angelina's abolitionist campaign that in mid-summer she published an "Essay on Slavery & Abolition," sharply criticizing Angelina's views. Angelina at once plunged into counterattack in a series of "Letters to Catherine Beecher," which were written in the heat of her speaking tour, one letter a week for a number of weeks. These were published in the antislavery press, then printed in a tract, and spread abroad throughout the North.[69]

Catherine Beecher had derided "immediate" emancipation. Angelina dealt directly with what she meant by the term.

> 1. It is to reject with indignation the wild and guilty phantasy, that man can hold *property* in man.
> 2. To pay the laborer his hire, for he is worthy of it.
> 3. No longer to deny him the right of marriage, but to "let every man have his own wife, and let every woman have her own husband," as saieth the apostle.
> 4. To let parents have their own children, for they are the gift of the Lord to them, and no one has any right to them.
> 5. No longer to withhold the advantages of education and the privilege of reading the Bible.
> 6. To put the slave under the protection of equitable laws.
> I have seen too much of slavery to be a gradualist. I dare not, in view of such a system, tell the slaveholder, that "he

is physically unable to emancipate his slaves." I say *he is able* to let the oppressed go free, and that heaven-daring atrocities ought to cease now, henceforth and forever. . . . Oh my soul is grieved to find a northern woman [Catherine Beecher] . . . thus framing and finding . . . soft excuses for the slaveholders' conscience, whilst with the same pen she is *professing* to regard slavery as a sin. "An open enemy is better than such a secret friend."[70]

Catherine Beecher had complained of abolitionists' "aggressive spirit." "Far from being a repulsive one to me, it is very attractive," Angelina wrote. "I see in it that uncompromising integrity and fearless rebuke of sin, which will bear the enterprise of emancipation through to its consummation."[71]

Like many, Beecher asked, why preach to the North? Why not take her message to those who held slaves? Here was familiar ground to Angelina—she had been dealing with it in speeches for months on end.

We are spreading out the horrors of slavery before Northerners, in order to show them *their own sin* in sustaining such a system of complicated wrong and suffering. It is because we are politically, commercially, and socially connected with our southern brethren, that we urge our doctrines upon those of the free States. . . .
Anti-slavery reformers did not begin their labors among slaveholders, but among those who were making their fortunes out of the unrequited toil of the slave, and receiving large mortgages on southern plantations and slaves. . . .[72]

Angelina had witnessed black slavery in all its wrongs; she made a point of it in her letters to Catherine Beecher, though, she admitted, she had not seen it at its worst. But whatever the gradation, it was evil to the core. Enslavement could exist only because the white man had the power, an arbitrary power enforced by violent means, a power that was used to hold its victims in subjection. As a result, the white man claimed his victims to be less than human, an inferior type of being, and hence deserving of their slavery. This notion, which had proved so useful to the slaveholders, had spread among whites and from it, root and branch, had come the "prejudice" in men's minds. Angelina pressed her point so that none might miss it: what she meant here was not "Southern prejudice" but "American prejudice," which was prevalent throughout the nation.

"And what is more ridiculous than *American* prejudice; to proscribe and persecute men and women, because their complexions are of a darker hue that our own. . . . Miserable Sophistry! Deceitful apology for present indulgence in sin. What man or woman of common sense now doubts the intellectual capacity of the colored person?"[73]

The ugly fruit of prejudice was denial of equality—Angelina asserted it unequivocally here. And when Catherine Beecher claimed that some white individuals who had treated colored people well in the past had become so embittered by the abolition movement that they had turned against the Negro, Angelina said bluntly, that it was not that they had changed; it was merely "that the cloak of benevolence had been torn from the monster Prejudice" by abolitionism.[74] "Now I would ask, could such people have acted from principle? Certainly not or nothing that others could do or say would have driven them from the high ground they *appeared* to occupy. No, my friend, they acted precisely upon the false principle, which thou has recommended; their *pity* was excited, their *sentiments* of generosity were called into exercise, because they regarded the colored man as an *unfortunate inferior*, rather than as an *outraged* and *insulted equal*."[75]

Hardly had the first letter to Catherine Beecher appeared when the woman's rights conflict broke out within the abolition movement. The argument had begun, but in a mild form, in June when the Grimkés had first arrived in Massachusetts. The State Anti-Slavery Convention was then under way so various abolitionist leaders were in Boston: Garrison, of course, Samuel May, probably Amos Phelps—who would so strongly oppose the sisters—Henry Stanton, Burleigh, Goodell, Colver, and James Birney. Weld was not present; in fact, he was ill and had gone to his brother's home in Connecticut to recover. Maria Chapman had a social gathering at her home, and there Angelina, surrounded by "the brethren" and strongly supported by Lydia Maria Child, Maria Chapman, and others, pressed the men for their views on the rights of women. Angelina was well pleased with what she heard, "a very general sentiment prevailing that it is time our fetters were broken . . . very many seemed to think a new order of things desirable." She reported nothing concerning any opposing views.[76] But this exchange had occurred before the Grimké lecture tour.

Within a few weeks the Grimké name was notorious; the sisters' lectures to large "promiscuous" audiences had made the news; the "Pastoral Letter," with its stern reprimand, had been read from pulpits throughout the state; there had been press criticism of the Amesbury "debate" and Angelina's condemnation of Catherine Beecher's stand. Within antislavery ranks many were distressed, and groups began to polarize around latent differences. Abolitionists of the Garrison wing urged the Grimkés to speak out, but the timid were feeling that the church should be placated, even those churches that compromised on the slavery issue. A number of male abolitionists who disapproved of "rights" for females were openly voicing their antagonism. Other men, while insisting they supported female equality and upheld the Grimkés in essential ways, began to deplore the intrusion of "extraneous issues" and the fact that "woman's rights" were linked to those of the slave. It was not that Angelina discussed woman's rights when she stood before an antislavery meeting. As she put it to Jane Smith later on in the autumn, "It has been really wonderful to me that tho' I meet the prejudice against our speaking *every*where, that still in addressing our audiences I never think of introducing anything about it."[77] By now both sisters felt a principle was at stake, nor was it something vague and in the distant future. Their very right to speak was at issue, specifically their right to address "promiscuous" audiences.

In fact it was Sarah who brought the issue to a head, although Angelina supported fully what Sarah did. Sarah could not leave the question of woman's rights alone, perhaps more than ever since she was speaking less on abolition. Angelina exclaimed, "Sister does preach up woman's rights most nobly & fearlessly & we find that many of our New England Sisters are ready to receive these strange doctrines." It was mid-summer when Sarah conceived the notion of a series of "Letters on the Province of Woman." These were sent to the antislavery press. The *New England Spectator* accepted the "Letters" and published them periodically throughout that summer.[78]

At last Amos Phelps could hold his peace no longer. In a sense he wrote as an official of the society, since he was an appointed "agent" to work in Massachusetts. He wrote to the Grimkés "remonstrating very earnestly" against their custom of lecturing to both men and women. Amos Phelps was himself a Congregationalist minister and perhaps all the more affected by the "Pastoral

Letter." Phelps did something further that could not have helped matters. He requested their permission, Angelina wrote Jane, "to publish the fact of his having [written to them] with a declaration on our part that *we preferred* having female audiences only." The reply the sisters sent was clear and unequivocal: Phelps was free to publish anything he felt right, but they could not consent to his saying in their names that "they *preferred* female audiences only, because in so doing we should surrender a fundamental principle, believing as we did that as *moral* beings it is our duty to appeal to all *moral* beings on this subject without any distinction of sex."

Phelps made another point that could not be ignored. He felt the Grimkés were injuring the Anti-Slavery Society by making it responsible for their "promiscuous-audience" stand, thus involving it indirectly in the woman's rights issue. Angelina took immediate steps on the matter. She wrote to Elizur Wright of the national office, saying that the Executive Committee should feel entirely free to throw off all responsibility for the Misses Grimké by publishing a statement that the Grimkés were "neither responsible to or dependent on them," the latter because they were paying their own way.[79]

There was much soul-searching in the New York office. Henry B. Stanton wrote from Massachusetts urging Elizur Wright to publish nothing that would appear to voice disapproval of the Grimkés. Theodore Weld immediately became involved, as he did in most decisions in the national office. Having searched the minutes of Executive Committee meetings, he found that the Grimkés were not official "Agents"; they were not supported by national society funds; they were in no respect under society control; the Executive Committee had not claimed or exercised any authority over them, in short, had not "officially certified" them in any way; at most they were "cooperators" in the general movement. He made these points in a letter to Angelina and Sarah.[80] What his letter was meant to accomplish is unclear. To Angelina and Sarah, it seemed as if they had been cast off by the society. Meanwhile, men and women of the Garrison group were urging the sisters to stand firm.

Angelina's convictions had fully crystallized. She felt she had no choice but to practice her "woman's right" to publicly advocate great moral issues and to do so before mixed audiences of men and women. She had learned what it was to have halls refused because she was a woman, to see herself attacked in the public press, to know she was upbraided from many church pulpits, and to read and hear the epithets that were hurled at her person, much as they had been at the male abolitionists: "Sabbath-breaker," "infidel," "heretic," "incendiary," "insurrectionist," "disunionist"; particularly for herself, "woman-preacher," "female fanatic"; and for them all, "amalgamationist."[81] She could comment dryly toward the end of the summer, "Since I have studied human rights & had my own invaded," the woman's rights cause had become her own. The conception she then expressed remained with her ever after. She saw no conflict between her two great causes.

> My idea is that whatever is morally right for a man to do is morally right for a woman to do. I recognize no rights but human rights. I know nothing of men's rights and women's rights. For in Christ Jesus there is neither male nor female. I am persuaded that woman is not to be as she has been, a mere secondhand agent in the regeneration of a fallen world, but the acknowledged equal and co-worker with man in this glorious work. . . .
> This is part of the great doctrine of Human Rights & can no more be separated from Emancipation than the light from the heat of the sun; the rights of the slave & woman blend like the colors of the rainbow.[82]

No rainbow graced the sky when Angelina wrote these words. The storm that had arisen was in full and noisy clamor, not only in the church and public press, and clouds were overshadowing the antislavery movement.

Perhaps it was in the hope of forestalling a crisis that Theodore Weld and John Greenleaf Whittier wrote to the Grimkés urging a different course—separate letters but sent the same day. Angelina had believed that both men were "sound" when it came to the issue of equality for women. What could she think when both men now deplored Sarah's published articles on the "Province of Woman"? These had already begun to appear. Whittier pressed the Grimkés, "You are now doing much and nobly to vindicate and assert the rights of women. Your lectures to crowded and promiscuous audiences . . . are practical and powerful assertions of the right and duty of woman to labor side by side with her brother for the welfare and redemption of the world. Why, then, let me ask, is it necessary for you to enter the lists as controversial writers on this question? Does it not look, dear sisters, like abandoning in some degree the cause of the poor and miserable slave?"[83] Weld's letter reached the sisters on the same day. He took pains to remind them, and in de-

tail, how he had always advocated equality for women. More ve-
hemently than Whittier, he deplored and regretted Sarah's series of
articles on woman's rights. And he also argued that their "best
possible advocacy" was the one they were making day by day:
"Thousands hear you every week who have all their lives held that
woman must not speak in public." They had work to do for the
anti-slavery cause, a labor that was unique because they were
southern women who had been slaveholders; and they would lose
their vantage point if they espoused another cause. "*You two* are
the ONLY FEMALES in the free states who combine all these facilities
for anti-slavery effort. . . . Now can't you leave the *lesser* work to
others . . . and devote, consecrate your whole bodies, souls and
spirits to the *greater* work."[84]

Although Sarah appeared to be the focus of the attack, Angelina
was the one who wrote the reply, nor was there any hint of dis-
agreement with Sarah; if she felt Sarah had been unwise, she gave
no sign. She seemed to understand that she, more than Sarah, was
the one some abolitionists really feared, because it was she who had
broken down the barrier that had prevented women speakers from
addressing "promiscuous" gatherings. Angelina was piqued at the
men's combined assault and plainly determined to treat it as
combined, so her reply, a document of some two thousand words,
was a joint communication addressed to Weld and Whittier.[85] In
effect she stood her ground, the burden of her argument that "the
time to assert a right is *the* time when *that* right is denied." "We are
actuated by the full conviction that if we are to do any good in the
Anti-Slavery cause, our *right* to labor in it *must* be firmly established . . . on the only firm bases [sic] of human rights, the Bible."
She reminded Weld and Whittier, "We never mention woman's
rights in our lectures except so far as is necessary to urge them to
meet their responsibilities. We speak of their *responsibilities* and
leave *them* to *infer* their *rights*." She sounded a stern note toward
the end, as if she felt these trusted men had failed her. "Can you not
see the deep scheme of the clergy against us as lecturers? . . . [to]
persuade the people it is a *shame* for us to speak in public, and that
every time we open our mouths for the dumb we are breaking a
divine command? . . . What then can *woman* do for the slave when
she is herself under the feet of man and shamed into *silence*?"

Angelina felt gloom as she watched the mounting tensions. In
mid-August she wrote Jane Smith, "My only fear is that some of our

Anti-Slavery brethren will commit themselves in the excitement *against woman's rights and duties*, before they examine the subject, & will in a few years regret the steps they may take."[86] For many weeks the argument continued, nor did either side appear to give real ground. Sarah's "Letters" in the *Spectator* were being widely quoted, and Angelina took no steps to quiet the abrasive conflict.

For a brief few months there had been profound fulfillment, the exhilarating experience of the whole person used—intellect, emotions, even physical strength, expended without stint yet never to exhaustion, for even as she gave, Angelina found more to give. She knew that she was moved by the growing throngs, the intentness of her listeners, both men and women, the rapt response to which she was so sensitive; and when some were apathetic or strongly hostile, she would sense the battle and put forth all her powers to win or isolate them.

There was no precise time at which these days of freedom ended, but Angelina became plagued by an awareness of old bonds, perhaps at first infrequently. The main source of her unease was made clear in her letters. Angelina had not flinched at opposition from the enemy, but when fellow abolitionists began to show disapproval, it was a new experience for which she was unprepared. She was wounded by the censure that had reached them from New York, and the Executive Committee actions she felt were a rejection. Most of all, she was shaken by Weld's strong disapproval when he defended the Executive Committee from the Grimkés' attacks. And at this juncture a new conflict arose. Henry C. Wright was still managing the Grimkés' tour, making their arrangements, easing their journeys. Wright had also continued his column in the *Liberator* on "The Misses Grimké," always lavish in his praise and always appending his name or initials so that his name was associated with the Grimké sisters. Then Wright committed a further offense; at least the piece was offensive to the men in New York. He wrote an article called "A Domestic Scene," which described the Grimké sisters in Wright's home with his family in attendance, the ladies' hands busy at sewing or similar tasks, while Wright and the Grimkés discussed their views on current divisive issues, not only slavery, but also peace and woman's rights. All in all, it was a personal, intimate picture, and Wright's name as always was signed to the piece. Hardly had this article appeared in the *Liberator*, when the national Executive Committee of the Anti-Slavery Society discovered that Pennsylvania stood in urgent need of additional agents, and Henry C. Wright was transferred to Pennsylvania.

Angelina was angered when she heard of Wright's removal. She knew there were reasons that had not been stated. Nothing had been said of Wright's labors for the Grimkés, no claim that he had neglected his own work, no criticism of his articles in the *Liberator*, no mention of the fact that he and Garrison had supported the Grimkés against the New York office on the woman's rights issue. While Weld was not a member of the national Executive Committee, he was on the staff of the national office, a powerful figure who, by his own preference, always remained behind the scenes. The Grimkés and Weld had been exchanging letters frequently. Angelina addressed her outraged letter to Weld.[87]

In her letter, Angelina made intemperate accusations, all of them directed at the national Executive Committee. The members were dishonest, hypocritical, double-dealing; they claimed that Henry C. Wright was more needed in Pennsylvania, which was sheer "pretense" since another agent was sent to Massachusetts in his place. Her indictment continued at length and in detail. And she concluded by asserting that the Executive Committee had clearly "parted company" with Garrison, Wright, and the Grimkés on the woman's issue and the issue of peace.

Weld answered promptly in scathing tones. He rebuked Angelina and belabored her for her charges against "those devoted men" who were members of the Executive Committee. Her "reiterated" accusations were "based on trifles thin as air" and directed against men "who have put everything at stake and counted all things but loss in this cause." He wrote a second letter, explaining to her at length (and, it must be said, in a patronizing tone) precisely how the national society operated, implying that her woman's ignorance was partly to blame. Again and again, throughout both letters, he invoked the way of Christ as the test of all he said: "A mighty easy thing it is for you my dear sister to sit down in your retired room and con and scan . . . and then gather inferences of dishonesty, deception, hypocrisy, double dealing. SO DID NOT CHRIST." And, "Perhaps you may *resent* what I have said. And yet I am sure that the fearful strength of your *pride* will restrain *exhibitions* of resentment, and I *must* believe that the spirit of Christ within you is not so stifled but it will *forestall* the feeling itself." In the end, he placed her firmly in the seat of the accused. "If I have wronged you dear sister, then indeed I have done you a *grievous wrong*. If so, pray Jesus to forgive me for wounding one of his little ones. If I have told you the truth, *lay it to heart*. Go to God: His searchings will bring to light every [thing], even the subtlest form of pride." Weld's grand conclusion was "never to be forgotten." It cornered Angelina, allowing no escape. "To KNOW and to RULE ones own spirit is the rarest and most difficult of human attainments, *that* in which deception is most *frequent* and fatal. I am neither a prophet nor a miraculous discoverer of spirits; nor does it take such endowments to discover that you have studied everything more than the *moral* elements of your own spirit."[88] Angelina found herself unable to reply, and for months she felt unable to re-read Weld's letter.

From this time on, she was more shaken when opposition arose. Even foolish rumors nagged at her mind, like the one from Phila-delphia reporting that she wore black gloves when she lectured. Jane Smith had written her of this. "There is *no* truth in my *black* hand, indeed I never have lectured with gloves of *any* kind on."[89] She had expected to meet hostility among New England Friends. Now it was disturbing as it had not been at first, especially when she found that Philadelphia Friends had sent a representative all the way to Uxbridge to urge a ban against the Grimkés. "Paul Newell [of Philadelphia] had been there & warned them against giving [the Grimkés] any countenance if they should come to the neighbor-hood, as their doing so would weaken the hands of Philadelphia Friends in dealing with us. So much for the bitter fruit of Sec-tarianism."[90]

By late summer, Angelina had begun to show fatigue. She often mentioned the hardships of travel now. True, this was at the time the conflict was beginning that culminated in Angelina's fateful letter from Weld. In mid-August, the sisters were to take a ten-days' rest; Samuel and Eliza Philbrick had invited them to their home, a "beautiful country seat" in Brookline, near Boston. In fact Angelina rested only three days and then was back at her lecturing in nearby towns.

Charlestown, Massachusetts, was regarded as a most important meeting, the first antislavery gathering ever held in the town. She rode six miles by carriage, spoke one and a half hours, then six miles back again at night. She said she had found it "hard to speak," yet people were attentive, nine hundred attended, and many were obliged to stand. She was perhaps too aware that Garrison was present: "This the first time he had heard me & I could have wished him to have a little better opinion." Though she felt it was "poor," she was urged to return, and she spoke there again five days later. Nor was Garrison's opinion in the least lukewarm when he wrote of the occasion in the next *Liberator*.[91] "No wonder that the Pastoral Association is filled with consternation, and the proslavery heads and tails of society know not what to do, when WOMAN stands forth to plead the cause of her deg:aded, chain-bound sex. We listened for the first time to a lecture by Angelina E. Grimké on the subject of slavery. . . . Unaffected dignity of carriage, propriety of gesture and manner, excellence of arrangement, and conclusiveness of reasoning, and beauty of elocution, it was all that the most fastidious could wish. We never listened to a more perfect and admirable performance."

Not even atrocious weather seemed to hold people back. On her way to Westford rain began to pour, the carriage driver was getting drenched, and Angelina and Sarah urged him to turn back, certain that few would brave the storm and mud. They found three hundred people awaiting their arrival. On their way to Concord, they made a stop at Roxbury, where the audience was small and she felt the "leaven of prejudice"—prejudice "against her womanhood." They left Roxbury at 5 A.M., rode eighteen miles to Concord, where she lectured at 2 P.M. Four hours of sleep the night before had left her "strengthened in body, but low in mind." Even so, she could say of this meeting, "It was one of the best meetings I ever held . . . the house full, about 650 present." She gave several lectures in Concord and its vicinity. "We had more invitations [to speak] than we could accept, and the week was a very fatiguing one."

After Concord came Acton, then Groton was to follow. At Acton a thousand came out to hear the Grimkés. Dr. Farnsworth of Groton then drove them fourteen miles to his home after the lecture. Next morning they were scheduled to take the stage to Ashburnham at nine, but it departed at twelve, with twenty miles to travel, and their meeting was called for two o'clock. They arrived at three, "stopped only long enough to change, ate half a cracker," then went to the meeting and found a full hall; the people had been waiting for more than an hour. Angelina commented, "Spoke with perfect ease one and one-half hours. Am I not *strong*?"[92]

They set out for Worcester in late September, a strategic center for antislavery work, traveling by stagecoach, with a stopover in Shrewsbury and an afternoon meeting. Five hundred were present: "one of the most solemn meetings we have had." They left immediately to continue to Worcester, where fortunately they were to stay at the home of friends. "Was very weary, had ridden 20 miles, and spoken 2 hours. So went to bed early." At Worcester a large Congregational Church had been secured, apparently in the absence of the minister, for when he returned he slammed the church doors shut, declaring he would never enter the church again if the Grimkés spoke there. The local people then obtained a Methodist Church that seated a thousand people, but as many more came, hundreds stood on window sills and in their wagons, straining to see and hear. Angelina disliked these overcrowded halls, certain that many came out of "*mere* curiosity." She spoke of the "feeling of unsettlement" these large crowds gave her: "it seemed like the rolling waves of the sea." Yet despite the throng, "it was remarkably still," except that now and then a bench would crash or the sound of creaking timbers break the spell. They were to have met in the same church again, but the floor was found damaged from so large a crowd. Angelina rejoiced in the smaller hall they moved to—"much more satisfactory" than the huge curious throng. Nor was this Methodist Church the only hall that suffered damage from overcrowding. At Woonsocket Falls, where a thousand had pushed in, the floor began to pop and crack as she spoke. The man who presided urged the audience to leave, fearful that the floor would soon give way, but they refused and she continued speaking—"excellent attention."

Rain was a constant affliction in the journeys of the Grimkés. It mired the roads, delayed the stages, bogged down their carriages, held up their arrivals. Yet inclement weather rarely held back the crowds. Rain was pouring one day as they were to ride in a chaise to a small town in the Worcester area. Angelina insisted that Sarah remain behind, for although Sarah was speaking rarely now, she was usually at Angelina's side. Abby Kelley, an abolitionist who would soon be well known, accompanied Angelina on this stormy night. The chaise nearly upset on a downhill piece of road, but the driver righted the vehicle, and they continued on. As they drove through the dark and rainy night, Angelina could see men "in flocks on the road," moving toward the meeting house where she was to speak, and despite the heavy rain, five hundred came out. "It seemed as if I could not realize that they were going to hear *me*."[93]

Angelina was accustomed to quiet in her meetings, even rapt attention to the message she brought. In rural towns especially, women often brought their children, much as they did when they went to church. "Have been somewhat annoyed by crying children. Mothers anxious to hear & having no one to leave their babes with, bring them along and try in vain to keep them quiet by nursing, dandling & walking them in the house, or out in the lobbies, & as my position is an elevated one, I not only *hear* but *see* all their contrivances; however, I go ahead and *try* to forget everything but my great cause, & succeed pretty well—sister says. We still meet with kindness wherever we go." "Some of these places are only villages," she noted, "so that the few hundred who have come out have been good for the size of them" and then exclaimed, as she wrote to Jane, "What dost thou think of some of them *walking* 2, 4, 6, & 8 miles to attend our meetings."

At Townsend the meeting was called for 5 P.M., "a very bad time"—it was mid-September—"for it became dark before I was half done, the blinds being closed. However, I kept on for the hour and a half as usual." Frequently she felt that the "leaven of prejudice" had been at work, sometimes that local people had been timid or apathetic; hence little had been done to publicize the meeting; sometimes she would hear that a slaveholder was present; and sometimes she was heckled and this required deft handling. At Fitchburg, with some six hundred in her audience, a belligerent man rose angrily to his feet shouting, "She should go South to preach her doctrine!" The presiding clergyman asked the man to be seated, but he refused and continued his abusive speech. Angelina waited until he had had his say, then put it to the people: should she continue? With their resounding Yes, she proceeded to address them on why she had left the land of slavery. The outcome she felt was excellent, the heckler having done "more good that I did."[94]

As winter approached, the hardships increased. They were due at South Scituate on November 28, with appointments scheduled for the next several days. They missed both the steamboat and the stage, so they hired a "carryall" and drove through in it, their driver a kind "abolitionist brother." "Set off at 4. Had 20 miles to ride, arrived at destination at 8 p.m." Fortunately their driver had brought along a buffalo-skin robe to protect them against the damp and bitter cold. They were expected at the home of Samuel May, where they found "a blazing fire & some refreshment & social intercourse, retired." Next day a storm made the going hard, and they expected few people to brave it for their meeting, but the hall was "well filled." For this she could be glad, though her lecture, she felt, had fallen short, as well it might, because the doors and windows were closed by necessity and the place was heated by a potbellied stove, the pipe from which ran just above the speaker's head, so that the heat was oppressive and her mouth dry.[95]

When their travels first began, Angelina was unsure as to how far their physical strength would carry them. They expected then to lecture three or four times a week in addition to the traveling. Actually it was often six times a week, for in some places they spoke twice a day. By mid-summer this grueling schedule had been altered, and thereafter Angelina lectured no more than every other day. Even so, her performance was truly phenomenal. Angelina left a fairly full record of when and where she lectured, together with the numbers attending each meeting. In June, seventeen lectures in ten different towns, a total of over eight thousand attending. In July, nineteen lectures in fourteen different places, the total present nearly twelve thousand. In August, Angelina was ill with a cold and fever and missed ten days of travel; even so, eleven lectures in nine different places, with nearly six thousand persons present. In September, she was back again in full swing, seventeen lectures in sixteen different places, with well over seven thousand persons attending. And in October, she reached a high peak again, fifteen lectures in as many places, and her hearers totaling nearly twelve thousand. In five months' time Angelina had lectured seventy-nine times to audiences totaling well over forty thousand persons.[96] Many of her lectures lasted nearly two hours.

As early as October, Angelina had begun to express uncertainty concerning her future. While at times she could say, "Sometimes I feel as if what I am doing is only the *beginning* of what He will call me to do," the question as to where she should go and what she should do next was ever-present in her mind. It seemed as if New England had lost its appeal, though invitations were pressing on her and new plans were proposed. Boston antislavery women, looking toward the coming year, were urging a series of lectures in Boston. Angelina had not accepted, but neither had she declined. She and Sarah discussed the future at length. They considered Pennsylvania, though they had been told that traveling facilities were far better in New England. Moreover, they had a "good foothold here," and "some think we had better keep it instead of going to a new field." Angelina decided at one time that she would go to Philadelphia and there await God's call. Sarah dreaded the thought; she would feel like an "outcast" there, but finally she consented, and then this plan was dropped. Meanwhile a new proposal had come from Massachusetts: "*Not* to travel over the country as has been done, but to go to Salem, New Bedford, and other cities, and deliver courses of lectures." Angelina acknowledged one reason for her distress, one that had haunted her since she had become an abolitionist. She was seeking "evidence" "that if I have faith to go, He would open the way into the Slave States. It is to these that I find my mind secretly but powerfully drawn. I feel as if I wanted to go right among the slaveholders, & that I could plead with them in the spirit of love to undo the heavy burden & let the oppressed go free." Beneath the surface of her mind there lay another reason—how free was she to be in the abolition movement? She had been deeply shaken by those antislavery men who had sought to silence her woman's voice and by the thought that Weld had defended them while rebuking her. Her estrangement from Weld was painful and undermining. While she still had settled nothing when winter arrived, she held to her work as to a strong and steadying guide. "I *must not* sit idle at such a time."[97]

On November 1 she lectured in Duxbury. She felt ill that day and rested until six, though when the meeting time came, she was on her feet again. "I soon forgot myself & spoke with great ease for two hours." She was at Hingham on November 3 and still felt ill, but since Sarah was also sick, it was left to Angelina to speak alone. "For one hour, I think my voice was clearer and fuller than I have ever known it." She was filled with emotion as she concluded this meeting, for it would be her last until the New Year, a quiet culmination to a triumphant five months for which there was no precedent in the annals of reform. She wrote, "Thus ended our summer campaign."[98]

When Angelina arrived in Brookline at the Philbricks' country home, where she and Sarah were to have an extended rest, she had a high fever and for weeks lay ill. Any engagements they might have made must be postponed, and her physician forbade all planning until after the New Year.[99]

5.

Certain antislavery leaders, both men and women, who had witnessed Angelina Grimke's power, believed that her talents should be saved for large centers in which the audiences would be strategic in influence and size. It was all the more apparent that a different plan was required because of Angelina's illness, and the leaders were made aware of how her health had been abused in the months gone by. Her fever continued for many weeks, a debilitating illness for which the doctor found no name,[100] and she was so physically exhausted and emotionally tense that her recovery dragged on until well after Christmas. Urgent invitations had been pouring in. Boston's antislavery women were pressing her to agree to a series of lectures in a large Boston hall to begin in April.[101] She had not made a decision when, in early February, a proposal was made that she perforce must consider since the occasion might come at any time.

Henry B. Stanton had been working in Massachusetts, a representative there of the national Anti-Slavery Society. One continuing focus of abolitionists' concern had been the existence of slavery in the District of Columbia. Congress ruled there and had the power to abolish slavery. Abolitionists' arguments were simple and telling. They knew well the recalcitrance of slave-power congressmen and knew that their only hope lay in the free states. So their forces were brought to bear on northern legislatures to air the issue, to win more support, and perchance persuade legislators to petition the Congress to abolish chattel slavery in the nation's capital. While such action would free few slaves, even so it would mark a signal victory. Stanton and his colleagues had made some headway in Massachusetts. A special committee of the legislature had been appointed to consider petitions from antislavery groups urging an end to slavery in the district, and several abolitionist speakers had been heard—Henry Stanton himself, Amos Phelps, Francis Jackson, John E. Fuller, and James Birney, who had been sent by the national office. The legislative chairman was on their side, interest was high, and attendance at the sessions had been unusually large.

The special legislative committee hearings were still in progress when Henry B. Stanton appeared at the Philbrick home, ostensibly to call but in fact with a proposal: would Angelina consider speaking before the committee of the legislature? She laughed at first—he was surely not serious, nor could she believe such a thing "would be required" of her. But Stanton pressed the matter before he left that day. After all, he argued, some thousands of women's names as signers of petitions were before the committee; it was surely appropriate for a woman to speak for them.

After Stanton left Angelina was thrown into unexpected mental conflict. It took her two days to gain her own consent, though at last she told Stanton she would agree to the plan, "if the friends of the cause thought well of it." The men abolitionists were not all in agreement. While most of them were for the plan, some were fearful. A committee of three was to consider the proposal. Amos Phelps was one, and they knew he would object. Maria Chapman reported that Quincy could be counted on and that Francis Jackson "was sound to the core." "He [Jackson] went right up to the State House to inquire of the Chairman whether Miss Angelina Grimké could be heard." "Wonderful to tell he said yes without the least hesitation & actually helped to remove the scruples of some of the timid hearted Abolitionists."

At this point even Stanton appeared to hesitate. Stanton and John E. Fuller* had come a few days before, Angelina reported to Jane, and she felt that they "seemed to dodge the question." She wrote Jane, "It seems that even the stout hearted tremble for the consequence when the Woman Question is really to be *acted out* in full & tho' he [Stanton] is right in the abstract on the subject, yet now he greatly fears the consequences of such a bold assertion of our equality." But now Angelina felt her principles were at stake, though she said little to the men and awaited further developments. The legislative committee as a whole had yet to vote. If, as she expected, they merely did nothing, she had decided that she must take the initiative. She would by-pass, so to speak, the abo-

*John E. Fuller of Boston was a prominent abolitionist in New England. At the time of the schism in the antislavery movement, he opposed Garrison, but that was two years later. In September 1837 the Grimkés were having mail directed in Fuller's care, so apparently by this time, they had come to know him well. (See Gilbert H Barnes and Dwight L. Dumond, eds., *Letters of Theodore Dwight Weld, Angelina Grimké Weld, and Sarah Grimké, 1822-1844*, 2 vols. [1934; reprint ed., New York: Da Capo Press, 1970], 1:333, n. 9; also Sarah to Weld, 20 Sept. 1837, ibid., 1:450.)

litionist men and personally make an independent application to the chairman "as a Woman, as a Southerner, as a moral human being." False rumors had begun to circulate, reaching as far as Philadelphia, that Angelina Grimké had already written the chairman of the legislative committee asking to be heard. She had not yet written, though she planned to if necessary, so great was the importance of this opening, "the most important step I have ever been called to take—important to Woman, to the Slave, to my Country & the World."[102]

Stanton and Fuller were indeed hesitating, but not for the reasons Angelina had supposed. Stanton admitted to Weld later what the true reason was. They had learned that Sarah had decided to appear. These men regarded Sarah as a dull, pedestrian speaker and feared she would bring ruin to their plan, yet they were unwilling to ask Sarah not to speak. Sarah meanwhile was referring to "our" lectures before the Massachusetts legislative committee. On February 12, after Stanton and Fuller had called, she was writing to Weld that the two men were "backing out" and that Stanton had even said he thought Weld would disapprove. "My heart refused to believe it," Sarah said. Four days later Sarah wrote Weld again. "As we had heard nothing from the Committee of the A.S. Society relative to our addressing the Committee of the Legislature, we concluded to write them ourselves." This Angelina had done and was assigned two dates, both in late February. Sarah said to Weld, "I expect to occupy the first and A. the second."[103] Then by whose arrangement was Sarah to lecture, since Angelina was the only one who had been invited? Angelina let drop the answer in a letter to Jane Smith. "Therefore X [struck out] we wrote to James Alvord the Chairman of the Committee of the Legislature," adding below, "Sister felt she had something to say also."[104] As matters turned out, Sarah had a violent cold and was not even present at the first hearing.

The historic date was set for February 21, 1838. Angelina was at work on her momentous preparation when, with shattering abruptness, the unanticipated occurred. The totally unsuspected was suddenly revealed, leaving her shaken to the roots of her being, so great was the tumult of heart and mind, so intense the joy.

Theodore Weld might never have spoken, and he made his declaration in a spirit of despair, convinced as he was that Angelina did not love him but only regarded him as a dear and valued brother. It was nearly a year since the Grimkés had left New York. Throughout those months there was constant exchange, though rarely between Weld and Angelina alone. Sarah was assiduous in writing her share, and sometimes most of a letter was hers, so that usually Weld had begun his letters, "My dear Sisters," "My very dear Sisters," "My ever dear Sisters Sarah and Angelina," or "My beloved Sisters."

It was a bitter irony, in retrospect, that what forced Weld's avowal was the letter he had penned in October 1837, in this instance to Angelina alone. Sarah, of course, had read it, as she did all of Weld's letters. Weld was a believer in the duty of criticism, the faithful pointing out of a fellow-being's faults, provided it was done "in the love of Christ," and he expected the same "faithful" treatment toward himself. The October letter was the one in which he had delivered his scathing rebuttal of Angelina's complaints against the Executive Committee of the society and, for good measure, had declared that she herself stood condemned for un-Christlike traits of pride, arrogance, and gross self-deception. Angelina had continued to write to Weld occasionally; why would she not, feeling toward him as she did. Yet she had waited three months to allude to his rebuke, and while her words were restrained and she "thanked God for such a friend," she said she felt that "in some things you wronged me *in that letter never to be forgotten.*" Also she felt his letter had not been written "in the spirit of love," though she would not assert she had read it aright. She admitted to a wound that "would not heal" and asked that they write no further on the matter, adding—and she wrote large to drive her words home—"WE CANNOT UNDERSTAND EACH OTHER."[105] Weld received this letter in early February. His reply reached her a few days later.

It gave her pause to see the letter was marked "Private" (the one and only time, as far as can be found).[106] It began abruptly: "A paragraph in your last letter, Angelina, went to my *soul*"; it was not merely that she had said she felt he had "wronged" her, but she had asked to have all her letters to him destroyed, save the one he had said she should "be ashamed of" and with it her assertion—they could not "understand each other." He spoke of the pain her words had given him, dwelt on it a little and his turbulent emotions, though, more importantly, he wrote of the pain he had inflicted on her, as he feared, "ABIDING PAIN." "Oh, surely the probe that finds the core need not be tipped with *fire,* nor leave a rankling poison in the wound. Just enough pressure on the probe to reach the seat of the disease is *kindness,* but to thrust through and through with a rude and lacerating violence." So he knew he had used violence of a subtle, personal kind, even though he could add, "What shall I call it? Have I indeed done this to *you* Angelina?" At last, in his letter, he came to his avowal: he must "fulfill an obligation" he was now convinced "should have been discharged long ago," "a sacred duty which I owed to you, to my own soul, and to our Father." After "long conflict" he felt impelled "to avow to you what until recently I had fully purposed should be made known to you only by the disclosures of another world. . . . I know it will surprise and even amaze you, Angelina, when I say to you as I now do, that for a long time, *you have had my whole heart.*"

He wrote of how long she had meant much to him, that her letter to Garrison in 1835 "formed an era in my feelings and a crisis in my history that drew my spirit toward yours by irrepressible affinities." He had read it many times, in the deep consciousness that he would find in her spirit, though he had not yet met her, "the searchless power of *congenial communings* which I had always been pining for." Ever since, "I felt as though *communion with your spirit* was a *law* and a *necessity* of my being." He strove against it, though from the time he had met her until this moment of writing, this same state of mind had continued, gathering in strength; "that affection for you, Angelina, has intrenched itself among my deepest susceptibilities and taken the strong holds of my nature." This might seem inconsistent after his letter rebuking her, and he had no explanation. "Thoughts and feelings long restrained and smothered only by constant conflict now crowd for utterance." Thereupon he made a statement he called "fact," "the knowledge of which *may spare you much pain.* It is this. I have *no expectation* and almost no *hope* that my feelings are in *any degree* RECIPROCATED BY YOU." Was he saying that on this account he had not declared his love? "When I found the strength of my affection for you, I strove against it till weary with conflict and convicted of sin." But he added, "It has often occurred to me that God might have ordered it in his providence as a crowning trial, to test my love to Him and see whether I would at His bidding cheerfully relinquish *all, but* Him and *for* Him. . . . I trust I *have* brought my insurrectionary spirit into captivity unto the obedience of Christ. . . . To God and the word of His grace I commit you and in submission to *His will* wait the issue."

This ended Weld's letter, except that there was a postscript, one all too fateful for the coming years. He had marked the letter "Private," "not however because I have the least unwillingness that dear sister Sarah should see it if it is your wish and desire." Sarah saw the letter, read it in full, and also she read Angelina's intimate reply.[107]

"Your letter was indeed a great surprise, My Brother, and yet it was no surprise at all," surprise because he had so controlled his feelings as not to reveal them, even to her. But no surprise, because "in the depths of my own heart *there was found a response* which I could not but believe was produced there by an undefinable feeling in yours." When she saw the "Private," "I tho't you had found it your duty to reprove me again. . . . You say that my letter revealed to you that you had inflicted 'abiding pain'; Yes! you did, and it was love for you which caused reproof to sink so deep. . . . It was impossible you could love me, save as a poor unworthy sinner. . . . You have broken the precious box of ointment over my wounded spirit, and it is healed."

She was deeply moved that he had comprehended why she had been obliged to write the letter to Garrison. "Ah! you felt then that it was written under tremendous pressure of feelings bursting up with volcanic violence . . . you felt that it was the first long breath of *liberty* which my imprisoned spirit dared to respire whilst it pined in hopeless bondage, panting after freedom to *think aloud*." And now she could tell him how a letter of his published in the *Liberator* before she knew him "drew my spirit to yours. . . . I felt that there was a kindred mind, a congenial soul and I longed to hold communion with you."

"You talk of the 'long conflict' you have had on account of your affection for me. I confess I have had the same on account of you. . . . I was frightened when I found that my happiness was becoming bound up in you, and I wrestled in prayer to be delivered from a state of mind which if it continued, must unfit me for the work to which I believed myself called." Now within the long weeks since his October letter reached her, her suppressed feelings had returned in full strength. "I have prayed earnestly . . . [asking God] if it was wrong for me to love you *as* I did; WHY HE had constistituted me a being imperfect, a *half* only of myself as it were; why He had created these restless longings of my heart after communion and union, deep and pure and chaste and indestructible? . . . my only hope that He had awakened corresponding feelings in your soul." At the end she reproached him a little: why had he suppressed his love so long, when the customs of society had given him the right to make the advances. "I was too proud to break the fetters which had been fastened on me [by society]. . . . But why have you so purposely and perseveringly 'smothered your feelings by constant conflict'?" This, she said, was as unaccountable to her as that he should say that he did not expect his love to be reciprocated.

Weld did not rush to Angelina's side. When her letter reached him telling him of her love, he implied that he was almost incoherent for a time and several days passed before he could even write. He told her he must wait until he had gained full self-possession—his inner tumult was too great, his emotions too volcanic. Moreover, Angelina was now confronting her greatest challenge—the opportunity of addressing an official legislative body to plead the cause they were both committed to. Both voiced trepidation lest their personal crisis should distract Angelina from the task she faced.

The question remained in her mind as to whether she should urge Weld to come. She both longed for and feared his presence when she spoke. No occasion hitherto could compare with her appearance before a committee of the Massachusetts legislature so that, at all cost, she wished to excel. Yet to see Weld, and on the eve of her appearance—her fear was that "these two things together will almost overpower me." She was acutely aware that Weld had never heard her speak. Yet her first obligation was to the cause she served. In the end she left the decision to him, but at least she had opened the door to his coming and, by so doing, had dealt with her fear. "After some sleepless hours and much fervent prayer I feel compelled by a deep sense of duty to you My beloved Friend just to say that if you feel it is *right* in the sight of God to come on to the Meeting of the Leg. Com. I am willing that you should." She added, "The only query is, is it right? . . . I have NO will in it, therefore *I shall not be disappointed* if you do *not* come."[108] Weld replied that it was best he not come. It was far too "momentous a juncture in our blessed cause." While he might master his feelings, Angelina would see his conflict "and it would distress and cumber you, and the dear cause might be perilled." Moreover, so overwhelming were his emotions at this time, "I need the severe discipline of *absence* from you for a season."[109]

Angelina's first lecture was on February 21. Several abolitionist women accompanied her; Sarah was still ailing. The crowd was so great that the committee moved its hearing to the Hall of Representatives, which in turn was filled to overflowing. There had been no announcement, yet the word had spread that the "Orator in Petticoats," as a Boston paper called her, would be speaking on slavery in the Capitol building.

Angelina wrote Weld the night it was over, fervently thankful he had not been there. Never had she dreaded a meeting more. "The novelty of the scene, the weight of responsibility, the ceaseless exercise of mind thro' which I had passed for more than a week—all together sunk me to the earth." Maria Chapman, at her side as she rose to speak, murmured, "God strengthen you my Sister." That she found strength was fully manifest, although momentarily she felt great weakness and said her limbs trembled, but these feelings passed. For two solid hours she held her one thousand hearers thoroughly captivated; most of those in attendance were men, and not a few were worldly-wise and very probably somewhat cynical about man's inhumanity.[110]

Angelina felt that she spoke less than well, but it was not so with those who heard her that day. The House was tightly wedged for an hour before the appointed time; the Boston *Daily Advocate* said the crowd was so great that at least a thousand persons were unable to enter the hall.[111] Antislavery papers were filled with superlatives. Abolitionist women were not easy critics, yet Lydia Maria Child, long a leader in Massachusetts, was carried away as she pictured the scene in a letter to an absent friend.

> I thought of you several times while Angelina was addressing a committee of the Legislature. . . . I think it was a spectacle of the greatest moral sublimity ever witnessed. The house was full to overflowing. For a moment a sense of the immense responsibility resting on her seemed almost to overwhelm her. She trembled and grew pale. But this passed quickly, and she went on to speak gloriously, strong in utter forgetfulness of herself, and in her own earnest faith—in every word she uttered. "What so ever comes from the heart goes to the heart." I believe she made a very powerful impression on the audience. . . ."[112]

Two meetings originally had been scheduled for the Grimkés' appearance—when it was thought that both Sarah and Angelina would speak. James Alvord, the chairman, who was thoroughly antislavery, seized the opportunity to have Angelina speak again at the second meeting two days later.

Following her first appearance, however, a storm arose in the House. A resolution was introduced which might have blocked the second meeting; ostensibly the concern was for the safety of the building. The Committee on Public Buildings was instructed to draw up regulations, if needed, to limit the use of the hall. There was heated debate, and nobody was fooled, least of all the press and the abolitionists. Those favoring the resolution did not name Angelina, though a number referred to the "lady in question," especially to deny that she was under attack. One spoke of the untoward incidents because of the great crowd, for example, one lady who was caught in the jam had cried out "Murder!"—and in the Hall of Representatives![113] Representatives from Boston declared "these curiosity seekers" had so packed the place that the galleries were in danger of breaking down, whereupon a Salem member dryly proposed that "a committee be appointed to examine the foundations of the State House of Mass. . . . to see whether it will bear another lecture from Miss Grimké."[114] A special committee was appointed, though too late to stop the hearing, and Angelina was heard again in the Hall of Representatives.

The second hearing reflected the new tensions that had arisen, and of these Angelina was fully aware.

> My heart almost failed me when I learned that in consequence of the excessive crowd & the complaint of the legislators, that they could not get in, it had been determined to appropriate the whole of the floor to men only except two or three of my friends. Some hundreds of people were waiting downstairs when we got to the State House, kept down by several Constables with their long poles & we could only gain permission to pass by announcing who we were. At length we reached the Hall & found it full of men—I had never had such an audience to address before . . . but the Lord was there and helped me thro'.[115]

Sarah had recovered sufficiently to be with Angelina at the second hearing. They were squeezed through the door and into the hall, and even then, to gain the front, they had to walk over seats. At last the chairman announced that Angelina would be heard, whereupon a dense crowd of men at the door began to hiss. "I never felt more perfectly calm in my life," she wrote Weld. She arose to speak, but the noise of booing and hissing was so great that she was asked to wait until order could be restored. When she presently arose again, the noise was renewed. This was repeated at least three times. The chairman then tried another tactic, asking Angelina to stand near the committee, since under the circumstances they could not hear. First she was placed before the speaker's desk; a moment later, she was moved behind the secretary's desk—now she stood at an elevated position. "I had just arranged my papers [on the secretary's desk], when I was invited to stand at the Speaker's Desk and my dear Sister occupied the *Speaker's chair*. At last I got fixed and recommenced, after which I was suffered to speak without the least interruption for two hours to the densest and most quiet crowd I ever spoke [to] before."[116]

Angelina's name had now become a Boston byword. Mrs. Child referred to it with some dry humor. "One sign . . . is that the 'sound part of the community' (as they consider themselves) seek to give vent to their vexation by calling her Devil-ina instead of Angel-ina, and Miss Grimalkin instead of Miss Grimké. Another sign is that we have succeeded in obtaining the Odeon, one of the largest, most central halls, for her to speak in, and it is the first time such a place has been obtained for anti-slavery in this city."[117]

The old Odeon, once the Boston Theater, had a main floor and four roomy galleries rising tier on tier towards its ceiling. Three thousand people could be seated here. The Female Anti-Slavery Society of Boston had dared to hire this great hall for a series of lectures on the immediate emancipation for the slave by Angelina Grimké. In fact, the notices read, "the Misses Grimké," though it was assumed that Angelina would do the lecturing, while Sarah would appear at her side.

Weld and Angelina had not seen one another since the exchange of letters that revealed their love. Angelina was outspoken in her longing to see him, but Weld had held back—he must gain self-mastery. "The truth is, Angelina (for you have a right to know my *weaknesses* and *shall*—the *whole*)—I have so long wrestled with myself like a blind giant stifling by violence all the intensities of my nature that when at last they found *vent*, and your voice of love proclaimed a *deliverance* so unlooked for, so full, and free, revealed what I dared [not] *hope* for, and what I have never for a moment dreamed to be possible—that *your heart* was and *long had been mine*—it was as a life touch to one *dead;* all the pent up tides of my being . . . broke forth at once and spurned controul."[118] Angelina replied swiftly that his letter had distressed her. Why "still 'warring against nature,' " she exclaimed. "I am alarmed that under such a conflict of feeling, you still feel it right to rein in your emotions. . . . Why this waste of moral strength? . . . For *my sake* you must give over this conflict and let nature act out itself—don't torture and strangle her any longer." Now the Odeon lectures lay just ahead, and they had agreed that Weld would not attend them. The lectures were scheduled one a week for six weeks. He must come at once, she wrote him, or wait until they were over. Weld replied, "I will be with you on Saturday evening." He made an urgent request that allowed of no exceptions. "And now my love grant me this boon—I know you will—when I meet you, let me meet you ALONE. For a little while I MUST be *alone* with you. Do I ask too much?"[119] Perhaps it was well that Sarah read this letter.

The Philbricks were skillful in the careful arrangements. Angelina would have supper in her chamber. When Weld arrived, he would dine with the family, then the Philbricks, with Sarah, would go into Boston for a lecture, and Angelina would descend to the parlor where Weld waited.

Weld had left Angelina before the first Odeon meeting. They had held to their agreement that he should not remain in town, nor did he seem disposed to, even when he learned that Sarah would give the opening lecture. The announcement appeared in the March 21 papers, put there by the Female Anti-Slavery Society.[120]

> NOTICE. The MISSES GRIMKÉ will lecture on Slavery at the Odeon TOMORROW EVENING, March 22, at 7 o'clock. The public are respectfully invited to attend.
> M. W. Chapman
> A. N. Weston
> Committee of F.A.S. Society

The same notice was repeated on the day of the lecture, and this procedure was continued every week for the six weeks.

Before Weld's visit, Angelina had been dreading the Odeon

meetings—it was always the case before her lectures that she experienced feelings of anticipatory stagefright, a sense of heavy burden, a fear that she might fail, a feeling of the great responsibility she confronted. Nor could she seem to remember that these fears evaporated the moment she stood before her audience. At the same time, she knew the Odeon was the peak of her campaign, and she knew that the Boston women had planned it to be, so all the more she felt she must do well. As on other such occasions, she told Sarah of her feelings. Sarah's response was altogether unexpected: she proposed that she give all six lectures herself. Angelina wrote Weld of what "dear Sister" had suggested, but of course she knew she must do her share. Then Sarah insisted that she would give the first lecture, and this she did, though it had not been the plan of the society. The success of the Odeon lectures might very well hinge on the first meeting.[121] The Anti-Slavery women were counting on Angelina, who had aroused so great an interest at the legislative hearings.

The Odeon was packed for that first meeting. It was a surprised and apparently resentful audience, since all had come expecting to hear Angelina Grimké. At the legislative hearings hundreds had been unable to gain entrance to Angelina's lectures, and many of these people were in the Odeon, as were hundreds of others who had poured out to hear her. Nearly three thousand men and women sat waiting expectantly. Angelina was in the hall, so they assumed her turn would come, but only Sarah Grimké lectured that night. She spoke at length, and the meeting was ended.[122]

What followed was all the more tragic since Sarah believed she had succeeded. "Last evening," she wrote Jane Smith, "we held our first meeting at the Odeon." She had "trembled" at the thought of the great responsibility, "& my agonized spirit continually ejaculated Help Lord Jesus, or thy servant perisheth," but she felt a "sweet and strengthening" response in her soul, and after severe conflict felt "calm & resigned & went to the meeting trusting in the Lord—I need not tell you Jesus was with me & gave me utterance." She must indeed have believed this, since she had lost track of time and spoke upwards of two solid hours, tracing, she said, the history of slavery and speaking fearlessly. She felt that the audience had listened with respect and attention. True, a few boys in the upper gallery had hissed, and some had clapped loudly though they had been requested not to. But with "few exceptions," the audience remained until she was finished. Sarah was euphoric as she wrote Jane Smith. "Peace unutterable has been my portion, may he who gave me strength to do this great work keep me humble, keep me little, keep me low—."[123]

All through their campaign, Sarah had shown ambivalence, wishing to lecture yet turning away. She had written friends on several occasions that Angelina was the one who possessed the special gifts; "the cause is better pleaded if left entirely in her hands. My spirit has bowed to this dispensation with prayer for resignation to being thus laid aside."[124] It appears, however, that Sarah could not feel resigned and chose these great meetings to insist upon being heard. A cold had kept her from the legislative hearing, and now she was battling for the Odeon.

Following the first meeting, Sarah had heard a rumor that Angelina would be asked to give all the remaining lectures—at least it is assumed that this prompted Sarah's next action. Unknown to Angelina, Sarah wrote to Maria Chapman, who answered Sarah's letter but also showed it to Anna Weston, who in turn wrote Sarah. What Sarah wrote is known from Anna Weston's reply, dated April 4, 1838.[125] Clearly, Sarah's letter was bitter and accusing; she felt she was betrayed and must have said as much. Anna Weston wrote Sarah of how mistaken she was. "I know all about our plans for those lectures. . . . I never heard it suggested that you were not to deliver a proportion of the lectures. The *Sisters* Grimké were invited to lecture. . . . [The Odeon] was procured for the Misses Grimké & our advertisements were written accordingly." Mrs. Weston told Sarah that the men were the problem. "I know that the brethren cannot seem to comprehend that this matter is not in outline and detail entirely in their honor— & I think them given to *gossip.*" She admitted that the men thought Angelina a better lecturer. "I know that Angelina is more popular with many of the brethren than yourself—as a speaker—and that they asked to have her appear." Anna Weston then attempted to soothe Sarah's wounds by insisting she liked Sarah's lectures "just about as well." "We thought your tone peculiar and monotonous" but decided "you would probably get over that."

Sarah had not received the reply from Anna Weston when a letter reached her from Theodore Weld. Angelina was then immersed in preparation for her lecture, the second in the series, announced for March 30. Weld had written from Hartford soon after he had left them, while visiting a brother on his way to New York.

Weld's letter to Sarah began on an ominous note—he loved her "like a brother" and asked to take a "brother's liberty" with her. "I have the fullest confidence that we all love each other well enough to *inflict* pain upon each other if high and holy interests demand it." It seems that, as he had traveled from Brighton to Worcester, he had met travelers who were abolitionists—some ardent, some luke-warm—and also travelers with proslavery views. Abolition was the topic of discussion as they rode. On one matter both sides were in agreement, that Angelina Grimké's lectures before the legislature "had done more for the abolition cause in Massachusetts than any —or *all other measures together* for the whole season." The aboli-tionists were distressed with the first Odeon meeting, where Sarah had lectured; the antiabolitionists voiced delight and expressed the hope that Sarah would continue to speak, for if Angelina spoke, she would build up the abolition cause more than ever before. The abo-litionists told Weld privately how Sarah had planned to deliver one of the lectures before the legislative committee; they had wished to dissuade her but feared hurting her feelings; also they had "strangely the impression" that Sarah was determined and would not give way. It was not for faulty matter that her lectures were so poor but "lack of an interesting and happy manner of speaking," a manner so "monotonous and heavy" that, Weld implied, people were lulled and went to sleep. So that "far from increasing the power of the *truth* uttered," she had weakened it to the detriment of the "holy cause." Now Sarah was insisting on lecturing at the Odeon, had already given the first lecture, and these men were ap-palled, fearing lest the series might already have been ruined. The crowd, they said, had gone to hear Angelina and had waited pa-tiently, seeing Angelina present; hence they did not leave as the great mass would have "if they had supposed she was not to speak."

Weld then told Sarah why he felt he must write. He had heard Sarah say to Angelina, in his presence the day before he left, that she intended to give three of the Odeon lectures, including the last, and that she wished Angelina to lecture in Dorchester on that last evening—in short, to absent herself. Weld then put the issue so there was no escape. "I could not love the slave as I love myself, nor the cause of abolition as myself, nor you as myself, if I did not tell you all these things. The immense, *incalculable* interest at stake in the results of the Odeon lectures do so bear on the precious cause that I should have felt as tho guilty of treason to it if I had not told you this. . . . Now my beloved sister," Weld pressed home his point, "I am persuaded you will agree with me that the *only* the *only* question to be thought of for a moment in settling the question between you as to *who* would deliver the Odeon lectures is this: *which* of you will produce the *best* effect. . . . I have little doubt, but the crisis is momentous in Boston and demands the highest effect."[126]

Weld added at the end a hopeless request, one that could not fail to further lacerate Sarah's feelings, all the more since his concern was to save Angelina's. He begged Sarah to make any excuse whatsoever to withhold the contents of this letter from Angelina, fearing it would afflict her greatly if she read it. Far from withholding the letter from Angelina, Sarah read it aloud, every single word, and it may be that she found some bleak comfort at the sight of Angelina's pained and stricken face. Angelina wrote to Weld, "She read it all out to me—O! that thou hadst written *Private* over it. I love thee unutterably for such faithfulness to her and yet beloved it pained me more than words can tell. I thank the Lord *she* had not *my proud* heart, for she would suffer a hundred fold more than she now will with her sweet humility."[127]

Sarah added a postscript to this letter of Angelina's. Her secret, bitter pride let her write a few lines only. "I received thy letter last evening dear brother and our adored A. shall deliver the other lectures at the Odeon. S." Two days later, she wrote more extensively.[128] She thanked her "dear brother" for his letter, knowing he did it as an "offspring of duty." "It spake," she told him, "as the voice of Jehovah and I trembled in his presence. It seemed like the thunders of Almighty wrath, but I fell at his feet and said 'Tho he slay me yet will I trust in him.' " She then added words that showed how a dream had been shattered. "It seemed as if God rebuked me in anger for daring to set my feet on hallowed ground. And I was ready to covenant never again to open my lips for the slave."

Having made Weld confront her open, painful wound, Sarah proceeded to demonstrate that he need never have written. "Calmly and prayerfully," she had reviewed what she had done and did not regret having given the one lecture, for she was right, she believed, to bear part of the burden: "I was anxious to relieve my precious child." But she had had misgivings as to how many she should give, and several days before receiving Weld's letter she had written Maria Chapman asking what she should do. Maria's reply, which was "received previous to thy letter, decided me not to speak again at the Odeon." She enclosed Maria Chapman's letter for Weld to see.

Ostensibly this ended the painful incident for them all. Sarah's "sweet humility" was soon uppermost once more. It would surely have been better had she not hid her grief or forced herself to be so generous and self-effacing; then Angelina might have perceived far sooner that this wound of Sarah's was one that would not heal.

Angelina delivered the five remaining Odeon lectures, and she gave them alone. Her last appearance was on April 19. Samuel Philbrick noted those evenings in his diary: "Five lectures . . . before an assembly of men and women from all parts of the city." Every part of the building was crowded, he wrote, every aisle filled, "as many as three thousand at every meeting."[129] Long years after, abolitionists who had heard her still carried vivid memories of those meetings. Robert F. Wolcutt declared that he never would forget

> the wonderful manifestations of [her] power during six [sic] successive evenings, in what was then called the Odeon, the old Boston Theatre . . . the four galleries rising above the auditorium all crowded with a silent audience carried away with the calm simple eloquence which narrated what she and her sister had seen from their earliest days. And yet this Odeon scene, the audience so quiet and intensely absorbed, occurred at the most inflamed period in the anti-slavery contest. The effective agent in this phenomenon was Angelina's serene, commanding eloquence, a wonderful gift, which enchained attention, disarmed prejudice, and carried her hearers with her.[130]

Wendell Phillips described it as if it had happened yesterday. "Her public addresses were remarkable for the fulness and clearness of the arguments they urged. . . . Gifted with rare eloquence, she swept the chords of the human heart with a power that has never been surpassed, and rarely equalled. I well remember, evening after evening [at the Odeon], listening to eloquence such as never then had been heard from a woman. . . . Were I to single out the moral and intellectual trait which most won me, it was her serene indifference to the judgment of those about her. Self-poised, she seemed morally sufficient to herself."[131]

Sarah had been reporting to Weld on the lectures, one week "superior to anything she has done in Boston"; another, "not the same power, but an excellent lecture." Finally, "Beloved, it is over, last night A. closed her arduous labors at the Odeon. . . . The end crowned all, full of solemn pathos and deep feeling. . . . John Tappan was there. A lady told me he said a fire had been kindled which would never go out."[132]

Angelina and Weld had planned their wedding for May 24, but Weld's brother Lewis found it difficult to come at that time, for his School for the Deaf and Dumb in Hartford required his presence then. They were to be married in Philadelphia, at the home of the Grimkés' sister, Mrs. Anna Frost. Mrs. Frost might detest her sisters' abolitionism, but family feeling overcame her distaste when a wedding was involved.* Angelina was to attend the Anti-Slavery Convention of American Women in mid-May. Weld had been invited to another occasion, the dedication of the new and beautiful Pennsylvania Hall, a building erected by the lovers of liberty for free discussion of the great causes of the day. Weld had declined to speak because of a throat ailment—he had not lectured for more than a year. Angelina proposed May 14 for their wedding. She thought it a better date in any event, since their friends would already be in the city for the women's meeting and for the Pennsylvania Hall dedication. It is true, she admitted, that the fourteenth was awkward, since the women's convention began the next day, but it did not enter her mind to miss the convention. "And mighty as this event [their marriage] is, I should go out to the meetings as tho' nothing had occurred, although I do not believe"—she was writing to Weld—"I can be much use at such a time, married or unmarried."[133]

Angelina and Sarah had set their date for leaving Boston. They would go by Rhode Island to deliver several lectures, then on to Philadelphia to make preparations. One crucial matter had already been settled—that Sarah would make her home with the Welds. Following the wedding and after the conventions, Angelina and Weld—Sarah in their train—would leave Philadelphia for a kind of honeymoon. They would spend a brief time in Manlius, New York, with Weld's aging parents on the family farm. From there the three would go to Fort Lee, New Jersey, where Weld had rented a small

---

*Mary Grimké sent her blessing to Angelina and Weld in a long, cordial letter, relieved that her daughter would now have a male protector and hoping that Angelina would withdraw from public life after her marriage. (Mary S. Grimké to Angelina and Sarah, 4 Apr. 1838, Gilbert H. Barnes and Dwight L. Dumond, eds., *Letters of Theodore Dwight Weld, Angelina Grimké Weld, and Sarah Grimké, 1822-1844*, 2 vols. [1934; reprint ed., New York: Da Capo Press, 1970], 2:617-18.)

cottage that would be their modest first home, still largely un-
furnished until the sisters could arrive and select what was needed.
Sarah was at peace in her sense of belonging—Angelina and Weld
had gone to great lengths to reassure her—so she seemed to feel no
qualms about this far-reaching change in which she could no longer
feel that she came first. A few weeks later she was exclaiming to
Jane Smith, "O Jane, it is almost too great a blessing for us three to
be together in some quiet humble habitation, living to the Glory of
God."[134]

The *Liberator* reported the Grimkés' departure on April 24 from
the Boston depot.[135] "On Tuesday last, these intrepid advocates of
the slave bade farewell to Boston, and to the Commonwealth. . . .
It is creditable to the people of this state that, often as these beloved
coadjutors have addressed promiscuous audiences, they have been
listened to with respect, always with interest, and generally with
admiration—brute violence having been awed into decency in their
presence." A considerable number of abolitionist friends were as-
sembled at the depot to bid them goodbye, and perchance the
women, as they gazed at Angelina, were wondering within themselves whether the marriage would work. Would she remain the
same in the years to come, the uncompromising public advocate of
equality for all? Several of her friends had voiced these questions to
each other.

Invitations to the wedding were written in Angelina's hand;
both her signature and Weld's were appended to the note. She
wrote on abolitionist stationery, which bore at the top of the sheet
a black and white engraving of a young Negro slave, kneeling, in
chains.[136]

Dear Friend,

Wilt thou grant us thy presence, sympathy & prayers on
the occasion of our marriage which (the Lord permitting)
will take place at 8 o'clock on the evening of the 14th inst at
Anna H. Frost's No 3 Bellmont Place. Pray for us that our
dear Master may be present with us, and spread before us
all who meet on that solemn occasion a spiritual feast.

Angelina E. Grimké
Theodore D. Weld

May 1st

The wedding ceremony was designed by themselves. They had inquired concerning Pennsylvania law on the matter, since they wished no priestly intervention in their marriage. They learned it would be legal to exchange their vows, provided twelve witnesses were in attendance, one of them a justice of the peace, and that the contract be signed by the parties to the marriage and the twelve witnesses. In addition, for the protection of property rights, they were advised to have the marriage contract recorded, although they seemed to have decided the latter was unnecessary. So the way was clear for the marriage they desired.[137]

Eighty friends were invited, and a good number of these came to witness this unique wedding on that May evening: Julia Tappan from New York; abolitionist friends from Philadelphia—Jane Smith, the Grimkés' Negro friend Sarah Douglass, and other women who were active in the local antislavery society; and of course the women of the Boston group. Some of the men from the Lane Seminary days attended—Henry B. Stanton, Amos Dresser, Hiram Wilson, George A. Avery; Thome had been invited but could not come. A number were present from the New York group —Gerrit Smith, Lewis Tappan, Charles Burleigh, almost all who had been close to both Weld and Angelina. William Lloyd Garrison was prominent among the guests. Several Negroes were present by special invitation, among them two liberated slaves who had once been owned by the Grimkés of Charleston. John Greenleaf Whittier was both absent and present—he stepped outside during the actual marriage ceremony to avoid being disowned by the Society of Friends, as Angelina and Sarah were later disowned.

Sarah described the marriage not many days after in a letter to their friend Elizabeth Pease in London. Since neither Weld nor Angelina felt they could bind themselves to any prescribed form of words and vows, they said to one another what came from their hearts. Weld "alluded to the unrighteous power vested in a husband by the laws [of the country], over the person and property of his wife," and he renounced "all authority" thus accorded him, except "the influence which love would give to them over each other as moral and immortal beings." Angelina promised to "honor him, to prefer him above herself," "to love him with a pure heart fervently." Then all knelt, and Weld began to pray "for the blessing of God on their union, that it might be productive of enlarged usefulness, and increased sympathy for the slave." Angelina followed

Weld with a brief prayer, asking God's blessing "and that their union might glorify Him." Next a Negro Presbyterian minister prayed, then a white minister. Then, unable to restrain herself longer, Sarah prayed fervently and at length. Sarah's prayer brought this phase of the ceremony to an end, for Weld, Angelina and the company then arose. William Lloyd Garrison, as had been arranged, now read the contract to the gathering. Angelina and Weld appended their names, and all of the guests signed as witnesses—all but Whittier, who still waited outside the door. The ceremony over, there followed a season of "pleasant social intercourse."[138]

The Anti-Slavery Convention of American Women opened next morning, May 15, with Mary S. Parker of Boston presiding. Officers for the coming year were elected, and Angelina Grimké Weld was chosen a vice president.[139] That day the convention met in Pennsylvania Hall, in a small meeting room that seated several hundred people.

So new was the hall that painters were still at work, though the "great saloon" had been completed. Dedication ceremonies had already begun in this large meeting place, a series of programs to demonstrate the founders' aims. There were discussions of science, temperance, literature, slavery, and the rights of working men, for the hall had been built by hundreds of contributions, not only from abolitionists, but also from mechanics and other workers, and from prominent citizens as well. It was to provide a forum for free discussion of any question whatsoever, provided it was not "of an immoral character." Abolitionists probably would make more use of it than others; antislavery organizations greatly needed such a place, shut out as they often were from other halls, and there was an abolitionist bookstore in the building. It was a handsome building, well designed, and the best materials had been used in its construction and in the furnishings in the great hall. Above the stage here was the motto, "Virtue, Liberty and Independence." Dedication ceremonies were to last three days and would end in the afternoon of May 16.

On May 15 word had reached Samuel Webb, president of the Board of Managers of the hall, that placards had been posted throughout Philadelphia, all written by hand, though not always the same hand, reading as follows:

> Whereas a convention for the avowed purpose of effect-
> ing the immediate abolition of slavery in the Union is now
> in session in this city, it behooves all citizens, who enter-
> tain a proper respect for the right of property, and the
> preservation of the Constitution of the United States, to
> interfere, *forcibly* if they *must*, & prevent the violation of
> their pledges, heretofore held sacred.
> We would therefore propose to all persons, so disposed,
> to assemble at the Pennsylvania Hall in 6th Street, between
> Arch & Race, on tomorrow morning (Wednesday 16th of
> May) at 11 o'clock, and demand the immediate dispersion
> of said convention.—May 15, 1838.

One set of placards said "in Philadelphia" instead of "in this city," making some believe the writer was an outsider.[140]

The leaders of the Convention of Anti-Slavery Women knew of the placards and the threats they contained. Even so, they handed a request to Samuel Webb, president of the board, asking for the use of the great saloon, a hall that could accommodate three thousand people, on the evening of May 16 for a public meeting, a "promiscuous" gathering (men and women, black and white), to be addressed principally by Angelina Grimké Weld, Maria W. Chapman, and Lucretia Mott. The request came from several members of the women's convention, though not "officially," as Samuel Webb learned, because a number of women delegates strongly disapproved of females addressing promiscuous assemblies. Those women who signed their names did so only as individuals.

Samuel Webb was present on that evening and recorded what happened in a careful report, the events not only of this gathering, but of subsequent days as well. There were many eyewitnesses to all that transpired, some of them persons close to Angelina. Others were reporters from various newspapers—and the events were described in the press to an extraordinary degree. Some were prominent citizens who recorded what they witnessed in their diaries. Some were southern slaveowners who, by strange chance, were in Philadelphia at this time.

Long before meeting time the great hall was thronged. It was reported that thousands were unable to crowd in. There was little confusion within the building, however, although all who came saw the mob that was gathering, and even before the meeting had started, stones had crashed against windows. William Lloyd Garrison had been asked to speak, but he had been ill and said only a few words. By this time some rioters had entered the building, though apparently had not got inside the great hall itself. There were frequent outbreaks of loud disorder—hissing, shouting, attempts to intrude. Maria W. Chapman of Boston arose, waving her hand, hoping to bring quiet. It had never been her practice to address large audiences. "Oh! for the strength . . . on such an occasion to speak for the truth————" Uproar from outside drowned out her words. She attempted little more—her voice could not be heard. After Mrs. Chapman, Angelina arose to speak.[141]

It is known that Weld was present in the meeting hall,* much as he disliked large public assemblies and would not, by this time, address them himself. It is certain that Weld heard his wife speak that night. For the first and only time he witnessed Angelina's power, hidden though he may have been out of sight. Without a doubt he would have stood close at hand, for he, like all the others, could hear the sounds of the mob as it beat against the building. Weld had met many mobs in former days as he had gone about his own antislavery crusade, and he was known as a man who showed not the slightest fear.

Angelina had begun, "Men, brethren & fathers—mothers, daughters and sisters————," a few more words then yells from the mob. "Those voices from without ought to awaken and call out our warmest sympathies. Deluded beings! . . . They know not that they are undermining their own rights and their own happiness temporal and eternal . . . . Those voices without tell us that the spirit of slavery is here, and has been roused to wrath by our abolition speeches and conventions: for surely Liberty would not foam & tear itself with rage, because her friends multiplied daily . . . . As a Southerner I feel that it is my duty to stand up here tonight and bear testimony against slavery. . . . I witnessed for many years its demoralizing influence, and its destructiveness to human happi-

*William Lloyd Garrison told of seeing Weld at the close of the meeting, and of Weld's coming up to speak to Abby Kelley, then a young woman, and an active abolitionist in Massachusetts. This was her first occasion to address a large "promiscuous" gathering. Weld, said Garrison, "urged her to take the field as an anti-slavery lecturer; and laying his hand upon her shoulder, he said, in his vehement way, 'Abby, if you don't, God will smite you!' She obeyed his voice (and her own internal prompting) in the spring of 1839." Thereafter she traveled widely as an abolitionist lecturer (Wendell P. Garrison and Francis J. Garrison, *William Lloyd Garrison, 1805-1879: The Story of His Life Told by His Children*, 4 vols. [New York: Century Co., 1885-89], 2:216n).

ness———." Just then stones were thrown against the windows, a great noise arose without, and some commotion was started from those who had slipped into the building. It is said that Angelina stood quiet, serene, merely raising her magnificent voice to be heard. "What is a mob? What would the breaking of every window be? Any evidence that we are wrong, or that slavery is a good and wholesome institution? What if the mob should burst in upon us, break up our meeting and commit violence upon our persons— would this be anything compared to what the slaves endure? No, no: and we do not remember them 'as bound with them,' if we shrink in time of peril, or feel unwilling to sacrifice ourselves, if need be, for their sake." A great noise welled up from outside. "I thank the Lord that there is yet life left enough to feel the truth, even though it rages at it—that conscience is not completely seared as to be unmoved by the truth of the living God." Another outbreak from the mob, and some confusion inside caused by those who had slipped in. "How wonderfully constituted is the human mind! How it resists, as it can, all efforts made to reclaim it from error! I feel that all this disturbance is but an evidence that our efforts are the best that could have been adopted, or else the friends of slavery would not care what we say or do." Shoutings from outside, and stones thrown against the windows. "There is nothing to be feared from those who would stop our mouths, but they themselves should fear and tremble. The current is even now setting fast against them." The sounds of the mob grew ever louder and more threatening, but Angelina continued speaking for more than an hour.

Abby Kelley arose and spoke somewhat haltingly, for she had never addressed a mixed audience before, though soon she would become the intrepid public lecturer. Then Lucretia Mott, ever stalwart and serene, spoke a few quiet words to close the meeting. True, the mob outside had grown to several thousand, yet where could people go except through the mob? Strangely, when the doors opened, the angry men grew silent, and sullenly permitted the members of the audience to pass through.

The women's convention met in the hall again the next day, not in the great meeting hall, but in a smaller room. The leaders were particularly concerned about the colored members, who were heaped with insults as they came and went, for remnants of the mob still milled around the building. The white women present took great care to accompany the black members to and from each meeting.

As a result there were press reports of "amalgamationism" and "blacks and whites on the streets walking arm-in-arm." Rocks were thrown at them and ugly insults were hurled.

When the women met again on the morning of May 17 in a smaller lecture room of Pennsylvania Hall, five hundred women were present.[142] The minutes told that Lucretia Mott "made impressive remarks respecting the riot of the preceding evening," urging the women to stand fast. Angelina and Sarah were both present at this meeting. All that day the building had been surrounded by an ever-growing crowd of threatening men. Another meeting was scheduled for the late afternoon. Meanwhile, the women's Executive Committee was discussing convention business at a nearby house, and Angelina was present as a member of the Executive Committee. In the midst of their business, several abolitionist men rushed in to say that Pennsylvania Hall was surrounded and that, if they planned to gain entrance, they must go at once. One who was present said they first knelt in prayer, seeking "the sure refuge in time of trouble," and feeling great calm, they then "passed through the crowd of 'gentlemen of property & standing,' [i.e., those who comprised the mob] and took our seats in the Hall." Once again, as they left, "the colored members of the convention were protected by their white sisters," all passing through the mob, ignoring its presence, although a shower of stones descended on them. The Executive Committee met again at 8 o'clock—this was a hard-working body of women—and they met again in a private home near Pennsylvania Hall. They had heard rumors that the house would be attacked, so their season of prayer that evening was longer than usual.[143] Their prayers were hardly ended when several men rushed in, shouting that Pennsylvania Hall was in flames; the fire might at any moment reach this house, and they urged the women to leave at once. At first the women continued their business, but presently they were persuaded to go quickly to their lodgings.

Angelina learned later how the fire had been set, how methodical the preparations, how thoroughly carried out, and with no genuine interference from the city authorities. The mayor had merely come and spoken briefly to the mob: "We don't call out the militia here. You are *my police*." The mob had cheered the mayor and went on about its task. Those who did the work, so many testified, were largely younger men who came armed with beams and axes. They broke open doors, jerked blinds down, piled up the beautiful silk-plush chairs and with these, of course, all the abolition books. Then the gas pipes were opened and the piles were set afire, while outside the hall stood a huge crowd of men. Local newspapers asserted there were upwards of thirty thousand, "generally respectable [so one paper put it] and well-dressed, and determined, almost to a man, to protect from interruption the immediate agents in the destruction of the building."[144] When at last the fire engines arrived, firemen from only one turned their hoses on the flames, and when their fellow firemen saw this, they turned their hoses on those firemen. The firemen did, however, play streams of water on adjoining buildings. One New Orleans slaveowner who was present on this occasion wrote his local paper that he was much moved. "The noble firemen to a man refused to throw one drop of water on the consuming building . . . . I was on the spot when the fire began—and during the whole time. Not one drop of water did I see falling on the burning mass." He urged the New Orleans firemen to quickly hold a meeting to vote commendation to the Philadelphia firemen. An Augusta, Georgia, native wrote to his paper of how he was there with another southern gentleman, "And we lent our feeble efforts to effect the demolition of this castle of iniquity . . . . [The fire] assumed an aspect it had never worn before combined with its terrible majesty, beauty and delight . . . . Those beautiful spires of flame gave undoubted assurance to the heart of the Southron that . . . he had friends . . . who will defend him—at any hazard."[145]

Angelina saw the flames leap toward the night sky as the women left the house where they had met, and she heard the hoarse shouts of the satiated mob. Would the nation in its turn be enveloped in flames if the men of this mob had their way and would the multitude of people stand passively by? Angelina had long known that there were men who would use any force to preserve human slavery. In these recent months, as never hitherto, she had felt in her own person how much was at stake, as though all her perceptions had been acutely heightened by the use of the powers she now knew she possessed and by the love of a man who, like herself, was committed altogether to achieve emancipation.

IV. Like a Dark Cloud

"Why is it that we are not happy?. . . The fear often comes over me like a dark cloud that . . . we are not fulfilling our destiny."

> ANGELINA GRIMKÉ WELD, *in a letter to her husband, in 1849, after ten years of marriage.*

1.

The hidden struggle had begun even before their engagement, when Weld had confronted Angelina with her "faults." Angelina, while wounded, had not feared for the future, for though she knew she loved this man, she then supposed her love was hopeless. Moreover, she supposed that she shared Weld's belief in what he termed the duty of "absolute faithfulness," the obligation, as he later put it to Sarah, "that we can not only *bear* to hear the whole truth of ourselves from each other but the mutual understanding that *we are to hear it* at all times and the *whole* of it to the very uttermost."[1]

The controversy that had arisen over Henry C. Wright and Angelina's accusations against the national Executive Committee,[2] which had brought from Weld unsparing and caustic criticisms of her, was Angelina's first experience with Weld's "faithfulness" at its harshest. His words might have gone unheeded; Angelina might have remained herself and not sought to force her life into a mold not her

155

own. But then, after many weeks, she at last had replied to the accumulated criticisms he had heaped upon her in that letter "never-to-be-forgotten," and Weld, appalled by the rejection in her response, had burst his self-imposed bonds and declared his love. Thus their union was assured, with all that was to follow.

Once they were engaged, Angelina had told Weld that she recognized her faults and added some to his roster. She deplored her pride, how selfish she could be, how often irritable and impatient of contradiction. "Such an impatient temper, such a *little* soul, such a selfish heart."[3] Also it appears that she had become sensitive to what Weld had said of the dangers of ambition. She revealed this in a letter written on the evening following her first appearance in the Massachusetts State House, excited exhilaration sounding in her words. She had described how she was finally ushered to the speaker's desk—she, a woman—and had spoken for two hours without the least interruption "to the densest and most quiet crowd I have ever spoken to before." "I think it was good," Angelina wrote Weld, then she suddenly grew fearful lest her spirit seem wrong, whereupon she voiced "deep humiliation of soul, for what am I?"—adding these surely fateful words: "I expect you to help me crucify the old man of sin and to crush down the first things of *pride* and self gratulation. O! Lord Jesus . . . purge out the old leaven and turn thy hand upon me until I am purified from dross. . . . I am sorely tempted to believe I have had a *triumph* this afternoon, but I pray to be delivered from such sinful, presumptuous thoughts."[4] After their engagement Angelina had written Weld that the wound he had inflicted was healed by his love. Yet could she ever erase from memory his climactic words, when he had insisted that she had studied everything more than the *"moral* elements" of her own spirit? "Long and desperate conflicts . . . have taught me that the soul's grand conquest is *self* conquest. . . . Whether or not as the old Greeks said 'Know thyself' came down from heaven, it is the gate to the entrance of the ONLY road that leads there. Oh Angelina! enter in! enter in!" Weld had never retracted his earlier criticisms, though the tenderness of love now suffused what he said. "I did not reprove you for anything which did not appear to me *real* defects and some of them *great* ones. . . . I saw these defects very clearly. . . . I longed exceedingly to do you good."[5]

It must be said for Weld that he revealed to Angelina, in the pas-

sionate tortuous letters following their engagement, all he knew to
tell her of the kind of man he was. And if he failed to say what he
had done to himself in the violence of his attempt to crush all self-
seeking and bend his rebel will to the dictates of his God, it was not
from any wish to hide himself from her. Of course Angelina might
have understood, as the man stood revealed in what he said and
was, except that her eyes were blinded by the joyful, brilliant light
that promised to transfigure all the years to come.

Admittedly the extremes of his expressions had given her pause—
"An untamed spirit—wild as the winds." His heart, he had told her,
had never been schooled, and "the leading strings with which he
sought to hold it had often snapped at its first wild bounds." "I look
back," he had written, "over the weary months and years since my
heart turned to you with such searchless power, and I feel come
over me an oppressive sense of . . . guilt and shame. Yes, I believe I
can say so. I now see and feel that I have laid violent hands on my
being and blindly striven like a very suicide to kill an inner life of my
nature while God quickened its vitality."[6]

Angelina had brushed aside his first revelations. "Can you say
nothing good about yourself?" He had insisted and persisted. "You
must know all the TRUTH." For page after page he had catalogued his
defects; in perverse fashion, though surely unaware, he had seemed
to find peace in the forbidding picture.

He was selfish, he had told her—not in its "gross, repulsive, vul-
gar forms," not in scrabbling for money or "scrambling after . . .
applause" but in "a secret meaner selfishness" that he did not
explain. He had a bad temper; though not malicious, he was often
irritable, often tempestuous. He was stern and severe; even children turned from him; and he quoted from friends whose very
words he remembered—"moveless severity," "deep wild gloom,"
"like a streak of lightning," "stern silent fierceness," and one had
said his countenance was like the inquisitor general. Sometimes, he
feared, he would cut her "to the heart by looks and tones and
words" that were unreasonable and cruel. He was impatient of contradiction, as she and Sarah well knew from his letters of past
months. He was intolerant, much prone, as she had witnessed, to
"put the worst construction on doubtful actions," though he knew
to do it was "unspeakably base." And when he did it, he was
"utterly unrelenting." "In two instances, I have broken the closest
and longest friendship in an *instant* and spurned from me those who

in a *single* instance blenched from principle." In some cases he was sure what he did was "unchristlike," though he sought at all times to live the way of Christ. One woeful trait was an "inveterate propensity to deal in sarcasm and contemptuous irony" when he was battling against opponents. "Contempt of opponents is one of the *trade winds* of my nature and very often it *blows a hurricane.*" He was willful, he had a "stupid and mulish preference for my own notions and my own way," so much so that there were times when he felt ashamed. Perhaps Angelina understood what Weld had told her of his loathing and disgust for artificial social life, the ways to be found among the upper and "middling classes"—"it is almost a martyrdom for me to mingle with them"—and many of these people supported abolition. Weld had told her he avoided their company if he could.[7]

He had spent a little time on less unlovely traits. He recognized himself as "poorly educated," contrary to the opinion his friends had of him. As a youth he had been an omnivorous reader and had sat up late reading in a poor light, until his eyesight had failed, and so for years he had read little. He had skipped the routines of the usual education, later concentrating only on the subjects he loved. Also he was self-indulgent, "downright indolent"; he procrastinated if he could. He was woefully absent-minded, never knowing the date or day of the week or where his pen was, though it might be in his mouth; often he would forget to wind his watch—he had had these traits for as long as he remembered. He was a dreamy man, often abstracted, not hearing questions put directly to him, taciturn in manner, inattentive to others' wants, not one who was thoughtful or who gave nameless services.

Personal habits—Weld had even dwelt on these—"many of them repulsive" to others he had no doubt.[8] He had said he scorned a mirror, yet how thoroughly he had observed himself: slovenly, he told her, careless in his appearance, a man of slouching gait and listless air, shoes slipshod and hardly ever blacked, coat rarely brushed, no fixed time for shaving, he simply wore the stubble until it chafed against his collar—or until friends begged him to make himself presentable. In pictures of Weld, his hair is flying wildly. He explained why here—because he rarely combed it, though he cared for it thoroughly in his own special way: every morning he doused his hair in cold water and then "frictionalized" it with a stiff brush, "letting it straggle in all directions like quills of a porcupine." His indifference to his appearance was notorious among his friends, so much so that he himself had begun to have misgivings. With it all, he reassured his love that he had a "mortal instinctive shrinking from *all dirt.*" Nor could he pass a single day, winter or summer, without washing his entire body—he would lose his self-respect if he ever failed to do it, though sometimes in winter he had to break through ice to get at the water for his daily bath.

Weld had said the love of daring was a passion with him—personal recklessness was of his very structure. As a boy no music had so delighted his ears as the roll and crash of a thunder storm; he would rush from the house into the field, whooping and hallooing in wild response. In childhood his reckless daring had nearly cost his life, and he had broken and dislocated so many bones, so bruised and lacerated his entire body, that the wonder was he had survived to manhood—"tornado boyhood" was the term he used. His perilous spirit had continued into adulthood. A few years before, while at Lane Seminary, he had often gone out at night into the deep woods to climb young trees and swing from them, fifteen or twenty feet, the higher the better. "Jumping, wrestling, leaping fences and chasms, standing on my head, diving into deep water" from high places—he loved these activities to this day. He said he feared he would often cause her anxiety, he could weep to think of it, yet it remained part of him, he could not deny it. He reminded her that she had seen him only in "grave discussion," in "investigations," or in "staid sober conversation," that she knew him only as "rigidly self possessed," "deliberate and stern and philosophical and solemnly contemplative." "You have never seen me unbend at all." Yet he was a man who loved "to cut capers," "all sorts of boyish capers with a perfect zest," every day, if possible, to find a place where he could not be seen and then "jump and hop and scream . . . throw stones," and he liked to play "tag" and "hide and seek." He added, there was simply no use to quote St. Paul to him; he had no intention of putting away these "childish things." "I cant," he had exclaimed in his letter to her. "They wont *go* away, and I dont want them to go; they are *part* of me; take them away and you destroy my *identity.*"

The most formidable "fault," the one Weld had greatly stressed, was the one he chose to call his "pride." It was almost an inversion of what is usually meant by the term, unless what it reflected was an inordinately high self-esteem, because he had been able, by the violence of his strength, to repress his normal ego needs. Consider Angelina's painful emotions as she read these reminders of his reproof of her ambitious nature. "Too proud to be ambitious," "too proud to seek applause," "too proud to tolerate it when lavished on me," "proud . . . that I can and do scorn applause . . . spurn flattery . . . indignantly dash down and shiver to atoms the censer in which others would burn incense to me." Too proud, he had told her, to "betray emotions, or . . . for an instant to lose my self-possession," or "to move a hair for personal interest," or "ever to defend my character when assailed, or my motives when impeached"; "too proud ever to *wince* even when the hot iron enters my soul."

Weld might call his pride "this great besetment of my soul," "the poisoned thorn that festers and corrodes." Even so, he was proud of the wreckage he had wrought, as he had met the crisis at his life's turning point. For what he had become began with his conversion. He had resisted the great revivalist, Charles H. Finney, although Finney had turned all the powers of his preaching on this young man until Weld's will was conquered. Weld was proud of his final submission. He told Angelina it was "grace" and the "power of miracles" that had brought him to "sit at Jesus feet." And when that conquest was accomplished "my pride raged like an infuriate fiend in the agony of a death struggle resisting unto blood, till finally in the unearthly conflict protracted thro a whole night, tho my bodily strength and power of endurance were great, they broke under me; and for hours I was prostrate on the floor of my room, *unable to stand*, writhing in agonies of proud, impenitent defying resistance to the Holy Spirit." Angelina knew some part of what had followed —that he had capitulated and had gone all the way, becoming one of Finney's "Holy Band," and that, still committed, he then gave himself fully and entirely to the antislavery cause. Perhaps she did not guess that it was then that he had learned what he believed he had most to fear, because his powers were those of a charismatic leader—"eloquent as an angel, and powerful as thunder," one who had heard him described him.[9] She knew that countless young men began to follow in his steps, eager, bold disciples in the abolition movement: Thome, Renshaw, Wattles, Stanton, Weed, and many others. Weld himself had named them, telling Angelina, "they strangely and stupidly idolized me . . . [and] implicitly . . . yielded themselves to my sway . . . the whole mass of [Lane] students who became abolitionists." And when, as was inevitable, he was called into the field to preach abolition to large throngs of people, was many times mobbed, stoned, and threatened, he would still remain in a town, quite unafraid, until opposition melted and he had captured the majority, enlisting them in the antislavery cause. She did not guess that he had felt exhilaration as he had used these powers with which he was endowed and that it aroused in him—there is some evidence of this—an overwhelming fear that ambition, applause, adulation, and success might rob him of his goal of the Christlike life, and Weld had been "too proud" to permit defeat.

What Angelina saw but could not comprehend, since all had been suppressed when she came to know Weld, was a man who was clearly aware of his powers yet had denied himself all the human satisfactions that he must have once felt when his followers responded. It appears that Weld had found a drastic solution that had reached its final phase when he was writing Angelina. Before he knew her he had already begun to make himself anonymous: refusing all offices in the abolition movement; avoiding conventions as though they were sin; voicing his unwillingness to lecture in large cities, as though he feared the great audiences might break down his will; refusing to let his letters from the field be published or to have his name appear on the tracts he had written. He hated to receive the recognition of a good salary and had accepted only enough to pay for room and board. Weld had had a major triumph at the Convention of the Seventy. Here Angelina had met him for the first time. For that stirring three weeks, he was the dominant figure—"Lion of the tribe of abolition," she had called him—lecturing, exhorting, training, teaching, for a brief time reverting to the man he really was. But the aftermath was catastrophic.

Weld had suffered difficulties with his voice when he was an agent, working ceaselessly and intensely for months on end to spread abolition in strategic states—Ohio, Pennsylvania, upper New York. When the Convention of the Seventy came to a close, Weld's voice was little more than a rasping croak. A tale went the rounds to account for this disaster: an accident at a certain Alum Creek somewhere in Ohio when Weld was on a lecture tour in 1831; the creek was swollen by winter rains of torrential proportions, and the stage he rode in had attempted to cross. Weld had almost lost his life in the icy waters, and it took him months to recover fully.[10] How this accident was related to his loss of voice no one then explained, but medical knowledge was somewhat limited in that day. It is surely conceivable that Weld had to lose his voice, his most essential instrument, if he would use his greatest powers. He may have found that he was unable to repress the whole of his normal human satisfactions, despite the ferocious demands of his "pride." One way he could win was by loss of his voice. In any event, he did win this way, and the Convention of the Seventy was his last appearance as a platform figure in the abolition movement.

Angelina Grimké could not have known such a thing was possible. The Weld she knew was the Weld of the convention, the Weld of Lane Seminary, the Weld who had swept the Midwest before him as he preached abolition in the field, the Weld of whom she had heard from the men who "idolized" him, and also the Weld of the steady correspondence from the time Angelina and Sarah had left New York.

While Weld had soon receded into full anonymity as far as the larger public was concerned, he, Angelina, and Sarah always attributed his withdrawal to his ailing throat, which they hoped and prayed would soon be healed.[11] In no sense was the man Angelina married a different man in other respects. His voice was stilled only for public speaking; in the quietness of small groups, in the classroom or the home, he continued through the years with constant use of his voice. His compelling personality went undiminished; the authority of his presence remained dominant and assured, and his unchanged principles were as adamant as ever. Unrelenting in his sureness that he knew Christ's way, he never faltered in his conviction that he must point out others' failures, admitting of course that he also had "faults."

Angelina knew the way of life Weld preferred, she knew his conception of what it meant to follow Christ, she knew his belief in human perfectibility* and that mutual criticism was a bounden duty, and she sensed the baffling violence of his turbulent nature. By his

---

*Since Theodore Weld was converted by Charles G. Finney and labored in Finney's band for some time, it may be assumed that his conception of human "perfectibility" was patterned after Finney's. It is said that Finney developed a theology of his own based on man's ability "to attain such spiritual stability as to become superior to his weakness and attain a state of perfection." This came to be called the "Oberlin Theology," since Finney was espousing it while serving as President of Oberlin College (William Warren Sweet, *Religion in the Development of American Culture, 1765-1840* [Gloucester, Mass.: Peter Smith, 1963], pp. 228-29).

own description she knew his "faults," though surely she did not comprehend them at once, in particular what Weld claimed his "pride" had accomplished in repressing satisfactions that she still enjoyed, though she prayed to be freed of the sin of self-love.

2.

If Weld and Angelina had set forth on married life as man and woman alone, instead of being "three," perhaps their great love might have brought them through to peace, despite the complications of Weld's repressed nature and the harsh and painful conflicts Angelina came to feel. There can be no doubt, it was Angelina's doing that Sarah became a member of the Weld family circle, even though it was Sarah who began the campaign. Once her sister was engaged, Sarah had not delayed. In a long involved letter to Weld (telling first of Angelina and of their joy in her engagement and rejoicing in his expressions of tenderness towards herself), she proceeded to make certain that Weld was aware of her own special claims on Angelina, the "child of my prayers" to whom she had been a mother as well as sister. She had told him she knew that change might lie ahead for her, for whom "the future was impenetrable . . . [but] the future is not mine it is God's, I am a little child whom he has led thus far & I know he will lead me still. I know," she told Weld, "if he separates me from you it will only be in tenderness to us because his blessed purpose can better be affected in & thro' us."[12] Angelina might have ignored Sarah's cues, though it is certain that Sarah talked explicitly with her sister of her lonely life, with its trials and sacrifices—this was often Sarah's theme in what she said and wrote, as was her submission to "God's holy will." A fortnight later Angelina was writing Weld,

> She has been a dear & tender & sympathizing sister with us. How can I ever be separated from her? O! Lord, wilt thou bind our hearts together & cast our lots together in this cold & desolate world, & bless us in each other, & make us instruments of good to the bleeding, heart-broken captives of our land. . . . If I am worth any thing to you, Theodore, then next to Jesus, render unto this loved one the love & the tribute of a grateful heart. She sacrificed every thing when she left Philadelphia 18 months ago to be my companion in that 'work of faith & love' to which I felt myself called in the holy cause of human rights.[13]

This letter had reached Weld on the eve of the first meeting since he and Angelina had declared their love. When Weld left Angelina, Sarah's fate had been settled. In a letter to Jane Smith directly after Weld's departure, Angelina was telling Jane of their future plans. "We calculate on getting HOME [their first home at Fort Lee] about the middle of the 6th month. Our dear sister Sarah expects to go with us & abide with us—this I regard as a great favor, for separation from her was my only fear, but Theodore loves her as a sister, & she is very much attached to him, so this arrangement is mutually pleasant to all of us."[14]

Angelina might have seen Sarah's tortuous traits—her compulsion to possess and her intensely rivalrous nature—even though these were hidden behind a self-effacing spirit. There had been ample opportunity in their life together. It was the easier course to accept the humble Sarah, the unselfish older sister who lived to serve others. Sarah's need to possess and to feel she belonged did not abate when Angelina found Weld. Sarah had sensed long before Angelina's engagement that Weld might declare himself and that separation from "her child" might thereafter be her fate, and Sarah's deepest dread was to lead her life alone. She had never left Weld to Angelina. Her letters to Weld were as frequent as Angelina's, or, if Angelina was writing, Sarah shared the sheet. Angelina had no privacy when it came to correspondence. Not only had Sarah read Weld's declaration of his love, but when Angelina had replied, Sarah had added her note, complaining that she had "bargained for more space." So Angelina had capitulated to Sarah's avid need not to be shut out from her intimate correspondence.

Not only had Angelina let Sarah feel she shared in Weld, but Weld himself had added a crucial element. He had done it in his zeal to try to save her pain when he had asked her to withdraw from the Odeon lectures: "and it is beyond expression a joy and strength to my spirit that God has so moulded *us three* into one spirit in *honesty* and *faithfulness* as well as in the *tenderness* of love." What Sarah seemed to desire, and what she won, was to be one of "three," not a mere appendage in a married sister's home. She had established a claim that she clung to through the years, a feeling of possession, and now when Sarah spoke it was "us," "our," "we," and Weld became her "Dearly beloved," "Beloved and longed for in the Lord," "Beloved," "Dearest."

Sarah's rivalrous nature had remained a hidden trait. Perhaps only in her journal was it glaringly apparent, and even there the religious expressions tend to obscure it as she poured forth her sufferings in prayer to God. Not until the sisters had entered public life did this feeling of Sarah's betray her overtly. She had many times said that Angelina had the gifts. Had she admitted to how unresponsive their audiences were to her? She surely was aware of the sudden transformation when Angelina approached the lectern: a stillness, yet an electrified excitement in the hall, and Angelina's powers to hold, to inform, to persuade, and to sway all those within the sound of her controlled and moving voice. Yet Sarah had shared some of the response that came by the mere fact of sharing the platform. As people had surged up to touch Angelina's hand, they had touched hers too, forgetting that she was dull, for she was an abolitionist and a Grimké Sister. And she had read and heard the "Grimké Sisters" acclaimed as pioneer females in the antislavery cause. Sarah knew she had failed as a Quaker minister; she had been rebuked by the elders for her faltering tongue, which to them seemed forced instead of an outpouring of the spirit within. As an abolitionist she had found a thrilling mission: she was a woman pioneer who had lectured numerous times, a public figure who had enjoyed recognition. She could tell herself that her former failure merely meant that she was never destined to be a Quaker minister and that the Lord had used that failure to help her find her present course. It was heady stuff for Sarah to have a career. Of course there was much else she could have done; she had considerable ability and great warmth toward individuals; and few female abolitionists ever became public lecturers. But Sarah wished to succeed as a public speaker, certainly in part driven by Angelina's great success. Perhaps she dreamed that a night would come when untapped gifts would suddenly emerge, and Sarah Grimké would captivate the throng. Had she hoped for this at her Odeon lecture? She assumed that she had succeeded when she wrote Jane Smith. Then Weld's letter came urging her to withdraw because her lecture at the Odeon had jeopardized the cause, and she wrote him, "I am ready to covenant never again to open my lips for the slave." Her sense of failure must have been overwhelming.

When Sarah began her life as one of the "three," she was a more crippled human being than she had ever been before. Outwardly she remained as she had always seemed, gentle, humble, deeply devout, unselfishly devoted to those she loved. Inwardly she was driven, as she had been since girlhood, by feelings of deprivation that had warped her deepest needs, these needs that again had suffered frustration and left their demands still unassuaged.

3.

The Weld home was established in June 1838 in a small house at Fort Lee, New York. It soon became apparent that Angelina, Sarah, and Weld were three disparate persons; each had a different expectation as to what a home should be. For a good many years none had known a home. During the long period since they had left Carolina, Angelina and Sarah had dwelt in friends' houses, sometimes well aware that they had worn out their welcome, and on their speaking tours of recent years, they were itinerant travelers, making short stays as guests in various homes. Weld had lived as chance decreed, most of the time in rented rooms, in neighborhoods of colored and white poor, as he strove to feel identity with the earth's disinherited. Weld, it must be said, had managed very well and had seemed to thrive on his hand-to-mouth existence.

Angelina was not so much enamored of a place as she was of the richness of her life with her husband. She wrote Jane Smith soon after their marriage of how confident they were that their union was of God. "We feel it every day. . . . Our love for each other is not of ourselves, its fountain head is from above, hence our faith in its endurance through all the changing scenes of life . . . the Lord has joined us together and made us *one* flesh," though even this early she sounded the poignant note, "far from my faults alienating [Theodore] from me [they] draw him still nearer."[15]

Sarah more than the other two spoke glowingly of a home and all it meant to be settled down at last. "O Jane, words cannot tell the goodness of the Lord to us since we have sat down under the shadow of our own roof and gathered round our humble board. Peace has flowed sweetly through our souls. The Lord has been in the midst, and blessed us with his presence." Sarah felt she must add that their daily aspiration was "Lord, show us thy will concerning us." In fact she hoped she would never be called forth. "I confess I do not love public work."[16]

Angelina and Weld believed in equality when a man and a woman married and established a home, and it had been their plan to live out their beliefs. But Weld was a man who lived by "principle," and he assumed that his preferences were what he had learned from Christ. Angelina believed that she supported these same principles, and Sarah was compliant. So almost unobtrusively Weld's way of life became dominant in the new household, as Weld's tastes and will set the tone of family life, and Angelina closed her eyes to what this might portend.

Weld had established them on the Graham diet system, a food fad he had practiced for a number of years. Angelina had turned to Grahamism shortly before her marriage. How strict Weld was is seen when later on Angelina's health required a helper in the home, and Weld asked Lewis Tappan to help them find a domestic. "Our peculiar mode of living as it may be to her quite an objection—she should know. . . . We *never have in our house* meat, butter, tea or coffee. We never provide them for any or allow them to be cooked in the house . . . nor tobacco, nor intoxicating drinks [are allowed]."[17] Sarah found that she had no choice but to live by this system and decided, as was her way, that it was pleasing to the Lord. She told of the Graham lectures they had heard and voiced her thankfulness that they had all been converted, that all were of "one heart and mind" in the matter. She decided it saved them much precious time. They could make good bread, which with milk, she said, made an excellent meal. One week she was cook, the next week, Angelina. Sarah liked to cook a week's supply in advance, which meant they often took their food "cool."[18] Angelina was never overly sanguine about her own cooking, but she declared that her husband liked what she prepared, especially if he was hungry from heavy labor in the garden. "Everything is sweet to him, so my rice and asparagus, potatoes, mush, and Indian bread all taste well, though some might not think it fit to eat."[19] This was written in the early months of their marriage. Weld gave no ground even for visitors, and there was a constant stream of guests, especially after they moved to Belleville, New Jersey, in 1839: the Grimkés' sister Anna Frost with her daughter and her daughter's husband; Weld's parents, aunts, uncles, brothers, and sisters; and a host of friends from their former active life, among them Jane Smith, Sarah Douglass, James Birney, John G. Whittier, Henry Stanton, and Elizabeth Cady. If the Welds' "simple meal" was rice and molasses, the visitors had it too; or it might be bread and milk, pie without shortening, hominy, or the vegetables Weld had grown. All guests were set down to the Welds' Graham diet and learned to accept it as a fact of the Weld home.

Weld cared little for the social amenities; he wished to be surrounded by the simple and austere, and even the household furnishings were adapted to his tastes, although Sarah, without thinking, had made curtains for the windows. It was Weld's wish that they do their own work, he on the outside, wife and sister in the house, though neither of the women had ever cooked before nor done much cleaning or scrubbing. Angelina felt that their home would be all the more blessed by doing their own work, and Sarah took it in her stride, as perforce she must. Both found themselves smiling at a letter from their mother, written from the ease of her Charleston slave household, "Pray, have you no servants? and do you mean among you, to perform all the offices of domestic employment? this my Daughter is like some of your other strange notions."[20] This regime went unaltered until children came, and Angelina became too unwell to carry a full load. Even then Weld insisted that they not have "servants" but helpers who were "friends" and members of the family, eating at the board, sharing their common life, and of course adhering to Weld's rigid taboos when it came to meat and drink. Angelina spoke dryly of her new role as she wrote her Boston friend, Anna Weston, before the antislavery schism had come between them: "We keep no help and are therefore filling up 'the appropriate Sphere of woman' to admiration, in the kitchen with baking pans and pots and steamers, etc., and in the parlor and chamber with the broom & duster. Indeed, I think our enemies would rejoice could they look in on us from day to day & see us in our domestic life, instead of lecturing to *promiscuous* audiences."[21]

Through these months Angelina was not entirely at peace. She knew she was torn by a nagging ambivalence: her desire for a home yet impatience with its restraints; her wish for Sarah's presence while disturbed by Sarah's claims; more than all else, her great love for Weld, with all he brought of deepest fulfillment, and an unacknowledged fear that he somehow curtailed her, though judging from his words he wished to place no restraints. Because Angelina, Weld, and Sarah were so strongly committed to a "Christlike life"— as each understood it—the issue soon became how to know God's will, how to be certain His voice called Angelina and not the desires of faulty human flesh. Hence the Weld home became an unacknowledged battleground as each of the three wrestled with the Lord and, in their joint life, contended with each other. Angelina's future was the principal issue, and Angelina alone expected and desired to continue her work as a public lecturer.

Before her marriage Angelina had sensed this dilemma and several times had tried to voice it to Weld. She would gladly, she told him, "change the exalted and public station I now occupy for the LOWEST, *private condition*," and in the same breath she added that "for woman's sake" she wished to prove that "well regulated minds can with *equal ease* occupy high and low stations and find *true* happiness in both."[22] Soon after they were married, she was groping once more, as she wrote an English friend, "I cannot tell thee how I love this private life—how I have thanked my heavenly Father for this respite from public labor." Even so, she could say that "whilst I am thus dwelling at ease I may not forget the captives of my land, or be unwilling to go forth again on the high places of the field, to combat the sin of slavery . . . if called to do so by Him who put me forth and went before me in days that are gone."[23] She voiced her belief that Weld would help her to go forth: "Dear Theodore entertains the noblest views on the rights and responsibilities of women, and will never lay a straw in the way of my lecturing."

Weld too was confident that he would never hold her back, nor did he feel that he had as time went on. Within their first two years together, when the calls would come and Angelina would exclaim that she must go, it was her duty, Weld would tell her to "wait," she must be sure it was God who called. "Wait on the Great Leader" was his admonition.

It was surely not deliberate that, during their first months of marriage, Weld, for a time, had diverted Angelina by proposing a major project that would absorb all of her time. He had found the writing of tracts to his taste, particularly now that his throat ailment precluded public speaking. He had written two important pieces anonymously, refusing to allow his name to appear as author. Angelina also had authored two pamphlets although, in her case, her name was attached. Weld now proposed to write another tract, *American Slavery As It Is*, which was published in 1839, months before the open split in the Anti-Slavery Society. It became perhaps the most famous of all antislavery writings. What Weld needed was current, telling material. He still worked in the New York antislavery office, going back and forth each day from Fort Lee. He enlisted Angelina and Sarah as his researchers, bringing them the material on which they could work at home.

This was not the first occasion on which Weld had advised such a course. Before the engagement he had urged the sisters, at a time when Angelina had been ill, to turn their energies away from public lecturing, as he had done since the difficulty with his throat. "I have never done half as much for Abolition as since I have stopped speaking." What was needed, he had said, was for some of the best men and women in the movement to turn to investigation, collating, compiling, gathering facts, writing. He could cut out work enough in half an hour to keep a dozen busy all winter long.[24] The proposal had appealed to Sarah at the time, though not to Angelina—so it seemed—for it had come on the eve of her greatest triumphs, her lectures in the State House in Boston and at the Odeon.

Now the situation was different. All were in a state of postmarital bliss, and the idea at the moment held great appeal—the three working together in behalf of the slave and working on a task that let the women remain in the home. The New York Commercial Reading Room kept its newspapers for a month before removing them from the shelves to sell to any buyer. Weld contracted to purchase all papers from southern states. These comprised the raw materials that he carted to his home. The design, he said, of *American Slavery As It Is*, was to make the South "condemn itself"; "slavery and cruelty were inseparable," "horrid brutality" was intrinsic to the system. All this could be proved from the mouths of slaveholders, not merely by editorials, letters, and speeches, but by advertisements such as "For Sale likely young negroes" and for a runaway—"my man Fountain . . . marked on the back with the whip." There were a few personal narratives by southern abolitionists, but the bulk of the contents of the tract came from the southern press. Angelina and Sarah gathered the material, and Weld put it together. Clearly, Angelina did a good deal besides. Weld's handwriting was atrocious, hers a beautiful script, so her intelligence, which any man would value in one who served as amanuensis, was put to good use as she spent hours recopying what he wrote, perhaps redrafting some of his notes, perhaps composing. Neither said so, but then Weld believed in anonymity.

When the work was completed, they climbed the attic stairs, curious to know how many papers had been covered. When the count reached twenty thousand, they let it suffice. Sarah believed she had never labored more assiduously for the slave than she had done that fall and winter. They were almost too busy, she wrote a friend, to lift their heads to see the winter landscape, beautiful though it was on their high bluff above the Hudson.

It was more than just the labor of gathering these materials that exhausted Angelina. Ten years had passed since she had left South Carolina. Since then she had experienced the exhilarating response from many thousands to her antislavery message, so she may have lost perspective on the old institution and believed that their people's movement could shatter the slave's bonds. She was brought to her senses as she read the southern papers, realizing with full force that slavery had never been more firmly entrenched or slaveholders more determined to maintain their way of life unimpaired. Sarah suggests the fierceness of the impact on them, "[We were] wrought up by our daily researches almost to a frensy of justice, intolerance, and enthusiasm to crush the viper that is eating out the vitals of the nation."[25]

There was another task in addition to clipping papers. Of the personal narratives in the famous tract, Sarah and Angelina were authors of two. First came Sarah's, on page 22, opening in characteristic tone and style: "As I left my native state on account of slavery, and deserted the home of my fathers to escape the sound of the lash and the shrieks of tortured victims"; then followed many tales of what she had seen and heard. Some twenty pages later, Angelina's account began. "I sit down to comply with thy request, preferred in the name of the Executive Committee of the American Anti-Slavery Society. The responsibility laid upon me by such a request, leaves me no option. While I live, and slavery lives, I *must* testify against it." While she disguised all identities, personal letters show that those of whom she wrote were members of her family, relatives, and friends, and many of them would recognize themselves in her stories, as did her sister, Anna Frost, who, when she read the tract, described it as "infamous."

The inhumanity of slavery could not be hid, even among those owners at the highest social levels. This was the point Angelina pushed and pressed. All of the stories were grim and unrelieved; many bore the imprint of her dark memories of the work house.

Angelina found the writing an acutely painful duty, as old recollections flooded her mind, and she relived the time when she, a child of a slaveowner, knew slave treatment face-to-face and was awakened to its cruelties. Some of the scenes she evoked were of her mother's harshness and her brother Henry's floggings of family slaves—though she did not identify her people by name, this she found impossible. Her writing at this time was all the more distressing because she knew that her mother lay close to death. Despite the gulf between them, home ties were strong; she yearned to see her mother after ten long years and to see her brother Henry; she still held to the hope that both might "repent" and renounce the "sin of slavery."

Angelina's mother died later that year, so she was never to know of *American Slavery As It Is*; that the book sold widely throughout the North—no less than a hundred thousand copies it was said; or that it became notorious even in the South, especially in Charleston where the Grimké name was known. The brothers and sisters felt the disgrace, and the bitterness of their estrangement was made more intense as they closed their hearts to their abolitionist sisters.[26]

In Angelina's account, she marveled at her escape. "Why I did not become totally hardened under the daily operation of the system, God only knows." As she wrote these words, her old dread of the violence bred by slavery, with its corrupting power, broke through. "Even were slavery not a curse to its victims, the exercise of arbitrary power works such fearful ruin upon the hearts of slaveholders that I would feel impelled to labor and pray for its overthrow with my last energies and my latest breath." She wrote this commitment in 1839, at the very threshold of those strange years to follow, when, to all appearances, she had withdrawn from her career as an active public figure laboring for emancipation.

4.

When Angelina Grimké first became a public figure, she was almost unaware of the simmering disagreements that were already apparent among antislavery leaders. She had read the *Liberator* eagerly and with zest; she had admired Garrison for his courage and outspokenness, and his principles appealed to her, the methods he advocated, especially nonresistance, for she continued to be haunted by the thought of "servile war." She admired the New York leaders, and she did not think it out of character that the national office of the American Anti-Slavery Society should invite Angelina Grimké, a single woman, to begin public lecturing for the abolition cause. It is true that their idea had been modestly conservative: they had invited Miss Grimké to lecture only to ladies in parlor meetings—the term "parlor meetings" had been used in their proposal. What actually developed has already been told.[27] Neither they nor Angelina could imagine her latent powers or dream that they would be unable to hold back her great talents or the growing crowds, men as well as women—those "promiscuous audiences" they so deeply deplored. As more and more men and women heard this remarkable female who could hold her listeners, even the merely curious, in silent absorption in her antislavery message, these conventional abolitionists became increasingly disturbed.

Only too soon had Angelina felt the opposition of the New York leaders to the practice of woman's freedom. Suppose that in early 1837 she had lectured in New York State, as she almost did, instead of joining the crusade in New England's freer air? New England had been freer because of Garrison and abolitionist men like him, and women abolitionists of the Boston area felt no qualms at arranging for "promiscuous" gatherings, opening meeting halls to all who would come, men and women, white and black. Once Angelina Grimké's name became known—provided local people had worked assiduously to publicize her—there was rarely any problem when it came to drawing throngs. Had she remained in New York, would any of this have happened? It is true that in New England there was outraged opposition to Angelina's and Sarah's unbiblical behavior, and this response came not only from the clergymen of the "Pastoral Letter" kind. Within the movement itself there were abolitionists like Amos Phelps who were sternly opposed to "promiscuous audiences" and perhaps, in their hearts, to female lecturers. As the disagreements sharpened into potential schism, Amos Phelps and some others joined the New York leaders in agreement with their principles, including opposition to equality of the sexes.

It should be remembered, when Angelina arrived in Boston in May 1837, she had already become committed to the cause of woman's freedom. So had Sarah. The New York leaders knew it, and some were apprehensive. Even Weld and Whittier, it will be recalled, wrote earnestly to Angelina and Sarah on the subject; both insisted that they believed in equal rights but that the cause of the slave was paramount at that moment. Angelina could assert that she took great pains never to mix the two causes in her lectures against slavery. However, Sarah's "Letters" on woman's rights, which were published during these same months, were not reassuring to the New York leaders.

Throughout this controversy of 1837-38, Angelina's staunch

support came first and foremost from the women, the stalwart Massachusetts antislavery group who had become her friends and most congenial companions. These included Maria Chapman, Lydia Maria Child, Anna Weston, Mary Parker, and Abby Kelley. There were also Lucretia Mott and others from the Philadelphia group who were outspoken on rights for women. Ever and always, there was Jane Smith, who, though not prominent in the Philadelphia female society, was important to Angelina for her unfailing friendship and unswerving loyalty.

When Angelina married Weld in May 1838, the crisis in the national society lay just ahead.[28] A premonitory split came in 1839, first in Massachusetts, then in the national convention. The question of woman's rights now became acute. When the American Anti-Slavery Society was formed and its constitution written in 1833, it provided that "all persons" could become members if they were nonslaveholders, supported society principles, and contributed money to carry on the work.[29] There was surely no intention of including women among the "persons" who could be full-fledged members, which meant those who could vote and hold office. Women were expected to have their own "female societies" in which they could be ever active and busy in the cause. By 1839 the Massachusetts society, taking "all persons" literally, had begun to admit women to all the privileges of membership, including the right to vote, to speak in discussions, to sit on committees, and even to hold office. This could hardly have happened without pressure from the female leaders who were prominent abolitionists in the state. Then the woman question, as it arose at this time, had to do with equality within the American Anti-Slavery Society. Garrison and his group, including women leaders, supported this right for female members. Some in the New York group strongly opposed it, while other leaders in this faction stressed various other questions that were at issue.

Among other crucial differences between the two factions, political action held a chief position. James Birney and Henry Stanton, in the New York wing, were leaders in urging the importance of politics; here, as they saw it, lay the best and surest means of gaining freedom for the slave. Garrison, for himself, was opposed to politics—"the political gulf which yawns to devour."[30] Garrison thought the hope for emancipation lay in a moral crusade. Moreover, a number of men on the Garrison side, with Henry C. Wright outstanding among them, frequently advocated a variety of causes. Some were ardent "peace men," some upheld nonresistance, a few pressed for what they called a "no-Government" doctrine, and some were so-called anticonstitution on the issue of slavery. In short, they were spreading their interests far and wide. Angelina and Sarah Grimké were briefly caught up in the multiple-cause idea during the period of their association with Henry C. Wright and were rebuked for it in severe terms by Theodore Weld in a letter he wrote them.

By the time of the 1840 national convention, the differences between the factions had fully crystallized.* Both sides had set to work to gain delegates for the convention. Several Massachusetts men chartered a boat and transported many delegates, especially Negroes, who otherwise could not have come. The Tappan men accused them of "packing the convention." Meanwhile, before the meeting, the *Emancipator*, the national organ of the society, had been taken over by the New York State society. Also national funds had been sequestered, allegedly to "secure its [the society's] indebtedness."[31] When the convention met, the chasm was deep. The delegates following Garrison were in a majority. A motion was carried to place a woman, Abby Kelley, on the convention's business committee, whereupon Lewis Tappan and Amos Phelps arose and led their delegates from the convention hall. From a separate meeting place, they formed a new society, the American and Foreign Anti-Slavery Society. The Garrison wing retained the old name, American Anti-Slavery Society and, having lost the *Emancipator*, established a new official organ in New York City, the *National Anti-Slavery Standard*, one of whose two editors was Lydia Maria Child, Angelina's warm friend in her New England days. When the Tappan men split off to form their new organization, this left some vacancies on the national executive committee of the old society. Three women were added: Lucretia Mott, Lydia Maria Child, and Maria Weston Chapman.[32]

---

*On the New York side were such well-known abolitionists as Arthur and Lewis Tappan, James Birney, Henry B. Stanton, Gerrit Smith, Amos A. Phelps, Elizur Wright, Jr., John G. Whittier, William Jay, Orange Scott, and William Goodell. Not all opposed the Garrison faction because of the woman issue; political action was of chief concern to some. On the Massachusetts side were William Lloyd Garrison, Wendell Phillips, Samuel J. May, Parker Pillsbury, Henry C. Wright, and virtually all the best-known women in the abolitionist movement. Weld had stood aside, so he is not included. The same was true for Angelina and Sarah Grimké.

One historian, Louis Filler,[33] believes it "incorrect" to view the woman question as either "helping or hindering" the abolition movement, since from the middle 1830s women were "strategic in every phase of antislavery"; the real question at issue was the "proper role of woman."* For the equal-rights women, this was indeed the basic issue that both then and later fired their efforts for full equality. It was not that these women failed to give prime emphasis to the abolition of slavery at any time. It was simply that they were seeking simultaneous emancipation for women. It seemed logical to their minds, and they said as much, that a movement laboring for freedom of the slave should accord equality to all its members, women as well as men. Naturally mere logic has never been very persuasive against long-embedded resistance that is born of custom and law. These women remained convinced, as subsequent events showed. It was not ten years later, in 1848, that a group of these leaders, with a few new names added, met at Seneca Fall, New York, to launch the first organization for woman's rights.

If the schism in the antislavery movement had not occurred, it is conceivable that Angelina might have responded to at least a few of the calls that reached her soon after her marriage and before she felt the hindrances that lay in wait. For a while she voiced thankfulness for the "respite from public labor," at the same time assuming that God would soon call her forth.

The very nature of schism placed Angelina, Weld, and Sarah in a

---

*It continues to be a question as to how significant the part played by the woman issue was in the split in 1840, since the opposing factions differed in other important questions. Dwight L. Dumond calls the woman question a "false issue" in the schism, in the sense that "slavery and the subordination of women did not equally violate basic natural rights of the individual." (*Antislavery: The Crusade for Freedom in America* [Ann Arbor: University of Michigan Press, 1961], p. 283.) Angelina Grimké once offered an answer to that argument, though it is doubtful that it convinced many antifeminist abolitionists. She stressed basic "human rights" and claimed that the rights of the slave and woman "blended," hence both should be labored for then and there, assuredly a view too far-fetched and idealistic for the practical reformers with whom she sometimes argued. (See p. 129.) Dumond also points to Garrison as a divisive influence. Louis Filler speaks of Garrison as "involuntarily" a pioneer for woman's rights, apparently suggesting that developments in the struggle between the two factions in a sense propelled Garrison into his strong support of an equal role for woman (*The Crusade against Slavery: 1830-1860* [New York: Harper & Brothers, 1960], pp. 129, 130-31). Filler's view on the importance of the woman's rights issue has been noted. Aileen S. Kraditor gives an illuminating appraisal of the whole issue of woman's rights in the antislavery movement in her *Means and Ends in American Abolitionism: Garrison and His Critics on Strategy and Tactics, 1834-1850* (New York: Pantheon Books, 1969), Chap. 3, "The Woman Question."

painful, wrenching dilemma. If they took sides, they would be on opposing sides, an unthinkable state for Angelina and Weld, who felt themselves one in the sight of God and felt they should be one where principles were at stake. Nor could Sarah have tolerated a separate course that would imperil the unity of the three, a unity she believed was straight from the Lord and a relationship from which she would not be torn.

Angelina's and Sarah's friends were of the Garrison wing, which included Garrison himself, Samuel May, Wendell Philips, Henry C. Wright, and other New England men, and the entire contingent of antislavery women who supported Garrison on the issue of equality. Especially, there were the Boston women, the Grimkés' warmest friends, and Lucretia Mott and others in Philadelphia. These were the men and women who had supported woman's freedom and full female equality in the Anti-Slavery Society. When, in 1837, the national Executive Committee had grown fearful of the Grimkés and in effect rebuked them for the course they took, the New England abolitionists had supported the sisters fully. Angelina felt at home with these New England friends. They agreed with her on the rights of woman, in particular on woman's right to address "promiscuous" audiences.

Weld's close associations were with the Tappan faction, the men on the national Executive Committee: Lewis and Arthur Tappan, who were the movement's main financial supporters, Elizur Wright, Arthur Leavitt, Beriah Green, James Birney, Henry Stanton, and Gerrit Smith. At the time of his marriage, Weld was working in the national office, where he had been stationed for two years or more. In 1839 he left his position, probably because the Welds had moved from Fort Lee to a farm at Belleville, New Jersey, which was farther from New York City. Angelina knew Weld's high regard for these men, knew it to her sorrow from the wound he had dealt her when she had sharply criticized the New York men and Weld had called her words "a railing accusation." "Your proof is merely your own construction put upon certain measures," and thus she had done "the Executive Committee *most causeless* and most *cruel* wrong." Once they were engaged Angelina had assured him that his harsh words had been wiped from her mind, but how could they be forgotten? Both would touch these still tender scars, but warily, when again the New York men became an issue.

The differences that split the movement made for harsh complications. For Angelina and Weld basic principles were involved, nor did these line up in ways that helped to ease their problem. Weld himself was "sound" on equality for women. He openly opposed the Tappan group's position. In late 1840 he was writing Amos Phelps, one of the more strident in the antiwoman group,

> As to the intrinsic question, that is, the doctrine of woman's *right*, as a moral agent to think & feel, her right to write what she thinks and feels, at the dictates of conscience, anywhere, to any person, & at all times, & to *act out* such thoughts & feelings—my heart has always cleaved to [illegible] it, and to repudiate the opposite doctrine. . . . On this account, the zeal which you and others feel & manifest in opposition to the doctrine is to me a mystery, which I can neither comprehend nor appreciate—at the same time, I must fully concede to you the [illegible] honest conviction that I claim for myself. . . .[34]

Then Angelina, Weld, and Sarah were of one mind on the general question of woman's rights. But the New York men opposed equality of the sexes within the society, while the Garrison wing demanded it in full, and Theodore Weld had long been at odds with William Lloyd Garrison and the methods he employed. As the conflict within the abolition movement grew acute, all voices grew louder, all charges more abrasive.

Following the final split, Angelina, Weld, and Sarah retreated to an uneasy neutral ground, perhaps the only tenable place given their different past connections. Sarah wrote a friend, "We feel it is almost impossible to judge in the case, our correspondents in Boston are all the friends of brother Garrison, and of course we know little except through them. We mourn that there are divisions amongst us."[35] And Angelina was commenting to their Negro friend, Sarah Douglass, "I do not wonder that your hearts are sick in view of the contentions and divisions in Massachusetts. I cannot read the *Liberator* now with any satisfaction. . . . I do not understand the controversy well enough to justify wholly either party."[36] Inevitably criticism was soon leveled against them, some of it harsh and unfeeling in tone. Angelina wrote Gerrit Smith, "We are hid here from the strife of tongues, and hear with equal indifference that our anti-slavery light has gone out in total darkness, & that Theodore and I have separated. O what a very little thing it is to be judged of man's judgment, & how preeminently do the signs of the times teach us to put no confidence in those we have been wont to

look up to as the princes of our land, in the great moral reforma-
tions of the day."[37] Sarah wrote of rumors reaching them from far
off England. "Elizabeth Stanton wrote us word that John Scoble
said we have changed our views on the subject of women's rights. I
am at a loss to imagine on what he founded such an assumption; we
thought we should have written ES & have told her that no one
had any just reason for saying so."[38] It was just as well that Angelina
no longer read the *Liberator*, at least one particular issue in 1842 in
which Garrison sharply attacked, on the grounds of inactivity in
the cause of the slave, some of those who had split off in 1840.
Where, he asked, were the Tappans, Birney, and Henry Stanton,
and he named others, among them, Weld. "Where is Theodore
Weld and his wife, and Sarah M. Grimké? All 'in the quiet', and far
removed from all strife . . . Once the land was shaken by their free
spirits, but now they are neither seen nor felt."[39]

One reason that the Welds and Sarah could be accused of being
"hid from the strife of tongues" was the move they had made in late
1839. The three together had purchased a working farm in Belleville, New Jersey, nine miles from New York City. Weld knew how
to farm, his father was a farmer, and a belief in manual labor had
long been a Weld principle. It was his intention to work the farm
himself and thereby solve the problem of supporting his family. The
three rejoiced in the large comfortable house on the place, the
peaceful and pleasant views, the adequate space, and the additional
rooms they would be needing as the Weld children came.

When they moved to Belleville, Weld had left his salaried work in
the antislavery office. The distance was too great for him to travel
each day, and in any event he expected to farm. Perhaps they felt
relief that the matter was settled for them, for if Weld had labored
for the new split-off society, it would have meant that he was
openly on the Tappan side.

Even so, Weld's relations with the Tappans were never strained.
He could feel towards them as he felt towards Amos Phelps,
though Phelps was a leader on the antifeminist side—these men had
the right, even as he did himself, to hold fast to their own honest
convictions. Through succeeding years Weld's close friendship with
the Tappans remained unclouded. He hated to borrow money, but
he borrowed from Lewis Tappan, not once, but several times. He
even did so around the time of the antislavery schism, perhaps to
help in the purchase of the Belleville farm.[40] While he refused to join

the Tappans' "anti-woman society," otherwise relations with them were unchanged.

As matters turned out, Weld was able to retain his old friends, something Angelina found difficult to do. Nearly all of her friends were on the woman's rights side. While the schism was acute, she felt herself unable to uphold them openly, even though in heart and mind she had not changed her views. Thus she held her peace when her friends felt she should have spoken. When they again began urging her to lecture, new obstacles had arisen for Angelina. By the early 1840s, some old friends had become estranged, because, as time went by, Angelina remained aloof, making no move to return to public life. To them she was abandoning her duty to the slave and betraying the cause of woman's freedom.

Three children were born to Angelina and Weld: the first child, Charles Stuart, in late 1839; a second son, Theodore, at the end of 1840; a debilitating miscarriage occurred two years later; and the last child, Sarah, came in 1844. During a part of this time Weld was absent in Washington, which made it all the more difficult for Angelina to be away.

Weld was called to Washington on a much-welcomed assignment in the winter of 1841. Joshua Giddings and other antislavery congressmen stood in need of Weld's help behind the scenes. A new "gag rule" had been passed in the House which forbade even the reception of petitions against slavery. The right of petition was thus crassly denied. Certain congressmen, led by Giddings, determined to fight the "gag" by bringing in bills and introducing resolutions that would open up the issue to debate on the floor. They had no time to assemble material, they needed information for their speeches, they needed guidance when it came to strategy, and they also needed lobbyists to win congressmen to their side. These would be Weld's duties, as they were described to him.

That winter Weld had planned to labor on the Belleville farm, work that was greatly needed to make the place pay a living. While the congressmen would pay for travel and his expenses while in Washington, Weld would be obliged to hire labor for the farm, for which the Welds had no funds. Ostensibly Angelina had an inheritance, and until recently the income had sufficed to support her. But a Philadelphia businessman had invested the money for her, had then lost his fortune in the economic slump, and now seemed to

have no funds to repay Angelina. Although he had promised to restore the entire amount, all he had sent was an occasional few
hundred dollars in interest. Sarah's independent income remained
intact, and she contributed her part to the upkeep of the home, but
Weld wished to be his own family's main support. How could he go,
he insisted, leaving the farm untended and his wife and children
without funds? Angelina was insistent—he must go. In the end
Weld again borrowed from Lewis Tappan to keep his family going
while he was away.

Weld was in Washington for two sessions of the Congress in 1842
and 1843, returning home as he could for the periods between the
sessions. In Washington he lived in Mrs. Sprigg's boarding house,
where Giddings and other like-minded congressmen rented rooms,
a dwelling that won the name of "Abolition House," a term of op-
probrium used by southern congressmen. It had been years since
Weld had engaged in such strategic work, so interesting, absorbing,
and demanding of great skill. His letters home voiced his deep involvement.

If Angelina were envious of this opportunity that came to Weld
which, under the circumstances, meant that she must remain at
home, she gave no sign in anything she said, no hint that her belief
in equality of the sexes was involved. She assumed there were times
when each must aid the other. Perhaps one other thought entered
Angelina's mind—the idea is implied though not made explicit—
she may have feared that she herself would never feel free to go as
long as her beloved refused to use his powers. Angelina was over-
joyed by her husband's opportunity: Weld's great talents would be
put to work again, work of such importance in the antislavery
cause. She heard from Weld frequently, reading eagerly of his
work, and was distressed because he worried about their burdens at
home. Her letters often showed her attempts to reassure him. Time
and again she voiced her pleasure in his work, telling him that she
missed him "comparatively little," so greatly did she rejoice that he
had been called again "to labor for the poor slave," but at the same
time she admitted that she sometimes trembled at the danger he was
in, living in a city of slaveholders. When Weld wrote her of material
he had furnished John Quincy Adams for a speech in Congress, she
exclaimed in pleasure, "Oh how cheerfully we give thee up." After
reading of his discussions with Joshua Giddings and Mr. Adams
about a certain crisis in the Congress, Angelina responded, "This is

the very kind of aid in great emergencies thou canst *not* render if thou art at home." And in another letter, "I expect thee to do as much good thro thy influence over a few minds in Congress as by the material."

Angelina had not been well and later suffered a miscarriage, so Weld was feeling strongly that he should be at home. This was in his second winter in Washington. Angelina pleaded with him to continue the work. "We want thee to consider *well* what duty is, before thou makest up thy mind *not* to return." She told him, "Thou art so exactly in the right place." She believed that soon he, in his own person, might be called upon "to plead the cause of the poor slave before a Committee [of the Congress]."[41] She never was at peace with Weld's desire for anonymity.

It is true that while Weld was absent a heavy load fell on the sisters, particularly on Angelina, who must manage the farm. She employed hired hands, purchased supplies, occasionally had to make decisions on where to plow and plant, though Weld had made most of the arrangments before he left, and she gave careful supervision for fear the precious borrowed funds would be frittered away. She also carried her share of household duties, along with some care of her two small sons.

5.

Admittedly Angelina was not without ambition and had recognized it long before when, apparently without guilt, she had said to herself, "My restless, ambitious temper, so different from dear Sister's, craves high duties and high attainments, and I have at times thought this ambition was a motive to me to do my duty and submit my will." It is true that she termed these feelings possible "temptations," and yet she did not fear them. While she responded to the approbation the world could give, she felt her deep desire was to let her God guide her, a commitment that had grown in the antislavery years. From her first public appearance and her rising fame, she had gloried in the freedom to use her gifts fully and had sensed how they seemed to multiply in power as her audiences increased in size and in the degree of their rapt attention. Angelina had voiced some fear that she might love acclaim too much, might think it was she and not her God who spoke through her, yet her fears were forgotten when she stood before the people and felt their response to the sheer power of her presence.[42]

In 1837 Weld had written Angelina, in his biting arraignment of Henry C. Wright, concerning the serious flaw of overweening ambition. Ostensibly his criticism had been directed at Wright. Weld's letter was brought on when the sisters had reproached Weld for his "unloving" attitude toward this brother in the cause. It seemed as though Weld had grasped at the chance to let Wright become the vehicle of a point he wished to make. From the time of his childhood, Weld had written, "exhibitions of personal vanity, ostentatious display, self-complacency, an overweening restlessness to show oneself and to be conspicuous and attract attention, had so excited my disgust and loathing that language could not express the repulsion." While he would not assert that Wright had such feelings, he seemed to have them—"itching to be known." Witness, Weld had urged, the number of articles signed by H. C. Wright in each issue of the *Liberator*, the *Emancipator*, the *Friend of Man*, and *Zion's Watchman*, sometimes two or more in the same week, and most of the articles required no name. "I have fairly hung my head and blushed for brother Wright." Weld had hammered away at the "famous 'Domestic Scene' ": "Brother Wright, with a preparatory note to herald the scene, walks leisurely out before the broad eye of the three thousand subscribers and hardly less than twenty thousand readers of the *Liberator*, and on that conspicuous eminence spread out his 'Domestic Scene.' . . . There is the table, the lamp, the Bible, the Grimkés, and here am *I* (i.e. H. C. Wright)." There were arguments back and forth, "and finally the *conquest* formally announced—'the conclusion was unanimous,' " they had all agreed with Wright. Weld's biting sarcasm could not be forgotten, nor the direct question he had put to Angelina: was "such a way of doing things, so apparently vain and ostentatious . . . ACCORDING TO YOUR TASTES?" He would not believe it, he had told the sisters.

Weld had then proceeded to make his central point, insisting that he did not write in a spirit of anger but "in sickness of heart, in mourning, grief and agony." For he hated all the ways in which abolitionists "seemed to be seeking fame and notice." "Oh what innumerable changes are incessantly rung and have been for years on the 'splendor,' 'eloquence,' 'irresistible power,' 'burst of sublimity,' 'profound argumentation,' 'logic,' 'power of appeal,' 'unrivalled,' 'peerless,' etc. etc. . . ." The winter before, he had reminded them, they had talked of these things—the perils to leaders of "the immense temptations, desire for applause, ambitious pomp and circumstance, the sickening eulogies of Speakers"; last winter the sisters had seemed to agree. How was it with them now? "As I look over our ranks, I sometimes ask myself how many of these brethren and sisters would do *just as much* in the abolitionist cause if they worked utterly in the dark, and they were never known as writers, speakers, the poets, the officers, the leaders? . . . Let him that thinketh he standeth take heed lest he fall—'Lord, is it I'?"[43]

Angelina could not doubt that Weld had pointed to herself. Once again she had learned the stern thrust of his "truth" and his implied insistence that she must change if she ever hoped to emulate the way of Christ.

She had not faltered in her lecturing but had gone on to greater triumphs, yet Theodore Weld's criticisms had left their scars. Thereafter Angelina did not wish him present when she lectured. After their engagement she would tell him, "Yes, come, if the Lord wills it," but then she would write, "O please do not come." Weld treated her reluctance as the result of their highly charged emotions; he believed that she might feel too conscious of his presence. Not until 1843 did he learn what she felt; he was in Washington at the time and put the question to her by letter. Angelina responded, "You ask in one of your letters why I cannot talk before you. Only because I have felt since I knew you such a crushing sense of my own inferiority that it has seemed impossible to rise above it."[44] Nor did she rise above it now, after their marriage, as she struggled to deny the needs that Weld deplored.

As far as can be known, Weld had heard Angelina lecture but that one time at Pennsylvania Hall, and even then, it is assumed, he remained out of sight. What Weld's thoughts were can never be known as he witnessed Angelina's powers on that extraordinary night. He had known what others said of Angelina as a speaker: sublime, clear and moving tones, marvelously persuasive, matchless powers that no woman had ever equaled, an unexcelled voice in the antislavery cause. It was not that Weld wished to silence that voice, not in his conscious mind—the thought would have been abhorrent. At the same time Weld himself possessed powers just as great and had once known the fame, the adulation, the success, so that thousands, through his influence, had been won to the cause. But he, by sheer violence, had suppressed his satisfaction and had come to condemn such satisfaction in others. Now his throat ailment would not allow him to speak. Conceivably, and quite unknown to himself, an element of envy might have played some part, when Weld, who was unwilling and unable to use his powers, was confronted with the possibility that Angelina, his wife, might go forth and, as before, win recognition as a famous platform speaker in the antislavery crusade. This much is apparent: Weld was self-convinced that Angelina should delay until she felt within herself that she had conquered self-seeking and what she called ambition—these particular traits that he thought must be suppressed.

It seems certain that Weld never comprehended the conditions under which Angelina's powers had been released or that she could never be as she had been before if she did not feel free to use her gifts, untrammeled by doubts of the rightness of what she did. Not only must she feel free and right in their use, but she must confidently believe that her God approved what she did. It was in this sense that her religion was the force that had thrust aside the almost insurmountable barriers of her day. She had felt God's approval at the height of her powers, and why would she not, when she was using her talents not, she was certain, for self-aggrandizement but for the slave and for woman, that all might be free. If this had brought her deep personal fulfillment, as she had felt for a time, what could be wrong with that?

It had long been Weld's practice to seek to remake others in his own image of the Christlike life. If he saw in Angelina, his best beloved, traits that seemed to him contrary to Christ, then he would seek to remold her if he could, not dreaming that what he did was fill her with self-doubt and undermine her cherished freedom.

Thus it was that sometime early in their married life—what Angelina later said indicates as much—Weld and Sarah, for Sarah was rarely excluded, told Angelina the "whole truth" about herself: her ambitious nature, her enjoyment of fame, her great exhilaration in an audience's response, and Weld probably repeated what he had written her before, of the curse of these traits to the abolition movement and his belief that God frowned on what Weld saw as self-seeking. Their criticism of Angelina was based on Weld's stern principle that all three, long before, had tacitly subscribed to, that the three were bound together in the understanding that they were to reveal to each other at all times the whole "truth" about each other. If this meant inflicting pain, so be it, "if high and holy interests demand it."[45] These were the terms, and Weld and Sarah were "faithful." They told Angelina directly that she had "sinned." "When thou and dear sister dared to tell me of my *sin*—I often had hard feelings toward you about it, thought you judged me very harshly and had a fault-finding spirit." Sooner or later they had pressed the point home that she must conquer her sinning before God could call her forth.[46]

Soon another "fault" of Angelina's was revealed, one that added complications of serious proportions. Both Weld and Sarah had been aware of this shortcoming, for Angelina had never hidden it but had spoken of it bluntly: the care of little children was a genuine "trial" to her. As she had told Weld before their marriage, she did not "enjoy their company" and to "mind them" was a burden.[47] At the time she did not speak of it in tones of guilt but to let Weld know that this was her nature.*

Now that she had children, she was directly confronted with her problem. She admitted to Weld that she found it "an inexpressibly great trial to take care of my children, it was a continual weariness to me, I had no pleasure in it . . . . I longed to sit down at my ease, read & enjoy the luxury of cultivating my mind." She came to admit her frequent "irritability," sometime "fretfulness," and "unloveliness of spirit" under the burden of constant child care. She would not admit, not for some time, that these were other than mere human failures that she could overcome with a little experience. Angelina spoke tenderly of each infant as it came, she was loving and affectionate though never sentimental. It was their constant care that remained a burden for her. In part, perhaps, one difficulty was sheer inexperience, for she had been the youngest in a slave-holding family in which nursemaid slaves waited on the master's children. Sarah, on the contrary, was a middle child, with brothers and sisters younger than herself, and from Angelina's early infancy she had adopted her youngest sister. In any case, the two were different human beings. Angelina found the company of little minds unstimulating. Sarah enjoyed the care and company of young children.

When Angelina had brought Sarah into her home, it appears she

---

*After writing in another letter of her love of the out-of-doors and the enjoyment of play, Angelina then commented, "Yet I have *no* philoprogenitiveness. I do not love the society of children—they have hardly any charm for me"—adding cheerfully— "this no doubt marks a moral defect in my character" (Angelina to Weld, [13] Mar. 1838, unpublished letter, Clements Library).

assumed that, when children came, Sarah would be an indispens-able adjunct. Knowing as she did how Sarah loved to "mother," she may have felt that Sarah's presence would enable Angelina the more successfully to combine the two careers she hoped for—the one in public life, the other in the home.

The predictable occurred. Sarah played a crucial part as she lived out her "nature" in the Weld family circle, pouring out love to each Weld child as it came, cuddling, petting, playing, and hovering, drawing these children to her with strong, dependent bonds. They were hardly out of infancy before they showed a strong preference for her, turning away from their mother. Once they could walk, they sought out Sarah to comfort them when hurt, to show her their treasures, to pull at her skirts so she would take them in her arms.

The children served Sarah in a profoundly personal way. She had long viewed herself as a lonely, tragic figure whose life hitherto had held much woe and pain. She had so induced this concept of herself that Angelina was ever vulnerable to Sarah's needs and had been since their life in Charleston. After five years in the Weld home, Sarah could still write a friend, "I tell thee I have passed through this ordeal before thee & agonized in my loneliness & rebelled against my God & thought my lot was hard." Nearly ten years later, when Sarah was sixty years of age, she still described her life as one of "deep disappointments," "withered hopes," "unlooked for suf-fering," "severe discipline." However, on these occasions, she also spoke of joy and how "God had bound up her wounded spirit."[48] "I have sometimes tasted exquisite joys and have found a solace for many a woe in the innocence and earnest love of Theodore's children." "Theodore's children," not Angelina's? How reminiscent the pattern of that time long ago, when Sarah's father was the loved one, and Angelina was Sarah's child. Thus the Weld children fed Sarah's ravenous need, as they grew ever more dependent on her possessive love.

The Weld children were a boon to Sarah in another way. She, as a single woman with an independent income and no family to keep her at home, had become sensitive to abolitionists' criticisms of her staying at home instead of continuing to lecture. Her letters to friends show how defensively she responded to this charge, as she argued her case and explained her views. She prayed to be pre-served in "watchfulness and prayer" so that she would know if and when the Lord called. She said she would not "dare to hold back," but she had yet to experience any "exercise of mind," which she was sure God would send if he wished her to "go forth." Since Sarah had failed on the public platform, the last thing she wished was to return to her failure. Angelina's children provided ample excuse, and while she would not say to friends that she could not leave home, that she must "mother" the Weld children because their mother was failing to do so, she could say as much to herself and argue it with good conscience. She derided the notion her friends held: that public action was the only satisfactory evidence of interest in the causes of slavery and woman's rights. "We believe that God calls us now to other duties, to assert our unchanged opinions as to equality of the sexes at the family altar, around the social hearth, and on all occasions which may arise in domestic life."[49] While Sarah said "we," she spoke only for herself. Angelina was not accepting any such dictum.

It appears certain that Angelina let matters drift during the first few years of Sarah's gradual usurpations. Often she was irritable and impatient with her children, demonstrating that she found it wearing when she must give them constant care. Yet her one source of relief now threw her into painful conflict, as she began to see Sarah as a bane as well as blessing—Sarah, who helped so generously to care for the children, while more and more she seemed to come between them and their mother. Some of these feelings she came to share with Weld. She was convinced that she should not accept blame yet felt in the wrong, and she was troubled night and day by this new threat to mental peace.

Angelina waged battle for many long months against these loved ones before whom she stood condemned. Her pride was strong, her spirit hard to break, she stubbornly believed in her own integrity, and she believed in her need to make use of her mind and her languishing powers. On principle she believed in a woman's equal right to work outside her home as well as within. When it came to her children, she knew she deeply loved them and recognized her mother's duties, while admitting she often failed. It was Angelina's fate, for a little longer, to continue to view "sin" much as Weld and Sarah did, and the more they judged her guilty, the more she lost her way.

When at last Angelina capitulated, admitting her "sins" at the judgment seat, her state was far worse than before. This proud and gifted woman became a stranger to herself. She accepted from her loved ones their "sentence of condemnation," feeling overwhelmed by a "sense of guilt" and like a "condemned criminal" when she knelt before her God—these were the terms she used about herself.[50] And yet, through it all, she continued to rebel as though the judgments of Weld and Sarah would deny her "human right" to live a full and whole existence. She carried herself in dignity and seemingly was composed on those occasions when others were looking on, yet in these years she withdrew into herself, and only Weld and Sarah glimpsed her inner conflict.

More and more Angelina's thought became focused on her children; before her eyes, they continued to reject her for Sarah. She could swing from almost abject expressions of how she valued them to humiliating admissions of her sense that she was failing. "I feel as though I never had anything to do in life of half the importance as tending my babes." More often she would tell of her weariness in the unceasing care of her children and that her "selfish heart loves not the *trouble*—and when the enemy comes with his temptations, I fall an easy prey," taken captive "by fretfulness, impatience, murmuring, complaining," until she drove these feelings from her by "fasting and prayer."[51] Sometimes she would force herself to count her blessings, how God had given her a husband, children, a sister who was "more than a mother to me & to them," and then below she would say that she had even turned blessings into curses by the feelings she had about caring for her children.[52]

Sarah soon became an open issue in the struggle. Weld, Angelina, and Sarah all admitted now that the children preferred Sarah, turning to her in place of their mother. Angelina's response was alien to her self-image, yet she seemed unable to deal with the growing rivalry. The more Weld and Sarah said the fault was hers, how wrong her spirit was in caring for her children "grudgingly & of necessity," and how, if the children were to love her, she must conquer these grievous faults, the more Angelina seemed to measure her self-conquest by the times when the children preferred her in place of Sarah. When she felt she had improved in her feeling toward the children, she thought she sensed a difference in little Charles Stuart's response as she tended him. "When I have been in the room with dear Sis[ter] and he has hurt himself, he has several times lately come to me in preference to her." By the time her youngest child, Sarah, had arrived, Angelina seemed to feel that she had won this child. On one occasion, when she returned with her son, Charles Stuart, from a visit with Jane Smith in Philadelphia, she wrote Jane joyfully of little "Sai's" welcome. The baby had been asleep when Angelina arrived at home. When the infant awoke she first saw Charlie, then Angelina came in and took the child into her arms. "She laughed with joy and hid her little face in my bosom. . . . I found her old preference for Mama was still alive, she refusing next morning to let Sister wait on her."[53]

Angelina had been fearful as she watched her children being weaned away from her. "If I know my heart," she wrote her husband, "I do not want him [Charles Stuart] to love me *more* than he loves her, because she has been a mother to him, and his love is the reward which God ordained and gives, and this renders her unceasing care of him comparatively light. But I want an equal share of his love, for unless I possess this I cannot exert that influence over him which as his mother I am solemnly bound to exert in moulding his character."[54]

Occasionally Angelina attempted a new scheme, such as dividing the children's care with Sarah, for instance, so that she and Sarah would take the children in turn, she in the mornings, Sarah in the afternoons. "Dear Sister helps me a great deal & would help me more, but I cannot believe it right to allow her to bear more than half the burden, when it is not *inability* in me, but a *selfish* love of my own ease which makes me restive under the care of my babes." She reported to Weld that all was going well; both she and Sarah were enjoying relief, because the plan afforded each of them a half day of rest and leisure. She was using her free time in the study of "mental philosophy," with the aid of Samuel Dorrence, a young minister whom they were befriending. Soon thereafter Angelina became pregnant again but, she wrote Weld, she could manage the fatigue of taking care of the children for whole mornings and then burst out, "I think physical weakness is the thorn in my flesh." Shortly thereafter, Sarah was writing Weld, her letter beginning "My dearly beloved," that Angelina wished her to say that she felt physically unable to care for the children for awhile, and within a week, she had a miscarriage. Angelina desired that they hire help for Sarah, and Weld wrote solicitously of Sarah's heavy burden. "As for my burdens, dearest," Sarah wrote Weld, "with the Lord's help they have been light . . . and I am sure if you looked in upon the boys and myself when we are having a game of romps, you would not think there was much to call forth sympathy."[55]

It was true, the Weld children were no burden to Sarah. The constant theme of her letters was what they meant to her. "I live for Theodore and Angelina and the children, those blessed comforters of my poor sad heart." When she was away they were ever on her mind. "I have enjoyed being with my friends: still there is a longing, a yearning after my children. I miss the sight of those dear faces, the sound of those voices that come like music to my ears." Her fervid tones showed the strength of her claims. "In our precious children my desolate heart found sweet response to its love. They have saved me from I know not what of horrible despair, or rushing into some new and untried and unsanctified effort to let off the fire that consumed me. Crushed, mutilated, torn, they comforted and cheered me, and furnished me with objects of interest which drew me from myself."[56]

It was consistent with Sarah's nature that she was blind to her motivation. She was surely unaware of how it soothed old wounds when she, at Weld's side, sat on the judgment seat while her gifted younger sister stood before them condemned. Nor did she realize how it was balm to her still painful wounds when the children turned from their mother and put Sarah first—Sarah the success, Angelina now the failure. This may possibly explain why, as far as can be known, Sarah showed no inclination to have Angelina return to the lecture platform even occasionally in the antislavery cause. It would have made the Weld children more than ever Sarah's. Sarah loved "her children," but what would happen to her pleasure if she were left at home, a mere sisterly convenience, while Angelina returned to her former public triumphs?

The Weld country house on the Belleville farm had some sixteen rooms, most of them in constant use, and there were fifty acres of land, some of which they planted. Throughout the winters of 1842 and 1843, when Weld was in Washington on abolitionist work, it devolved on Angelina to manage the farm, secure farm help, buy farm supplies, continue her management of the family finances (with funds always in short supply), and keep the household in running order. They owned horses and a surrey and purchased a sleigh, so they could get about in winter and summer. Angelina often drove, and some of Weld's favorite tales were of runaway horses, with the children in the vehicle, and of how Angelina handled the terrified beasts.

Perhaps Angelina's most depleting physical task was to serve as nurse and doctor in her home. There was an undrained meadow near the Weld dwelling, a breeding place for the ubiquitous mosquito, and Weld, Angelina, Sarah, and the children were subject to intermittent spells of malaria. Weld could not be persuaded to take his quinine regularly, so his attacks were frequent, and Angelina nursed him. She also nursed Sarah through chills and fever and the children, as they came, though Sarah helped when she was able. Even the neighbors began sending for Angelina, as Sarah wrote a friend, "Yesterday she was sent for by a sick neighbor, had to nurse her and bathe her."[57] Sarah was also sent for, especially for help with the mentally ill with whom she seemed to have a knack. She spoke of one such visit to "the most beautiful maniac I have ever known," referring to the poor woman's loud praises of God. When they had a cook, if she failed to come, the sisters must take over. Life was especially rugged when critical illness struck. On one bitter December day, Sarah, despite a cold, had foolishly insisted on crossing the river in a boat. Angelina, awakened in the night by Sarah's call, supposed the trouble was the usual chills and fever but realized it was something more serious when the searing pain continued. The nearest physician was eight miles away, and rough country roads lay between. In the emergency Angelina perforce fell back on her own skills. She consulted the medical book they kept for such times, and "We found it was pleurisy—treatment well described." Apparently her diagnosis was correct, and Sarah's pain subsided in time, yet for many days Angelina was nurse, sleeping in Sarah's room at night to minister to her.[58] When Angelina gave birth to her last child, with no time to secure a physician or midwife, Sarah was obliged to assist her sister. Sarah reported, with awe and admiration, Angelina's calm, matter-of-fact instructions —fortunately this birth was easier than the others—even to reminding Sarah to tie the cord before she cut it.

The Weld home during the 1840s was overrun with visitors, some of whom appeared with no notice at all. Some were relatives; certain old friends came and many new ones; and there were also many acquaintances, some of whom became friends. They might come for a meal, for overnight, for a week, and there were a few who stayed for several weeks. Except for relatives, most of these visitors were abolitionists, Angelina's tenuous hold on the world she had once known. Sarah's letters to friends told of her weariness, "I have been very busy cleaning house, and feel almost too

tired. . . . So I hope on, year after year, that there will be less occasion to overexert our physical powers," adding dolefully that
"the house has been full of company and this afternoon [a Sunday]
we shall probably have twenty to supper."[59] Angelina knew their
visitors depleted their small income, to say nothing of their
strength, yet she was adamant that all must be welcomed. Hospi-
tality must be extended to any who sought them out, as if by this
means she somehow assuaged her need to be at work for the causes
she believed in.[60]

Despite this active life that Angelina led at home, a rumor circulated in the middle 1840s—was it among those old friends who had
rejected Angelina?—that the reason for her failure to return to public life was a vague, unidentified illness. This notion persisted in
later years. For one thing, Weld himself lent substance to it when, in
1879 following Angelina's death, he purportedly explained what
had happened in the 1840s. He spoke of "two injuries" that occurred early in her married life, as though these held the answer to
the question. He described one injury as "internal" in nature; the
other was "a deep wound that never healed." Though they were
"unlike," one "caused" the other, intensifying a "life-long weakness."[61] Weld deepened the mystery by this kind of talk, for certainly one injury was well known. Angelina developed a hernia in
the early 1840s; she and Sarah spoke of it frankly and often. She
also suffered a prolapsed uterus, a fact well known to some; Sarah
wrote Dr. Harriot Hunt of it and probably had mentioned it to
others too. Angelina claimed that she had cured the uterus condition, but the hernia at times gave acute trouble, though Angelina
never let it restrict her activity for long. Sarah, more than once,
took note of this fact. "My dear sister," she wrote friends with
whom she had been visiting, "is very much worn by her labors in
the kitchen since Bridget's illness. . . . She had a slight attack of
spasms [from the hernia] since my return." While Sarah could see
no improvement in the hernia condition, she described a strap that
Angelina had contrived which had relieved her greatly, so she had
"resumed her household occupations and moves about the house
with ease and alertness." Angelina's first two pregnancies were difficult and depleting, as was her miscarriage in 1842. Yet even during
these years, there were long periods when she was physically able
to lead her exacting, even strenuous, life at home. Then it was
surely not the periods of physical disability, painful though they

were while they lasted, that prevented Angelina from returning to occasional public lecturing.[62]

Weld based too much on these two injuries in his attempt to explain Angelina, and a portion of what he said was strangely contrary to fact. "These several [physical] injuries with the morbid ailments resulting, unbraced for life her nervous system. All special anxiety and distress produced . . . such faintness and sense of sinking, that from the first she could say, 'My mission is over, He who gave it has taken it.' She never afterward spoke in public." But she spoke occasionally after she had returned to public activity, although she never was the famous crusading lecturer again. Also, he continued, she would not speak of certain topics, especially those for which she had once crusaded. "Together they [the injuries] shattered her nervous system. . . . Ever after she was forced to avoid exciting scenes and topics, especially slavery, its effects upon the slave and master, also the wrongs of women."

Had Weld through the years so buried certain memories as to let himself believe that this had really happened? Or was there so much that he felt he could not say, words from the intimate outpourings of Angelina's heart as she had sought his understanding of her misery and mental conflicts?

In one regard Weld's memory brought forth a picture of Angelina as she must have seemed in the 1840s, especially to those who had known her before.

> The morbid unrest caused by these injuries, she bore in silence. The exceptions were rare; yet, when greatly worn, life's corrosions would occasionally strike out a momentary flash of impatience, causing a grief which would not be comforted.
>
> Very few of her most intimate friends knew of the sufferings caused by these physical injuries, which she endured silently, making no sign. Indeed, none but her husband and sister knew them as they were, and even their knowledge came almost as much from inference as otherwise. Her instinctive reserve and reticence about personal discomforts and trials, however severe, were absolute.[63]

Why was Weld still insisting on the "physical" injuries? It may have been his way of protecting her memory. After all, when he wrote these words he was attempting to give a reason for the fact that one so greatly gifted, so committed to human rights, had withdrawn for a time and had not offered an explanation. It is conceivable that Weld never comprehended why Angelina had so greatly changed, the part he had played, or Sarah's part in the scarcely hidden struggles of those ravaging years.

Around the mid-1840s Angelina had reached a point of major crisis in her dealings with herself. Reticence, reserve, work—endless work within her household—these marked the outward aspect she presented to the friends who saw her. Within herself, it seems, she felt entrapped, as though the course she had taken led into a morass. How could she force from memory all it had meant to know that she possessed unusual gifts and powers and had experienced in full the freedom of their release? Now she could not escape the pain of frustration as self-doubt engulfed her and would not let her be herself. There were times when she fell into despair; this is known because at times she broke through her reserve with her husband. It is easy to believe that at some such passing moment—it was in the early 1840s—words escaped from her that Weld remembered and wrote down over thirty years later. "My mission is over, He who gave it has taken it."[64] Weld became deeply troubled while still in Washington, so much so that he refused to continue his work there. Before returning home he apparently had written Sarah of the doubts he was feeling about their course and their need to take stock. Sarah's reply had hewed to her hard line: "I do not exactly agree with thee as to the causes which have operated upon her [Angelina] and us since your marriage. I see clearly that whatever appears to us to hinder the growth of the soul, we are bound to remedy if we can."[65]

Small wonder Weld was filled with guilty doubt as he witnessed the abjectness of his once proud Angelina, who now could find no worth within herself. "O how my married life has developed the hidden evil of my heart. What unexpected revelations of character. . . . My soul is weary . . . weary because I am ever warring against the sins of my heart and never able to conquer . . . sinning and repenting—heavy laden continually with the oppressive intolerable weight of condemnation at the least impatience felt toward our precious little ones. Dearest, how am I ever to be delivered from the bondage of sin."[66]

6.

When Weld returned from Washington, he opened a boarding school in his home, the students—both boys and girls—sharing the large dwelling with the family. He knew he could teach and needed the income, and he had long held strong views on the subject of education. Angelina also taught, which proved an unexpected balm. At one time teaching had been her hoped-for profession; she now taught history, her favorite field, and had ample reason to give time to reading to prepare her lessons. Here was an occupation that made use of her mind. Sarah learned with displeasure that they expected her to teach also. She was competent in French, and this became her task. She hated teaching but felt obligated to do some teaching, which still left her ample time for the Weld children. Once the school was under way, there were a hundred other duties, so life in the household became even more demanding than before.

It appears that Sarah had become more self-assertive during Weld's absence in Washington, as though she had sensed a lack in the Weld home and felt she must fill it with her moral leadership. Sarah felt it was her duty to keep Weld informed of the progress they were making in helping Angelina. If Angelina felt hostility, she gave no sign then—it was not until later that she disclosed what she felt. So Sarah felt no hesitation in continuing to report on Angelina's growth in grace, words sometimes appended to Angelina's own letters, even, on this occasion, cross-written on the sheet. "I rejoice to tell thee that our precious Nina is reaping the reward of her change in her temper. I have been watching little Charlie with great interest, and can now clearly perceive a great change in his feelings towards his mother, he loves her a great deal more than he did, I think scarcely knows the difference between us, often goes from me to her when he gets hurt. . . . Our sweet babes are daily more interesting."[67]

While Weld was still in Washington, Sarah saw another duty, probably one she found somewhat harder to perform. She felt she must tell Weld the "whole truth" about himself, even as they had "faithfully" told Angelina. Weld had written home "rejoicing" in his work and in the "calm & peaceful state of his mind." Sarah felt his peace of mind was premature, since Weld had serious "faults" that needed his attention. Already, it appears, she had spoken briefly to him, and he had made excuses that Sarah considered insufficient. She wrote to him in Washington, at length and in detail. He was selfish, inconsiderate, slovenly of dress, unneat in appearance, and of careless table manners; in general, he disregarded the social amenities. She gave an example: if he went to a meeting he left his desk in disorder, clothing strewn about, one thing thrown here and another yonder, so that she or Angelina had to pick up after him, and he had, when she spoke to him, said he was absent-minded, that his mind was "generally occupied" with "great trains of thought." Sarah termed these excuses "insufficient and selfish." She chided him on inconsistency concerning equality: his inattention at home, but when it came "to the poor," no matter how occupied his mind with noble thoughts, he would stop immediately to give the poor his time. Why could he not be equally considerate of his family? All in all, she told Weld, he had certain bad traits that were "frequently trying to their patience, & making unnecessary draughts on their forbearance and love." Sarah closed her long letter with words of how she loved him, how hard it had been to write this letter, how sure she was he had the power to do better, and finally how thankful she was that God had "strengthened her" to do her duty, "& that He has so knit our hearts together that our faithfulness makes us love each other better"—these words were almost identical with those from his letter to her five years before when he had urged her not to speak at the Odeon.[68]

Of course Angelina saw Sarah's letter—this sharing of correspondence continued as before. It can surely be assumed that Angelina had found some of Weld's ways trying, though of course he had warned her of his faults. But as far as can be seen, she did not criticize, not in the presence of others, and whatever they may have said in the privacy of their chamber is not revealed. No doubt she had hoped that her beloved would grow considerate for equality's sake, as well as other reasons. But Sarah had said "we" in criticizing Weld, implying that Angelina had joined in the attack. It was one of a succession of fateful actions on Sarah's part that helped to arouse Angelina from her abject mental state. Thus began—it later would come to light—times of harsh and seething condemnation, unspoken but recognized, when Sarah intervened, as she continued to do between parents and children.

Both of the Weld sons had kept on turning to Sarah, but the second child, Theo, "Sody" she called him, in a special way had become Sarah's own. When Theo was an infant, Sarah had lavished her care on him, and when he grew into childhood, she had sought to keep him near her. She once wrote Angelina who was absent on a visit—Theo was hardly three at the time—"Dear, I think I have no selfish feeling about keeping this darling boy [to sleep in her room], but my judgment is that for his sake and your sakes he had better remain where he is." He woke, she went on, about the time she did, "bright as a bird," and in the Welds' chamber, he would wake his mother and his father, and the latter "needed his morning sleep," since he sat up late working. Letters from the time the boy was entering his teens contain a stark revelation of all that happened in his boyhood. Theo was sensitive and had been growing more disturbed, and it was to Aunt Sai that his worries were revealed. It is not surprising that these letters were passed on to Angelina.

> How your letters, my precious Sody, stir the depths of being and give birth to hopes for the future that I am sure will find realization—O yes I will strive to bring back the winter home of your childhood. How blest was I when I watched your infant steps and ministered to your infant wants, the sun beam of your love and smiling face gave me ineffable delight. Sody you never can know I trust you never will know how much you have been to me—how you called me back to duty and gave life and enjoyment and zest, for when you came I had a purpose, something to live for, and since then I have felt as if it would be base ingratitude to God to complain of anything.[69]

Sometimes Sarah's letters dealt directly with the parents, and her unconscious undermining became starkly clear. On one occasion when Theo was visiting the Gerrit Smiths in their lovely country home in upper New York State, Sarah wrote urging the boy to pay attention to "the amenities," "the way to sit at table," "the way to dress," "keeping nails clean," "hair neatly arranged." She then capped her advice by a reference to his father: "You may see in your dear father, noble and true and above most men as he is, how unpleasant are habits we acquire through carelessness. The friends you are now with are refined." Ostensibly she sought to bring parents and child closer. This was her spoken aim in another letter, written to the boy when she herself was absent. "How I rejoice that you are getting 'nearer father in spirit'—I feel a sweet reassurance that you will help him and be helped by him." Then she added, "You have a work to do with your dear mother. I think if you could ever feel like telling them how your soul yearns to enjoy the fulness of home love, they will feel it too and will be thankful for this incentive to make the circle of Home a temple of bliss." In closing Sarah told him how hard it had been to leave him, though she felt reconciled because she cherished "the secret hope" that, while she was away, her Sody would find "other bosoms on which to rest, other spirits with which to commune."[70]

Angelina had been slow in perceiving that Sarah was not a passive agent in what had happened to them. Perhaps she should have known what lay in store when she had insisted on Sarah's presence in their family circle. Angelina, to some degree, had remained attached to Sarah in a lingering dependence from childhood years, and while several times she had sought to break these bonds, when Sarah pleaded her loneliness, Angelina could not forsake her. Also, it must be said, Sarah had her uses, and while Angelina would have been loath to admit the advantages, there were certainly times when she lent herself to them. With it all, Angelina had long accepted Sarah's picture of herself as a self-effacing person, humble, deprived, one who had suffered untold sorrows yet had humbly submitted to God's will. Angelina had not seen how Sarah was driven by deeply hidden needs to assert her claims even though her demeanor obscured her aggression. Sarah said that what she did was under the leading of the spirit, that it was for the good of others, never for herself. This was especially true with Angelina's children: Sarah's image of herself was one of selfless giving.

By the late 1840s Angelina saw Sarah as a woman she had not known before. She believed that her sister had come between her and her children, particularly between her and her two sons who, as they grew older, were showing their estrangement from both parents, especially from their mother, who found she could not reach them. She was certain that her sister's usurpation, however blindly it may have been pursued, had undermined her husband and damaged their marriage. Angelina sensed that Sarah dreaded and resisted the younger sister's desire to become the public figure she had been. While Sarah may not have let her feelings speak directly, surely Angelina was in her mind when she expressed this view a little later: "I more and more feel that woman's work is inside, that the great battle must first be fought within, and the conquest obtained over her love of admiration, her vanity, her want of moral courage, her littleness, ere she is prepared to use her rights without abusing them."[71]

Angelina felt guilt for her unworthy part—she voiced it later in speaking to her sister, and she could not escape the humiliation and bitter pain. Even so, she found release from Sarah's condemnation so that Sarah was deposed from the judgment seat. Yet, for a time, this was not an outward deed, only an act within Angelina's mind, and it remained as such until 1854. Thus, for some years longer, Sarah was oblivious and continued much as she had before.

How Angelina came to terms concerning her husband has never been revealed—she dealt with it alone. Weld was her beloved, dear as ever to her; he too had suffered greatly, as she well knew. She would not lay bare what this struggle had cost them. Her eyes had grown clearer and she was now more her own person, so that Weld's way was no longer the one and only way to follow; she found herself more able to think her own thoughts, assert her own strength, know her own belief in what was right—this much stands revealed by 1849. It was in that year that she could at last speak, to voice her deep foreboding that their course had been wrong. "The fear often comes over me like a dark cloud that we are not doing the will of God, we are not fulfilling our destiny."

This could only mean that by this time Angelina was ready to accept these words as stark fact, to perceive her own part in the debacle of their lives, not, it appears, because her faults were "sins" but because she had been vulnerable—weak, she now felt—in allowing the pronouncements of her loved ones to overcome her. Further, she now admitted to herself that it was not only Sarah but also Weld who had been faulty in judgment, so that they, she, life's circumstances, and even slavery in its corrupting power had all acted together to make them what they were, had been their undoing.

Weld had grown restless and disheartened in the late 1840s. He labored for a living on the farm and in his school, but nothing went well, they were often in debt. A man of unique powers, he was frittering away his days, even home and family now spelled failure to him. In this same letter of 1849, Angelina spoke to her husband from her new-found comprehension, surely words that reflected what she had set herself to do. "Stop worrying about this thing and that thing—let things go . . . say with one of Old—here am I, send me. You *greatly mistake me* if you think it pleases me to see *you* working as you do on the farm—in such a state of mind—because you feel constantly you are *not* in your right place, you are not *now* doing the will of God. . . . It grieves me sorely dearest. . . . I entreat you no longer to kick against the pricks of conviction and

and condemnation that are tearing and wearing your spirit *all* the while."[72]

In this same year she took her first steps, uncertain though they seemed, toward recovering her former public life. A movement for woman's rights had taken form in the late 1840s, and its first convention was held in 1848. Angelina could scarcely have known the plan was pending, since a small group of women decided to call the meeting on short notice for Seneca Falls, New York, where Elizabeth Cady Stanton had just moved. Although small, the meeting was historic, as Angelina recognized, when later she read the "Declaration of Sentiments" and the familiar names that were signed to the document. Here were her beliefs; she knew her name should be here. Apparently a correspondence began—Angelina reaching out to have these women know she was with them. Within two years she was once more recognized as concerned and active in the movement for woman's rights.

In 1854 Angelina, Weld, and Sarah decided to sell the Belleville farm and move to Perth Amboy, to the Raritan Bay Community that had just been established in an attractive location. Raritan Bay was begun by a breakaway group from the old North American Phalanx in New Jersey which had established their own idealistic community. Weld had been invited to head Eagleswood School, which was to be associated with the community. The school would be coeducational, as Weld desired, and he had been promised full freedom in applying his own ideas, advanced though they were, in both curriculum and the school regulations. The Welds were to have an apartment in the school building; Sarah would have a room, though separate from "her family"; the Weld children would be pupils in Eagleswood; there would be no family meals—all would eat in the common room. By this time the Welds and Sarah had modified their Graham diet. Angelina was to teach, as she wished very much to do. The move was planned for September 1854.[73]

However plainly Angelina had acknowledged to herself that her relationship with Sarah had brought disaster, she had not yet dealt directly with her sister or purged herself of the feelings she had harbored. Clearly, until she acted, she could not find peace or be certain that her life could take the course she believed it should. The decision to leave Belleville somehow let her speak. Angelina wrote to Sarah who was then absent on a visit.

The long first letter was probably destroyed, at least no trace was found, nor is this surprising. Sarah could not have wished posterity to see the contents, since no possible interpretation could have reflected well on her. By chance, Angelina's second letter remains and readily makes known what was in the first letter, that at last Angelina had dealt directly with their joint life and the damage that had been done to them all.

> My own dearest Sister
> I thank you from my heart for reading my long letter; it cost me a great deal to write it. I knew I was telling you things that would astonish you. I felt that I had had deep rooted feelings which I thought you did not suspect, and yet which it seemed to me you *ought* to know. I felt self condemned, mean, hypocritical in concealing them from the very one who of all others had a right to know them.
> There are times dear Sister when I feel humbled in the dust, because I never have been willing to share my blessings with you *equally*—Often, very often, when I look at all the sorrows and disappointments you have met with in life and all that you have done for me, I feel ashamed and confounded at my ingratitude and selfishness. Then again it seems unnatural that a wife and a Mother should ever thus be willing equally to share of the affections of her dearest ones with any human being—and my heart refuses its assent and struggles on in darkness and death, for I know these feelings wither and blight and keep me from growth and yet it seems impossible for me to overcome them—O! how many nights I have laid awake and prayed God would give me *a right heart*, I really did not know what feelings would come with it—but I do earnestly desire it above *all* things else. I often feel weary of a conflict which has lasted 15 years and wonder when and what will be the end of it.
> As to self defence—dear Sister, I do not feel that you need any—You never meant to do me any wrong. You have lived out your own (in many respects) beautiful nature. I would not, could not *blame* you although I have suffered so intensely, that had I not had a pretty well balanced structure, *i am sure* I should have been a Maniac long ago. I am fully satisfied of this, for the conflicts thro' which I have passed have been terrible. But we shall yet see the why of all this.
> I am glad your future is a blank to you—I would not on any account have you decide *not* to live with us. We *all* feel this to be *your right place*, the home of your heart—We all want you with us and would feel a great blank if you were not with us at the Bay. . . .[74]

Sarah's shock was extreme, and for months she floundered. She did not go with them when the Welds first moved but visited friends, first the Gerrit Smiths, then Dr. Harriot Hunt, a Boston physician who was an active figure in the woman's rights movement. Sarah's letters to Dr. Hunt[75] showed her profound confusion and the dread of what might confront her now; she might be required to find an occupation and live the lonely life she had always feared. A surprising letter addressed to Sarah—a reply to one she had written—shows the lengths to which she went; at the age of sixty-one she had written to a Philadelphia medical school to inquire about studying for a medical degree.

In the end Sarah followed her family to Eaglewood, swallowed her pride and joined them there, anticipating a new life that would be appalling: a community of strangers so unlike her dear ingrown home where her influence had been felt each time she spoke or prayed. And she would be obliged to teach, since all who came must work. "I cannot teach," she wrote, "I have no capacity for it, I have an aversion to it."[76] Furthermore, she admitted to a "mighty temptation to live at ease," although she never spared herself in the care of her dear children. Even the children would no longer be hers. They would be like the other children there, just pupils in the school.

Angelina, on the contrary, found the new life healing. She had always liked teaching, and she had been assigned the subjects she loved, history in particular. The pall of Belleville began to lift a little. Before Sarah joined them, Angelina wrote her sister, "It is certainly the happiest winter I have spent since my marriage. I shall renew my youth, if my mind could be relieved of the heavy load it has had to carry in secret, silent bitterness for many years."[77]

V. Driven to Do Battle

"I recognize no rights but human rights. I know nothing of men's rights and women's rights. . . . I am persuaded that woman is not to be as she has been, a mere second hand agent . . . but the acknowledged equal and co-worker with man. . . . This is part of the great doctrine of Human Rights, & can no more be separated from Emancipation than the light from the heat of the sun; the rights of the slave and woman blend."

ANGELINA GRIMKÉ, *in a letter to Jane Smith, 1837.*

"In this war, the black man was the first victim . . . and now *all* who contend for the rights of labor, of free speech, free schools, free suffrage, and a free government . . . are driven to do battle."

ANGELINA GRIMKÉ WELD, *"Address to the Soldiers,"* Proceedings *of the Meeting of Loyal Women of the Republic, 1863.*

1.

As she began her going forth, Angelina seemed unsure, as though her public life had never been. Inevitably those years of misery and self-distrust, as she had strained to accept others' judgments of her-

self, had changed Angelina in noticeable ways. Not alone was there
reserve, a kind of tight constraint, a strong reluctance to be thrust
into the limelight, but there were no signs of her one-time brilliant
talent as an eloquent, spontaneous, unselfconscious platform
speaker. Had her gift indeed been crushed by her burden of self-
doubt during those years of her withdrawal? Only this is certain:
when, in the early 1850s, she more and more ventured forth toward
an outside active life, she showed no disposition to include public
lecturing. When asked to speak, she would equivocate or urge that
others be asked, as she did for a meeting to be held in Boston, suggesting that Lucy Stone, Wendell Phillips, or Theodore Parker be
called upon, "and they would no doubt speak for the cause nobly
and they could do *better* than I could, still if *Duty* calls me I will do
the best I can under the home pressures that rest upon me."[1]

Her feeling of unsureness may have had a further cause. Perhaps
she feared rejection from those former warm co-workers who,
throughout the 1840s, had not spared themselves or let their efforts
lag in the causes they believed in. Some were public speakers who
had once feared the lecture platform: Abby Kelley Foster now
traveled far and wide, speaking both for the slave and for woman's
rights, her husband with her, as ardent as she; Lydia Maria Child,
ever active in the work and always with her "good mate's" strong
support; Lucretia Mott, whose zeal had never flagged, with her
husband, James Mott, also firm as a rock; and Elizabeth Cady
Stanton, wife of Henry Stanton, who had become leading figures in
the woman's rights movement. These and many more Angelina
had known, and there were numerous newcomers whom she had
never met. So many had followed where Angelina once led; now
they led, and somehow she must follow.

She attended few meetings in the decade of the 1850s, as her circumstances remained restricted through this time. While still at
Belleville, the old ways had persisted, nor could she bring much
change in the established home patterns. In 1854 came the move to
Eagleswood, and with it Angelina's daily life perforce was altered.
She and Weld lived in the school, as did their children and Sarah;
their meals were with others at the common table; and Angelina
had other duties in the Raritan Bay Community. Above all, Angelina was a devoted teacher and remained so thenceforth—the
teaching of history her absorbing vocation. Sarah sensed what this
meant at some point in these years, voicing it to their friend Abby

Kelley Foster, "Angelina . . . has reaped a rich harvest from her school occupation. . . . Her great interest in her scholars and her devotion to her work, the contact with many noble spirits and elevated, cultured minds, have opened new sources of enjoyment and rejuvenated her body, mind and spirit."[2]

Well before Eagleswood, Angelina had reached out in an effort to play a part once again in the movement for woman's freedom. At the second general convention for woman's rights, Angelina Grimké Weld was elected a vice-president and to serve on the Central Committee, and although not there, she had sent a stirring letter. Similarly, at the meeting in 1852, the third national gathering at Syracuse, New York, Angelina again was on the Central Committee, and this time she sent a long disquisition, her contribution to the main issue that year: should the movement be crystallized into an "organization." A good many leaders opposed the change, as did Angelina, and the opposition won. Angelina's lengthy argument today seems odd and dull, a kind of "moral philosophy" that had developed in her mind, no doubt in the years when she was isolated. However, so warm was the response to her "Letter" that it was published as "Woman's Rights Tracts . . . No. 8."[3]

Once at Raritan Bay, the way opened up. The community was a center for reform-minded people, many of whom lent support to on-going social movements. In the early 1850s the "bloomer" costume appeared. Amelia Bloomer, the principal dress-reform leader, was urging on her fellows the drastic new-style garment, with its shortened full skirts half way to the knee and voluminous trouser-"bloomers" gathered at the ankles. Angelina at once adopted the new style, symbol as it was of woman's right to freedom. In doing so, she was bound to attain notoriety: bloomers were conspicuous, women who wore them were singled out, and the press attacked them for an evil radicalism, associating with the bloomer the beliefs conventional people abhorred—woman's "rights," "strongmindedness," "free love," "amalgamation."[4] Elizabeth Cady Stanton, staunch soul though she was, gave up the bloomer costume after two years, deciding that her symbol of liberation was hardly worth the discomfort. Angelina was still wearing bloomers in 1857. That year she wrote a message to a dress-reform convention, calling on the women no longer to be man's "petted slave whom he coaxed and gulled with sugar-plum privileges, whilst robbing her of her . . . rights as a human being."[5] She told the convention that she regarded the bloomer costume as only one approach to a true womanly attire that was sure to be inaugurated in due time. "We must experiment before we find the most suitable dress." First, women must win their freedom to achieve and with it the right to spend their own earnings. Then women would have an "indefeasible right to dress elegantly if they wish"; meanwhile they should discard "cumber-someness and a useless and absurd circumference and length."

Sarah had not adjusted to their life at Eagleswood. She went so far as to wear the bloomer costume, as did other women in the community, for it was in keeping with the advanced ideas of the place. While at first Sarah said the costume was convenient, she never really liked it. It was ugly in her eyes, "it violates my taste," she found it a nuisance to make the garments, so she went back to skirts, finding them more comfortable. Sarah taught both French and bookkeeping at Eagleswood and was thoroughly unhappy. "I am driven to it by a stern sense of duty. . . . I never hear the school bell ring with any pleasure, and seldom enter the schoolroom without a sinking of the heart, a dread as of some approaching catastrophe."[6] These were some signs of the wretched mood that dogged Sarah's life in these Eagleswood years. Time was when Angelina would have been shaken by Sarah's misery, even ignored her own good judgment to comfort and assuage.[7] Not so any longer. Angelina's course was set. She believed life at Eagleswood was best for them now—best for her husband, her children, and herself; she welcomed Sarah to be with them if Sarah so chose; otherwise it was for Sarah to find another way. Outwardly and inwardly, Angelina was reaching out to find a place again in her chosen public work; this time she would not be deflected nor would she again lose her way.

When Weld asserted that Angelina withdrew from public life because of an "unbraced nervous system," he claimed she was forced "ever after" to avoid "exciting topics"—the "wrongs of women" and "especially slavery." Weld clearly erred on the "wrongs of women," as Angelina's active efforts from 1850 on show, and he was also in error on the subject of slavery.[8]

Even the 1840s had not been entirely barren, though these, it is true, were Angelina's worst years, so deep was her absorption in her alleged "sins" and the self-recrimination that accompanied her mental state. This too was the period of greatest physical limitation—

pregnancies, miscarriage, hernia, prolapsed uterus, and bouts of malaria thrown in for good measure. But Angelina did not "avoid" the topic of slavery, not even where her emotions were most acutely involved—in the ownership of slaves by members of her own family. Before Mary Grimké died in 1839, Angelina and Sarah had begged their mother to will them the family slaves so they might set them free. Before her death, their mother circumvented this request by bestowing the slaves on her slaveholding chidren.

Stephen, the family cause célèbre, who suffered seizures presumably resulting from Henry's beating, had been brought north in 1840. Back in Charleston, Stephen was a miserable wreck, unable to work, living on a small dole or else in the poor house when he was ill.[9] After he had come to live with the Welds, Angelina and Sarah told of his joy. For several years he lived at Belleville, helping about the farm as he grew stronger and his seizures became less frequent. As he began to realize his new manhood, he asked for help toward independence, so Angelina and Sarah helped him find work in Philadelphia. He wrote from there of his desire to buy a little land where he could build a home. Angelina, with young Charles Stuart, journeyed to Philadelphia and visited with Jane Smith while she looked into the matter. She talked with Stephen and with the woman who employed him, from whom Stephen proposed to buy a small lot. After a proper title search, she arranged for Stephen to borrow five hundred dollars so he could buy the land outright, fearing he might be cheated by the woman's heirs.

One curious incident, which was later revealed, comes out of this time. None knew of it except perhaps Henry, and how ironic if it were Henry. Not even Weld knew until Angelina's death, when he opened a sealed envelope that she had left him and found a letter written many years before, at a time when she was ill and uncertain of her survival.[10] While what she told Weld had happened before the 1840s, she had carried the obligation all through the years. The letter told of four slaves that she had set free in Charleston by some legal circumvention that apparently her brother had helped her with. This may have involved—Weld does not make this clear—the guarantee by Angelina of financial support if, by ill chance, these former slaves fell into destitution. While she lived, Angelina could deal with what might come and did deal with it without any doubt when the need arose. She kept this action to herself, but with it went an opening and continuing concern. Then how could Weld say that she avoided slavery?

The 1850s confronted antislavery people with conditions very different from those existing formerly when Angelina Gri.nké had been publicly active. Though few might guess that outright war was imminent, many were aware of the ever-rising tensions, the harshness of the issues, the fears of bitter conflict, the mob violence wherever emancipation was being preached. This was the decade of the Fugitive Slave Act and of resistance by abolitionists both white and black, often a resistance that resorted to force in order to wrest fugitives from the clutches of a hateful court. Civil disobedience had long been the rule with men and women agents in the Underground Railroad who had conducted their operations as much as possible in secret. Now antislavery activists felt they had no choice but to defy the law openly, when legal action failed, to save escaped slaves by whatever means they could from forced return to the hands of their former masters. The instances of rescue by force were numerous and notorious. They were occurring throughout New England, New York, and the Midwest and were faithfully reported in abolitionist papers. All concerned abolitionists watched with anxiety to see whether a victim had reached Canada safely. This was the decade of the Dred Scott decision, of the Nebraska Act, of John Brown. Where was Angelina in these bleak and dreadful times, when her "cause of human freedom" had never been more threatened?

There are ample signs that she was now fully ready. She had turned her back on those miserable years, no longer submitting to others' dubious judgments but able to render judgments on herself. She now had the power and confidence to strip from herself the spuriousness in her old guilt, so that she could see the real and deal with it directly. If she often feared that it was too late to fulfill her rightful destiny, she also perceived that fear fed on itself and that to deal with fears she must go forth to meet them. Angelina had long been undergoing a religious change, a change that was crucial in what was happening in her life now. The process had begun in her Charleston years with those who sought to bind her to Presbyterianism; had continued in her life among the Orthodox Friends and their attempts to curtail her freedom of thought and action; and it had continued in 1831, when she and Sarah were disowned by the Friends because of her marriage to Weld, a non-Quaker. Angelina had long decried "sectarianism"; more than ever in recent years she had regarded it as wrong, so that former religious formulas had lost their hold on her. By the 1850s, and the same was true for Weld, she was increasingly free-thinking in her beliefs, but her religion remained for her a personal, living force, undergirding her every push toward freedom.

It is true that, as she again joined the crusade against slavery, Angelina did not rush to the public platform, nor did she repeat her old triumphs of nearly two decades before. The old spontaneity was gone, her progress was slow at first—it would be hard to find a niche in these changed times among the abolitionists who now were caught up in a different kind of work. But she was not changed in the depth of her concern. Anything touching slavery, the South and the North, conflicts in Congress, fugitives in the courts, decisive court cases, and the frequent mob violence she followed in any way she could. The *Anti-Slavery Standard* was habitual reading now. She talked with men and women who came, as many did, to the Raritan Bay Community, where abolitionist sentiments were strong and outspoken, and advanced ideas in general were the climate of the place. Their good friend Gerrit Smith was in the Congress in the 1850s. Weld must have seen the letters Angelina wrote to Smith, so how could he assert that she had hidden her face from slavery?

In 1854 she wrote Smith of a speech. "Truly it was fearless, faithful, great. . . . Go on, my brother, & a new era must dawn upon the history of Slavery in this country. I rejoiced that you opened your career in Congress just as you have done. Slaveholders know now *where* you stand. . . . God grant you entire restoration to health & ability to do his holy will at this momentous period." Angelina continued, "We are approaching change," and the times require "new instrumentalities." In essence, she told him, the old ways were past, "more efficient" ways are called for in this latter day "in the winding up of the great drama of anti-slavery."[11]

Six months later she wrote Gerrit Smith again. Word had reached them that he might resign from Congress. Because she was disturbed lest his public voice be lost, her letter stressed the vital issues then at stake. She was grieved, she told him, that the Nebraska bill had passed; she was appalled at the surrender of two fugitive slaves, Pennington in New York, Burns in Boston; and now came announcement that Smith planned to resign.

> Dear Brother, why is this—I know the Slave has other friends there. But not one who can exert the benign moral influence you have in this vital question. Chas. Sumner &

others can speak well—but there is no man there to whom God has given so large a heart, who strikes immediately at the Wrongs & upholds the Right in its naked beauty and sublimity. . . . Your speeches at Washington are read by many thousands who would never see them if they were delivered anywhere else. You speak to the Nation now. You come into the immediate presence of Slavery into personal contact with the Slaveholder, whilst you greet him as a Brother, you faithfully discharge your duty to him, as well as to the slave.

Angelina had more than slavery on her mind; she kept herself informed of decisive current happenings, she pondered all of these, and she discussed them with others. Moreover, and here is the first outward sign, Angelina's thinking was undergoing a basic change in the mounting crisis of these stirring years.

I have long hoped that the South could be reached by moral power, & your presence in the Congress brightened my hopes—but I begin to despair. . . . It is base to surrender the helpless who fly to us for Refuge. My heart was very full on this point after that terrible day in Boston [when the escaped slave Burns was delivered up to his former owner]. All my old feelings about Slavery came back again—& it seemed as tho' the bloody scenes of the Revolution *must* be reenacted before Slavery could be abolished. It is clear to my mind that the Fugitive Slave Act *ought* to be, *must* be resisted even unto blood. This surrendering to such a wicked law with all the solemn pageantry of Law for its protection . . . as was the case in Boston *last week*, is a horrible mockery, an insult to common sense, an insult to God. . . . This [the Fugitive Slave Act] is *not* the *Voice of the Nation*. I do *not*—I *cannot* believe it. If Traitors to the cause of Humanity who stood as the Senators & Representatives of this Nation, abused their power by making such a law, that is no reason why those of the people who utterly loathe it should stand by & see it executed in the midst of them. . . . It ought to be resisted, let the consequences be what they may.

She closed her long letter, "If you do indeed resign—then I should believe that the great crisis is near even at the doors."[12]

In the early 1850s her brother Henry died, a respected Charleston lawyer, a slaveholder to the end. For years Angelina had clung to the hope that someday Henry might free his own slaves. Perhaps her hopes were strengthened by those confidential letters when Henry, as it seems, had helped her emancipate four Charleston slaves. It is certain that his death was a painful bereavement, and the fact that she had not seen him since she left her home made it harder to bear.[13]

The decade of the 1850s was moving to its close when John Brown and his men appeared at Harper's Ferry, a brief but fevered crisis brought on by a mere handful of "fanatical" human beings. Was it true they dreamed that they could arouse and arm slaves and march them to their freedom in the free northern states? Some say this was the vision in the old man's head. But John Brown's men were armed, and blood was spilled, their blood most of all; and a terrible irrational fear spread through both the slave and free states that the most dreaded eventuality might occur, that black men rise in open insurrection and demand equality. How else could the military measures be explained, the force that was mustered to repel a few armed men, the sudden drastic closing of white ranks to combat this threat to their white hegemony? Not until nearly every man of them was killed or hanged did white men feel safe to be contentious again. Their miscalculation was speedily apparent; their divisions were too deep and would soon burst forth in tragic open war.

The Raritan Bay Community felt the impact of Harper's Ferry directly. For one thing, its members were almost all abolitionists. They might sharply disagree on the wisdom of John Brown's plan, yet they watched, as did abolitionists everywhere, with compassion, admiration, and profound anxiety, all that came to pass: the stand at Harper's Ferry, the capture of some men, the trial of John Brown, the trials of his men who were taken, and when their fates were sealed, the awful waiting for the hangings.

Rebecca Spring, wife of Marcus Spring and daughter of former abolitionist leader Arnold Buffum, was the one who involved the Raritan Bay Community. She was zealous and indomitable in abolitionist causes. Her position was strategic, since her husband, Marcus Spring, was a principal figure in community affairs, one of the main founders and financial supporters. As John Brown lay wounded in jail in Charlestown with several of his severely wounded men, awaiting their trials and expecting to be hanged, Rebecca Spring wrote to him, asking that she be allowed to nurse him in the time that remained. Indeed, she made the journey in the company of friends, gained permission to see the prisoners, and talked with Brown. It appears that she also talked with Aaron D. Stevens and Albert Hazlett and made them a promise, which she later fufilled, with no slight effects on the Raritan Bay Community. Upon her return to Raritan Bay, she poured out her account of Brown and his men, so that all through the trials Raritan Bay abolitionists—Angelina, Weld, and Sarah among them—felt the tensions, the horror of the almost certain executions.[14]

Before the executions occurred, Raritan Bay had a visitor. Rebecca Spring had found Brown's wife waiting out the dreadful days with abolitionist friends in Philadelphia, because her husband had felt it wise that she not come to him for a time. Rebecca brought Mrs. Brown to Raritan Bay, where she remained for several weeks until her husband said, "Come." The entire community, and with it Eagleswood School, for days and weeks felt the presence of John Brown in the person of his quiet, unassuming, grieving wife.[15]

Nor was this the end of the community involvement. Mrs. Brown, by permission of Governor Wise, was allowed to claim the body of her hanged husband and take it for burial to their old home. It appears that Rebecca Spring, when she visited John Brown, found that two of the men, Stevens and Hazlett, had no one to claim their bodies when they were cut down, so she had promised the two that she would lay claim, bring their remains to Raritan Bay, and there give them proper burial. Perhaps Rebecca Spring did not read the times aright, or it may be she had and ignored the risks. The two bodies, in due time, arrived at Perth Amboy and were met there by men from Raritan Bay to be transported the short distance to the community. Excitement was high in Perth Amboy. A threatening mob gathered to intercept the coffins—these bodies of "traitorous men" should not defile this place. The ugly moments passed, and the funeral was held, the grave sites in a spot that overlooked the lovely bay. Word reached the community that Perth Amboy was still aroused, that men proposed to come by night to steal the hated coffins. So night and day, men and boys of the community, including pupils at Eagleswood, stood guard at the graves until the crisis passed.

Needless to say, no one went unscathed, whether in the school or in the community as a whole. It is certain that Angelina, Weld, and Sarah were more shaken than others there, more aware of the meaning and the portent of the time. Sarah wrote a few words that remain extant, but nothing has been found from Angelina on John Brown, though Sarah reported that Angelina was made ill by these events—Sarah failed to mention when, why, and in what way. It is apparent that Angelina came to grips with the John Brown events and understood what they portended in the nation's life—not so much the impact of the man himself but the feelings he aroused, in North as well as South, among those who judged him. The fact that her long-held convictions were shaken to their roots is implicit in a comment she made not long thereafter in a letter to Theo, her second son, who was ill and absent from Eagleswood. "The South is dissolving the Union in order to prevent the abolition of Slavery," she wrote. "Things look very dark and gloomy and as I have given up all hope of its [slavery's] abolition except thro blood and insurrection, I feel willing it should come in my day, for the longer it is put off, the worse it will be."[16] How different were her words from those of a former time, when she had declared to Garrison, in her momentous letter of 1835, that only nonviolence could ever bring freedom. "If persecution is the means which God has ordained for the accomplishment of this great end, EMANCIPATION . . . I feel as if I could say, Let it come. . . . LET IT COME—let *us* suffer, rather than insurrections should arise." Had she now lost hope "except through blood and insurrection"? Closing her letter to her son, she exclaimed, "My dearest Son, may God grant all of us the blessed privilege of helping on this glorious work."

2.

So it was war, in all its violence and fury, that seemed to cleanse Angelina so old wounds might better heal. She did not like war or any violent means and had said so repeatedly. But if the conflict was inevitable, as she now believed it was, because slavery itself was maintained by violence and those who maintained it were committed to force, the choice was plain in Angelina's eyes. She put it this way on the eve of the war: the nation stood "on the brink of a terrible Revolution," and this was the last massive effort of the slaveholding South "to strengthen and enlarge the foundations of her great Bastille . . . [in her] attempt to carry out her plans to reopen the Slave Trade and establish Slavery on a wide and permanent basis."[17]

   The Welds were leaving Eagleswood at this time, disappointed by unfulfilled promises of support, although the school had won an excellent reputation, and by the growing financial burden that had been thrust upon them. Sarah left with them, happy to go. These had been wasted years where she was concerned, her heart clinging still to their former close-knit home. She voiced her nostalgia to her friend, Harriot Hunt, on the eve of their departure from Eagleswood. "Oh I do so long for a little private home, bread and water with quiet and love would be infinitely better than the penitentiary life I have had here for seven weary years."[18] In a few more years— and she would then be in her seventies—Sarah's wish would be fulfilled in the home the Welds purchased in Hyde Park, Massachusetts. Here Sarah would live, seemingly content, feeling loved and wanted.

When the Welds left Eagleswood in late 1862, they first rented a house in Perth Amboy, where they could wait out the time until future plans could be settled. The second son, Theo—Sarah's "Sody"—was now an invalid, though why, no one knew; physicians could find no physical basis for his trouble. Sarah's letters to friends often spoke of their anxiety. For a while Theo remained with his family, but soon it seemed best for him to be away for extended periods, as different treatments were attempted by his pained and baffled parents.

It was while at Perth Amboy that Weld's chance came. He had sought war work with the Sanitary Commission, where some of his abolitionist friends had found opportunities. As he waited in vain, letters began reaching him that urged a return to public lecturing, so great was the need for an aroused public support in this time of national peril. William Lloyd Garrison was one who wrote; moreover, Garrison set a definite time and place, an invitation that demanded a prompt decision. For three full days Weld hesitated. There was not the slightest doubt of where Angelina stood and with what urgent enthusiasm she used her influence, fearing Weld would falter and withdraw again. He wrote Garrison accepting. There had long been differences between Weld and Garrison, but now these seemed to melt away. As time went by, Weld could write, "My dear friend and brother," and once he closed a letter, "In the old time love."[19] On the second Sunday in November 1862, in the Music Hall in Boston, Weld returned to public lecturing. "My last public talking," he wrote Garrison, "was at the Anti-Slavery lecturers' convention of two weeks in New York City twenty-six years ago."[20] For some two years Weld went on lecture tours, some of them sponsored by the government in Washington. He covered all of New England, New York, Pennsylvania, then swung into the old territory he loved best, the midwestern states of his one-time great triumphs. Angelina's delight was outspoken and free. She wrote Gerrit Smith, "I am very happy in his absence. He is doing the very thing my heart wants him to do. *Now* is the accepted time and the day of Salvation from Slavery."[21]

For Angelina also it was "the accepted time," and she plunged into multiple activities for the cause. It was as though a quarter of a century had not intervened. She was working for the slave as she had worked before, feelings and beliefs fully committed, the great difference being that now the day of emancipation was at hand.

Abolitionists and others who wished slavery to be ended were demanding immediate emancipation of the government, and this time "immediate" meant what it said. Women abolitionists, the former woman's rights stalwarts who had quickly formed themselves into what they called "loyal leagues," were insisting that the president should proclaim all slaves free, wherever they resided within the slave states or lived as so-called "contraband" within Union lines. The *Liberator*'s pages were filled with the demand; so were the columns of the *Anti-Slavery Standard*, the official organ of the Anti-Slavery Society.[22] Petitions were drawn up; Angelina helped to frame them, urging that the government proclaim emancipation. Angelina, like her fellows, went from door to door, to secure signatures to be sent to President Lincoln. When the president, in late 1862, issued the proclamation that was to take effect in 1863, abolitionists found it wanting, a mere wartime measure, affecting some slaves while leaving others in bondage. Emancipation, as a principle, had yet to be achieved. In 1863 a new petition campaign began to secure one million signatures of women over eighteen years of age, to be addressed to the Senate and House of Representatives. What the president had not done, they hoped the Congress would do, pass an act emancipating "all persons of African descent held to involuntary service or labor" wherever they might be in the United States. Again, this meant a door-to-door campaign, and again Angelina began to tread the streets.

When regiments of Negro troops began to be formed, Angelina, greatly stirred, found her spirits lifting. She "rejoiced . . . in the heroism of the colored troops." Word had come of their action at Port Hudson and their successful raids in Carolina and Florida. "Joseph may yet save his brethren of the North who stood by and consented to his being sold in slavery by the South." At times these black troops gave her hope that perchance slavery's "curse" might be avoided. "Instead of *our* fighting for the Negro now, he is fighting for us, and will yet save us and himself too. His heroism and self devotion and spirit of forgiveness will save us from the curse of Slavery and the twin curse of Prejudice which like heels of iron have trodden him in the dust beneath our feet."[23]

Angelina, in her heart, had never shunned conventions, though she had stayed away in the years of her withdrawal. Now even Weld no longer scorned them, not in these stirring times when every effort counted. The antislavery movement called several conventions, and Angelina and Weld were usually present. On one occasion Weld took a seat on the platform, something he had not done in nearly thirty years. The two were present at an antislavery anniversary, where Weld spoke from the platform. The chairman then called on Angelina—Mrs. Angelina Grimké Weld, who had to be explained to this 1860s audience, most of whom had never seen her. Angelina spoke strongly and directly on the theme of "[The South's] rebellion had laid the axe to the root of Slavery's tree."[24] In 1863 when the American Anti-Slavery Society celebrated its thirtieth anniversary, Angelina, Weld, and Sarah were asked to come. Garrison himself sent the urgent invitation. They had just moved to Massachusetts, so the trip was impossible, but they sent a long letter, eloquent and full of feeling, a letter that was written in Angelina's hand.

A time came when the war was enveloping the Carolina coastal area. Angelina began to dream of a return to Charleston, not to remain, but to see it again. She had not seen her city since 1829. A few family members still lived and were there, suffering proudly under wartime deprivations. What Angelina dreamed could hardly have pleased them, for it meant that Charleston would be in the hands of Union troops. Now that Weld at last was lecturing again, she wrote him, what a splendid thing it would be if a day might come when he "had a mission" there, to lecture and teach in her "birth city." "If it is ever under Federal control, I hope the way may open for me once more to see my aged brother and sisters and breathe her balmy air once more."[25]

Principally Angelina worked for a wartime organization called the Loyal Women of the Republic or sometimes the Woman's Loyal League. The woman's rights movement had suspended operations, its members turning all their energies toward the war. The names of the leaders of the Woman's Loyal League were familiar—Susan B.

Anthony, Elizabeth Cady Stanton, Lucy Stone—and these women would return later to the cause of woman's suffrage. While the war lasted, they had but one aim in view, to help win the war in behalf of human freedom. Angelina was a vice-president of the league, served on committees, helped promote local leagues, and was completely caught up in the numerous league activities.

In 1863 the league called a convention of "loyal women of the nation" to meet in New York in the Church of the Pilgrims on Union Square. The convention began on May 14, 1863; the church was full, chiefly with women, and some had come from distant places. Angelina was present when the convention opened and remained until the sessions closed.

By a striking coincidence, the date of this convention was a memorable anniversary for Angelina Grimké Weld. Twenty-five years before, on May 14, 1838, she and Weld had been married, and the following day she had attended a convention of antislavery women. This was the convention that had culminated in the huge meeting in Pennsylvania Hall, a gathering addressed by Angelina Grimké Weld, while a furious, shouting, proslavery mob had hammered on the doors and thrown missiles at the windows, the same mob that next evening had set fire to the hall and burned it to the ground. As it turned out, this had been Angelina's last appearance as an antislavery crusader on the public platform. Surely she was thinking of that former time when she left Weld and Sarah at Perth Amboy to attend this convention in New York on her wedding anniversary, and surely it was symbolic of how far she had come since those hard years that had lain between. It was Sarah who, though unknowing, conveyed the meaning of the occasion in a letter to Theo. "The 14th (of May) was your mother's silver wedding day 25 years since she was married. Your father and I were at Amboy so we celebrated it with a kiss, and your mother by attending the meeting of 'Loyal Women' and opening her mouth once more for the oppressed."[26]

Angelina found pleasure in every moment of the meeting, an older woman now by twenty-five years, but still vivid, alert, informed, and outspoken. She spoke from the floor and made a platform speech, her remarks recorded in the official *Proceedings*. Then at the behest of the Business Committee, she prepared and presented a stirring "Address to the Soldiers." The women were appealing to the ordinary soldiers in the ranks, those who were completing their terms of service and returning home, asking that in this critical time of war they reenlist, because so much was at stake. "To you especially," the "Address" urged them, "whose terms of service have expired, or are soon to expire, we desire to speak of the shifting scenes, now acting in the Nation's Tragedy." The "war of slavery against freedom" had not begun with the recent crises, Angelina said to them, it began "when the first slave-ship landed its human cargo in Virginia. Then for the first time, liberty and slavery stood face to face on this continent. From then till now these antagonisms have struggled in incessant conflict." This was her theme. The "Address," which was later printed and widely distributed, was plainly a reflection of her deepest convictions.

> This war is not, as the South falsely pretends, a war of races, nor of sections, nor of political parties, but a war of PRINCIPLES; a war upon the working classes, whether white or black; a war against *Man*, the world over. In this war, the black man was the first victim; the working-man of whatever color the next; and now *all* who contend for the rights of labor, for free speech, free schools, free suffrage, and a free government, securing to *all* life, liberty and the pursuit of happiness, are driven to do battle in defense of these or fall with them, victims of the same violence that for two centuries has held the black man a prisoner of war. While the South has waged this war against human rights, the North has stood by holding the garments of those who were stoning liberty to death. . . .[27]

When Angelina rejoined Weld and Sarah in Perth Amboy, she must surely have returned with a sense of great serenity and of some exhilaration deep within herself.

3.

Three years after the war had ended and all slaves had been freed, Angelina, Weld, and Sarah were living near Boston, in Hyde Park. Angelina, with Weld, had continued as family breadwinner, both of them teaching in a Boston school, a fourteen-mile drive for them several days a week. The Weld children, grown now, were in and out of the home. Angelina assisted Sarah, as she could, in housekeeping. The exhilaration all had felt at the war's end had long since left them, and in its place was anxiety and a heavy apprehension. Abolitionist newspapers, in reporting recent events, had been torn between hope and a rising alarm: "Black codes" meant to "re-enslave" the freedmen—Freedmen's Bureau sent in to aid—Johnson "reconstruction" and the rise of Old South men—amendments that should forever set the black man free—a "Radical" Congress and its proposed "reconstruction"—a rumor, as early as 1868, of a masked secret power bent on "white supremacy." The uncertainties and grim portents had been increasing day by day, and there was fear among abolitionists that the South had not changed and was determined to restore the white man's sole control. These tensions and forebodings pervaded the Weld household.

Even after war ended and slaves were free, the *Anti-Slavery Standard* had continued publication. Angelina for years had been a reader of the paper, so she saw the issue of February 8, 1868. A heading caught her eye, as it was bound to do, "Negroes and the Higher Studies." The article stressed a point that had long been her belief: that in an age when Negro inferiority was assumed, "the Negro intellect, in the matter of scholarship, does not appear inferior to that of the Caucasian," and cases were cited from various institutions. One of those speaking was a Professor Bower of Lincoln University in Pennsylvania, who told of his experience in this Negro institution, a school Angelina had not known existed. "Last Wednesday one of the Literary Societies celebrated its anniversary, with essays and orations, in the University Chapel, and performances were just as good in manner and matter as those you generally hear from College students. One of them by the name of Grimkie [sic] who came here, two years ago, just out of slavery, was thrillingly, powerfully impressive." Angelina's thoughts can only be imagined, as she read the misspelled name and the lines that followed through eyes blurred by the rush of emotion.

It is known that Angelina withdrew to her room and spent a good while alone and that, at some time within the hours that followed, she shared what she had found with Weld and Sarah and acquainted them with the decision she had made.[28] They at once concurred, nor did they feel hesitation; if they had, both knew it would be of little use. In recent years they had learned to recognize the signs indicating that Angelina's decision would not change. She composed the letter, showed it to them, and posted it without further delay to Lincoln University, Oxford, Pennsylvania. Of course she spelled the Grimké name correctly.[29]

Fairmount [Mass.] Febry 15 [1868]

Mr Grimké
  Sir
    In a recent number of the Anti-Slavery Standard I saw a
notice of a meeting at Lincoln University of a Literary Society at which a young gentleman of the name of Grimké deliver'd an address. My maiden name was Grimké. I am the
youngest sister of Dr. John Grimké of So Carolina, & as this
name is a very uncommon one it occurred to me that you
had been probably the slave of one of my brothers & I feel a
great desire to know all about you. My Sister Sarah & myself have long been interested in the Anti Slavery cause, &
left Charleston nearly 40 years ago, because we could not
endure to live in the midst of the oppressions of Slavery.
Will you therefore be so kind as to tell us who you are
whether you have any brothers & sisters—who your parents were etc. etc.
    We rejoice to find you are enjoying the advantages of
such an institution, & should be glad to know how you
came introduc'd into it, & whatever you are willing to tell
me about yourself.
    My husband Theodore D. Weld was one of the earliest
Anti Slavery lecturers at the West.
    Hoping soon to hear from you
                  I remain Sir
                  Respectfully,
                  Angelina Grimké Weld
                  Fairmount
                  Massachusetts

She had not long to wait; the reply was prompt, dated February
20, and the letter was specific as far as it went. It was signed Archibald Henry Grimke.[30] A brief courteous opening, voicing pleasurable surprise at receiving a letter from Angelina Grimké, a name so
famous in the antislavery cause, then proceeding at once, as the
writer put it, to give a simple sketch of his history and his connections. "I am the son of Henry Grimké, the brother of Dr. John
Grimké, and therefore your brother. Of course you know more
about my father than I do."
Sarah said that Angelina was "prostrated" when Archie's first
and fateful letter came, that for a few days she found it necessary to
remain in seclusion in her room. Angelina herself, when she answered the letter, said she had been delayed by "indisposition" and
an unavoidable absence from home—evidently she had returned

within a few days to teaching and this meant a fourteen-mile drive three days a week. In fact, she answered Archie's letter within the week.

She was stunned; she must recover and take counsel with herself. She must come to a grave and far-reaching decision, or better, she must accept her inevitable decision and gain her full consent to assume responsibility. It was no problem to her to acknowledge these nephews because their darker skin meant Negro ancestry. Any hint of color prejudice had long been absent from her nature and abhorrent to her when she saw it in others. They were her nephews; she felt an obligation and that they, in turn, had a claim on her. Yet in acknowledging them, as of course she would do, she would be saying to the world what her brother had refused to say: that these three who were his slaves were in fact his sons. She knew and could reply, "the facts it [Archie's letter] disclosed are *no* surprise to me. Indeed had I not suspected that you [the brothers] might be my nephews, I should probably not have addressed you." She could also say, "I accept all you have told me as the simple truth."[31] It was one thing to understand what could happen under slavery, and another, a dreadful and painful fact to face, to know that the instruments of these inhumanities were a dearly loved brother and his white son. Here then is the story as Angelina learned it from Archibald and Francis Grimké.*

Archibald said that when Henry's wife died, "he took my Mother, who was his slave, and his children's nurse; her name is Nancy Weston. I don't think you know her." Henry had three sons by Nancy Weston: Archibald Henry, born in 1848; Francis James, born in 1850; and a third son, John, born just after Henry's death. "He [Henry] told my Mother he could not leave her free, i.e., he could not give her 'free papers,' because he favored a certain law forbidding Masters to leave their servants free, 'but,' said he, 'I leave you better than free, because I leave you to be taken care of.'"

Henry had three children by his legal wife. His oldest son was named Montegue. "In his [Henry's] words, speaking to my Mother, 'I shall leave you in the hands of my son [Montegue], in whom I can

*This account was put together from several sources, chief among them the 1868 letters to Angelina from Archibald and Francis Grimké; also gleanings from the author's interview with Angelina Weld Grimké, daughter of Archibald (see Bibliography). See also Carter G. Woodson, ed., *The Works of Francis James Grimké*, 2 vols. (Washington, D.C.: Associated Publishers, 1942), Introduction, for a sketch of Francis Grimké's life.

place confidence.' " Consequently Montegue owned them all, his three half-brothers, together with their mother, although Henry, as they believed, had stipulated that none of them should be sold.

While Henry was alive, Nancy Weston and her three sons lived in a small cottage and were provided for. After his death they found they must fend for themselves. "My poor Mother, a defenseless, woman, [was] crippled in one arm. . . . By dint of hard labor working her finger nails to their very quick she kept us from perishing . . . and sat by us when we were sick. . . . Thus she continued until 1860." All this while, they believed they were safe from separation since, as they supposed, Henry had made provision that neither mother nor sons would be required to serve as slaves.

In 1860 Archie was twelve. Montegue's first wife had died, he had remarried, "and he wanted a boy to wait on him; he informed my Mother that he wanted me, and that she should send me to his house. His mandate was irresistible . . . a severe shock to my Mother . . . unlooked for . . . unprovided for." So Archie served for a while as Montegue's slave. Then one day his mother, Nancy Weston, slipped her son away, dressed him as a girl, and for a time kept him hidden, until he escaped from Charleston. He remained out of sight until the city was captured.

When Frank was eleven, Montegue sent for him. "He tried to enslave me," Frank said. War had come, and Frank escaped, finding his way to the Confederate Army, where he served as an officer's valet for two years. Once when his regiment was near Charleston, Frank slipped home to see his mother. Montegue heard of it, and Frank was thrown into the work house, and there he became dangerously ill—"probably would have died"—had he not been taken home for his mother to nurse. Before he was well enough to run away again, Montegue sold him to a Confederate officer, whom he served as a slave to the end of the war.

Their mother meanwhile had lost her youngest son. John was also taken to serve Montegue—taken despite her bitter protest and defiance. Her sons told their children of Nancy Weston, describing the grandmother as "indomitable," "fiercely protective of her sons." "She was thrown into a loathsome cell," Archie said, no doubt in the work house, the usual place of punishment, "and kept there for six days, eating nothing . . . until at last sickness prostrated her," and the physician who was called insisted that she be removed.[32]

These were the facts, bleak and unembellished, as they came to Angelina during that long spring. Several times she wrote her nephews that she must be told all, she must be spared nothing, and gradually she learned much more about those harsh times in her nephews' lives when separation threatened and they were enslaved by a master they knew to be their half-brother. Sarah described her sister as "half-sick" that spring. She may have seemed so, abstracted as she was, in the days when she was at home and seeking solitude as much as she did, so Sarah might well have assumed that Angelina felt ill. In fact, to be alone was an urgent necessity, for Angelina felt impelled to find her way again, a way she thought she had long since known.

What Henry had done, as his darker sons told it, could come as no surprise to Angelina; what he had done was not uncommon, a usual bitter fruit of slavery. What Montegue had done, Angelina knew this well, was not unusual in a slaveowner's behavior, merely the normal procedure with his chattels, even to the use of the work house for punishment. And if, as seemed certain, Montegue knew that Nancy Weston's sons were his half-brothers, this situation was not unique. It would not necessarily have entered his calculations, despite the request his father had made; perhaps the truth was that he did not feel related. Angelina believed she understood how all this could be in men who otherwise seemed good and humane; she long ago had expressed it. "The exercise of arbitrary power worked . . . fearful ruin upon the hearts of slaveholders,"[33] so that they were corrupted by the enforcement of slavery and without conscious guilt accepted these inhumanties.

Yet there were people like Birney, Thome, and a dozen other men whom she knew personally who had been slaveholders and had not been made callous, for sooner or later they had turned their backs on slavery; she and Sarah, who had once accepted slavery despite their hatred of its cruel force, had also "escaped." There was her memory of Henry on that painful night, now forty years ago, when she had appealed "to the witness in his own bosom to the truth," and Henry had turned on her, bitterly wounded: did she not know that he felt something within himself which fully responded to all she had been saying and that she made him completely miserable? Then, in later years, Henry was apparently the one who had helped her free the four slaves. Yet it was this same brother who had refused to free his sons. She might say, as she did in her second letter to her nephews which was written within a week of her discovery of them, words that surely held a special poignancy for her, "I will not dwell on the past—let all that go—it cannot be alter'd—our work is in the present & duty calls us now, so to use the past, as to convert its curse into a blessing." Yet she did dwell on the past for a time until she had wrung from it all the meaning it held for her. Some weeks later, in writing Archie and Frank again—this time replying to their most painful revelations—she had found some vague insight returning: "I feel more & more, that slaveholders are by nature no worse than nonslaveholders & are the *victims* [her underscoring] of the very system they have clung to with a death-grasp."[34] It was as though Angelina had confronted an old dread and, after all these years, had come to terms with it: that all who had ever been a party to the slave system were, in some degree, its victims, even those who had escaped.

There was a light in all this gloom—what Nancy Weston had done.[35] Angelina's spirits lifted at the thought of the fierce battle this mother had waged to prevent her sons from serving as slaves and the conviction that she had instilled in her sons of their right to be free. Then after the war, when they were all free and reunited again, the old dangers past, Nancy Weston had sent her sons to a newly opened freedman's school established by northerners. Later in 1866, when the chance came through a teacher in the school, Archie and Frank were able to go north to continue their education. Then had come their opportunity to enter Lincoln University, where they had fulfilled all the promise others had seen in them. As she pondered all this, Angelina could feel that they too were her kinsmen, sons of her brother, and that she could take pride in them. She declared in a letter, even before she met her nephews, how glad she was that they bore the name of Grimké, "a *once* honored name." "I charge you most solemnly, by your upright conduct, & your life-long devotion to the eternal principles of justice & humanity & Religion to lift *this name* out of the dust, where it now lies, & set it once more among the princes of the land."[36]

Angelina was not content, however, with what letters could tell her. When she answered her nephew's first letter in February, she told Archie and Frank that she wished without delay to meet them in person and planned to come to their commencement in June. In mid-June, her teaching year ended, she immediately set out with her elder son, Stuart, at her side (not Weld, not Sarah—this was her choice), and she remained a full week at Lincoln University. She saw much of her two nephews during this time; they sometimes talked for hours, she asking searching questions as they called up memories, for she insisted that she must know everything.

With it all, Angelina had a crisp practicality. She had managed the Welds' meager funds in their frequent ups and downs between poverty and a living, and she was now intent on the future of her new-found nephews; every opportunity should be opened wide to them. She learned that Archie's support came from a church in upper New York State, where six young men were raising the funds, and Frank's came from a Squire Hotchkiss of New York. No support had been found for the youngest brother, John; and he still remained in Charleston with their mother. She talked with the two of the state of their finances, how much they might require, and told them of the aid their relatives would try to give—she and Sarah and her husband.[37] Archie looked ahead to the legal profession; Frank hoped eventually to study for the ministry. Neither clothes nor books were provided in their support, so Archie and Frank had worked winters and throughout summers. They hoped John could be brought north to college—somehow support should be found for him. So years of educational help lay ahead to equip her nephews for their promising careers. Angelina talked with the president and faculty members of Lincoln, and all spoke with enthusiasm of the gifts of these young men. As President Randall wrote her two years later, on the eve of her nephews' graduation from Lincoln, "Archie and Frank are still our foremost students."[38] Angelina appeared to feel that they were her peculiar charge, her chance to do what their father might have done. A number of months later, Sarah voiced it to a friend. "Ever since [she was at Lincoln University] she has been so deeply interested in them that they are in all her thoughts, she is always planning how to help them."[39] Before she left them in that June of 1868, Angelina assured her nephews of how her home would welcome them and then and there made plans for them to come. As matters turned out, they became frequent visitors.

When Angelina and her son returned from Lincoln University, Sarah met them part way. She had insisted on joining them in Newark to accompany them on the remaining journey home. Sarah reported that she found Angelina "exhausted and excited," so much so that Sarah voiced "alarm." In the months that followed, Sarah insisted in letters to friends that Angelina's health had suffered "since that fatal visit to Lincoln University," and she continued for months to sound the same lugubrious note—"she . . . has never recovered from that ordeal."[40] But Sarah also told of a different state. More than once, she spoke of Angelina's joy in finding their nephews, in being able to make the journey to Lincoln University, and in her confidence that now the way lay straight and clear, as she continued to work and earn to help them prepare for their careers.

4.

In these later years, Angelina spoke little of her inner thoughts as she dealt with all that came. If she wrote in a journal, its pages were lost. Among her letters that remain, few are intimate in their nature, and even here the reserve that had grown with the years rises like a shield against others' eyes. Yet in beliefs and in acts she was open to all, articulate, outspoken, bold in her stands. Her body was frail, more than hitherto—she was nearly sixty-five when she found her nephews—but there was no sign of a flagging spirit or dilution of her goals. She continued as committed as when her crusade first began—"I recognize no rights but human rights . . . the rights of the slave and woman blend."

Moreover, she continued in this later time to give no sign of any slackening in her effort, no willingness to let others become complacent or inactive, nor was there any task too minor if it served her beliefs. The range of her activities was as varied as ever. Teaching was still her profession, and she continued in it as long as her strength would let her do it well. She maintained her concern for the sick and helpless; just before her own lengthy illness, she had spent many hours nursing a bedridden consumptive neighbor.[41]

The woman's rights movement had been reorganized since the war, and Angelina maintained her contacts with national woman's rights affairs, with the women she knew well, and with the new leaders who had come later. She also headed various activities in her own locality. A petition campaign for woman's suffrage was afoot and signatures must be collected to be sent to the Congress. Angelina, Sarah, and others—Sarah had long since returned to her old interest—went from door to door throughout Hyde Park, Massachusetts, petitions in hand to gather names. Once she headed a march of Hyde Park women, sympathetic menfolk at their sides, to the polling place on election day, demonstrating symbolically their right to vote.[42] Through all this she knew again the familiar opposition and its old weapon ridicule.

There may have been moments in the long ago when, in exuberance of spirit, Angelina had felt a hope that emancipation, whether of the enslaved or of woman, could come swiftly by proclamation. If she had ever known such feelings, they were long since behind her. In those hard years of the 1840s, she had learned in her own person how entrenched were the obstacles, how resistant, and sometimes how concealed. When Angelina herself at last felt free, despite restrictions life had laid upon her, she still knew that emancipation had continually to be won.

Now she looked out on her world and was all the more aware. Human slavery had been ended for a number of years, at least the system had been crushed. Angelina's apprehension had grown, year by year, that slavery's violence was not ended when the institution was abolished and that what she had been witnessing since the war was the white South's determination to control black people by denying them the rights a free people should possess. She voiced no hope in the white men who held the power—she had said it before—neither those in the South nor those in the North "who had stood by holding the garments of those who were stoning liberty to death."[43] The direction of her thoughts can be glimpsed when, in wartime, she spoke of the black soldier and his bravery in the field, a man just out of slavery who knew what freedom meant —"he . . . will yet save us, and himself too." She had voiced it also to her nephews in clear and definite terms; she prayed God, "as He gradually removed by death the petty tyrants of the South, that he will raise up a generation of true and loving ones from the ranks of the oppressed who would labor as fearlessly for the great Christian doctrine of Liberty, Equality & Fraternity of all races as the Slaveholders had labor'd and lived—fought and died for Slavery."[44]

In her young womanhood in Charleston, when her minister had said sadly that all they could do about slavery was "Pray and wait," and Angelina had exclaimed, in passionate indignation, "Pray and work!"[45] she voiced the drive that would become the strength of her days. It was this, perhaps, that saved her, since it would not let her go. Work infused with meaning became her way of life, so that in later years Sarah could write to a friend that Angelina "is working until she is ready to drop, sustained by her nervous energy and irresistible will."[46] Here lay the sure means in Angelina Grimké's eyes, and she asserted it continually regarding emancipation—that work, even battle, would be constantly required to win and keep freedom.

By the mid-1870s abolitionist men and women who had known the fears and hopes of the early crusade were in a state of anxious foreboding. They had seen reconstruction draw to its close as, one after the other, the old slave states once more were in the control of former slaveholders. Much that they had counted gained they now saw as lost. William Lloyd Garrison, writing to Weld in 1875, used terms reminiscent of the old flaming *Liberator*—language Weld had never felt at home with, although since his wartime work that had been spurred on by Garrison, their former barriers had fallen.[47] "An uprising of Rebeldom . . . audacious, malignant, defiant"; "air resounding with the yells of Rebel exultation"; "dreadful events . . . in the not far-distant future."

At the end of Garrison's letter were some personal and sober words. "We have been pained to hear of the illness of your blessed Angelina." Angelina had suffered a stroke when she was almost seventy, not long before her birthday on February 20, 1875. She was partially paralyzed when that birthday came, a condition that continued for several years. It seems the final irony that toward the end she was deprived altogether of the use of her voice, the voice that once had been the prime symbol of her fame. Death came in October 1879. Sarah, at eighty-one, had died six years before. So only Weld was left of the three whose fateful joint life had lasted nearly forty years.[48]

There was a veritable ingathering of old abolitionists, as they came together "in memory" of Angelina Grimké.[49] One after the other, they spoke of what they knew—Elizur Wright, Robert Wolcutt, Wendell Phillips, and many others—"I heard"; "I saw"; "I shall never forget"; "We were comparatively a handful"; it was the "most inflamed period of the anti-slavery contest"; there appeared "this mild, soft-spoken woman, then in the prime of her beauty"; "high bred . . . beautiful . . . [yet] such solemnity and power." One told of Angelina's "moral and spiritual greatness." Wendell Phillips said, "She brought the anti-slavery cause greater help than any other person." But chiefly they spoke of her "magnetic power," of "those six evenings" in the Odeon Theater in Boston, "six galleries rising above the auditorium, all crowded"; of her audiences, "quiet, intensely absorbed," although sometimes outside could be heard threatening mobs. It was "Angelina's serene, commanding eloquence . . . which enchained attention, disarmed prejudice, carried her hearers with her," as one said, "eloquence such as never then had been heard from a woman." In their thoughts, all seemed to dwell on the past. It was as though, in remembering this southern woman who had come among them, they themselves were carried back to the glorious 1830s, those golden years of antislavery's crusade, dangerous, thrilling, zestful with life, a time when they too were at the peak of their powers.

It is certain that Angelina would not have been pleased could she have heard these friends speak in these terms of her life. She had known that in the 1830s she glowed to their response and had felt exhilaration in the full use of her potential. One gift had been lost—she had inwardly dealt with this—the power of her voice that once could move and mold great audiences of people. Not so her other gifts—they were never lost, nor were the gains she had wrung from subsequent experience: her supreme qualities of intellect and spirit wherein lay the essence of her drawing power, the tenacity of her principles of human rights and equality, her insistence on action to accomplish these goals, her courage and boldness against dangerous opposition, her belief in solitude and in hard-won independence, and her incomparable strength that would not let her fail. Here was the stuff of which her greatness was made, and because these friends knew it, even after long years, they could still hold in memory the moving power of her voice.

Notes

Explanatory Note:
In references to the letters and diaries of Angelina Grimké, Sarah M. Grimké, and Theodore Weld, after the first reference, Angelina's and Sarah's first names and Weld's last name are used. In the case of others, full names have been recorded.

Throughout these references the customary form is used, but when a full letter is quoted in the book, it is quoted precisely, including its form of dating. After Angelina Grimké became a Quaker (even before she became a member), she began to use the Quaker form of dating, as her sister Sarah had done for a longer period. Later Angelina reverted to the customary form, except that frequently she failed to put down the full date, even sometimes the year. Fortunately, at some point, Weld recorded the year of letters written after their marriage; in the case of other letters, it was usually possible to date them from the contents.

All italics used in quotations from letters and diaries of Angelina, Sarah, and Weld, appear in the originals; none were supplied. Angelina, Sarah, and Weld underscored freely.

All unpublished letters, diaries, and other papers referred to in the notes are in the Weld-Grimké Collection, William L. Clements Library, University of Michigan, unless otherwise indicated.

Foreword

1. For a history of the antislavery movement see Louis Filler, *The Crusade against Slavery, 1830-1860* (New York: Harper & Brothers, 1960). Also Aileen S. Kraditor, in *Means and Ends in American Abolitionism; Garrison and His Critics on Strategy and Tactics, 1834-1850* (New York: Pantheon Books, 1967), deals especially with important issues within the movement. Dwight L. Dumond, *Antislavery: The Crusade for Freedom in America* (Ann Arbor: University of Michigan Press, 1961). Chaps. 21 and 22 treat "Theodore Weld: The Agency System" and "Angelina Grimké: Woman's Rights," and elsewhere in the book there are substantial portions dealing with Angelina and Sarah Grimké. Articles by a number of writers will be found in Martin Duberman, ed., *The Antislavery Vanguard: New Essays on the Abolitionists* (Princeton: Princeton University Press, 1965). Leon F. Litwack, *North of Slavery: The Negro in the Free States, 1790-1860* (Chicago: University of Chicago Press, 1961), provides valuable insights on the free Negro in the North during the slavery period. See especially Chap. 7, "Abolitionism: White and Black."

Chapter I
   1. Mrs. St. Julien Ravenel, *Charleston: The Place and the People* (New York: The Macmillan Company, 1906), Chap. XXVIII. See also Frederika Bremmer, *Homes in the New World*, 2 vols. (New York: Harper & Brothers, 1853), 1:263-64. This Swedish novelist and feminist gives her impressions of the homes and streets of Charleston at the time of her visit of several weeks between 1849 and 1851.
   2. [Theodore D. Weld, ed.], "Testimony of Angelina Grimké Weld," in *American Slavery As It Is: Testimony of a Thousand Witnesses* (New York: American Anti-Slavery Society, 1839), pp. 54-55.
   3. Angelina in [Weld], *Slavery As It Is*, pp. 54-55.
   4. Ibid.
   5. Catherine Birney, *The Grimké Sisters: Sarah and Angelina Grimké, the First Woman Advocates of Abolition and Woman's Rights* (Boston: Lee and Shepard, 1885), p. 6. "Landgrave" apparently was a title given to a small number of large-scale landowners of the aristocracy in early Carolina. See Ernest M. Lander, Jr., and Robert K. Ackerman, *Perspectives in South Carolina History: The First 300 Years* (Columbia: University of South Carolina Press, 1973), pp. 8-9.
   6. Mary S. Grimké to her daughters Angelina and Sarah (after they were abolitionists), 1 Jan. 1839 and 11 Nov. 1838. See also Birney, *Grimké Sisters*, pp. 6-7.
   7. From a Grimké family Bible in Clements Library, University of Michigan.
   8. Ravenel, *Charleston*, Chap. XXVIII. See also Ulrich Bonnell Phillips, "The Slave Labor Problems in the Charleston District," *Political Science Quarterly*, 22, no. 3 (September, 1907): 416-39.
   9. [Weld], *Slavery As It Is*, pp. 54-56.
   10. See, for example, Angelina, Diary, 12 Apr. 1829. Also see Birney, *Grimké Sisters*, pp. 7, 14-15.
   11. Angelina, Diary, 31 May, 12 June, 20 Jan. 1829. Mary S. Grimké to Angelina, 18 June, 16 Nov. 1838; also to Sarah, 23 Mar. 1838, and Angelina to Sarah, 7 Dec. 1828.
   12. Birney, *Grimké Sisters*, pp. 11-16.
   13. Angelina to Weld, [n.d.], 1843.
   14. Birney, *Grimké Sisters*, pp. 8-14, for Sarah's stories of her girlhood.
   15. Angelina to Sarah, 2 June 1828, 18 Jan. 1829.
   16. The *Charleston Courier*, 5 Dec. 1811, gives an extended account of the impeachment proceedings against Judge Grimké before the House of Representatives of the South Carolina Legislature, citing the eight charges brought against him, some dating back to 1801. All charges had to do with specific court cases. The votes were close: for instance, on the first charge, 43 Ayes (to impeach), and 50 Nays.
   17. Mary S. Grimké to her daughter Angelina, [n.d.] July 1838.
   18. Angelina, Diary, [n.d.] Sept. 1835.
   19. Sarah, Diary, "story of her life," dated 3 June 1827. Sarah called this lengthy special entry a story of her life, but in fact it dealt chiefly with her tortuous religious experiences, including conversions and lapses back into the gay social life of Charleston. She touches briefly on having turned against slavery in the early 1820s, or so it appears, probably about the time that she became a member of the Orthodox Friends. She tells here and in other entries in her Diary of how Quakerism repelled her when she first encountered it.
   20. Birney, *Grimké Sisters*, pp. 14-15.
   21. [Theodore D. Weld, ed.], *In Memory of Angelina Grimké Weld* (Boston: Press of George H. Ellis, 1880), pp. 35-36. The Dedication, "To the Old Abolitionists," is signed T.D.W.
   22. Sarah, Diary, "story of her life," dated 3 June 1827.
   23. Birney, *Grimké Sisters*, pp. 39-40.
   24. [Weld], *Slavery As It Is*, p. 53.
   25. Bremmer, *Homes in the New World*, 1:281-82.
   26. Angelina, Diary, 12 June 1828.
   27. Many entries in Angelina's Diary reflect her feeling that her mother ruled with "fear."

28. [Weld], *Slavery As It Is*, pp. 52-57. A few of Angelina's stories of treatment of slaves here seem to make reference to her mother, judging by letters later exchanged and incidents referred to in Angelina's Diary.

29. Mary S. Grimké to Angelina and Sarah, 12 Feb. 1838. See Angelina's reference in [Weld], *Slavery As It Is*, p. 56, to the Charleston matron who required her personal slave to sleep on a pallet at the foot of her bed.

30. Angelina, Diary, 23. Apr. 1828.

31. [Weld], *Slavery As It Is*, p. 55.

32. Angelina, Diary, [n.d.] 1828.

33. For the impact of the attempted Vesey uprising on slaveholders in and around Charleston, see the following accounts: Lionel H. Kennedy and Thomas Parker, *An Official Report of the Trials of Sundry Negroes, Charged with an Attempt to Raise an Insurrection in the State of South Carolina* (Charleston, S.C.: James R. Schenck, 1822). Also James Hamilton, Jr., *An Account of the Late Intended Insurrection among a Portion of the Blacks of This City* (Charleston, S.C.: Authority of the Corporation of Charleston, 1822). Both may be found in the Library of Congress, Washington, D.C.; and a second edition of the latter report, with Appendix, is in Cornell University Library. Accounts of the court trials of those apprehended were given in the Charleston press. No doubt these accounts were widely read among slaveowners, including the Grimkés. See *Charleston Courier* 29 June, 1, 3, 10, 12, 19, 26 July 1822; also *City Gazette and Commercial Advertiser* for the same period.

34. See Phillips, "Slave Labor Problems," pp. 416-39. Population figures in table on p. 426.

35. From Angelina's historic letter to William Lloyd Garrison, "Philadelphia, 8th Month, 30th, 1835."

36. Sarah, Diary, "story of her life," dated 3 June 1837.

37. Frederick P. Bowes, *The Culture of Early Charleston* (Chapel Hill: University of North Carolina Press, 1942), in Chap. II, "Churchmen and Dissenters," discusses the Anglican church and other religious influences in eighteenth-century Charleston. W. J. Cash, throughout his book, *The Mind of the South* (New York: Alfred A. Knopf, 1941), touches on the prevalence and significance of evangelicalism in southern life. Clement Eaton, *Freedom of Thought in the Old South* (Durham: Duke University Press, 1940), deals in various places with religious influences; see especially Chap. XI, "Decline of Skepticism," and pp. 282-83; also Clement Eaton, *The Growth of Southern Civilization, 1790-1860* (New York: Harper & Brothers, 1961); William Warren Sweet, *Revivalism in America: Its Origin, Growth, and Decline* (New York: Charles Scribner's Sons, 1944), see especially Chap. 6, on revivalism in the early 1800s.

38. Sarah, Diary, "story of her life," dated 3 June 1827, tells in detail of her several experiences with revivals that she felt had a long-time effect on her development.

39. Mary S. Grimké to Sarah, 5 Oct. 1835; Angelina in [Weld], *Slavery As It Is*, pp. 52, 53.

40. Mary S. Grimké to Angelina and Sarah, dated Charleston, 10, 12 Feb. 1838.

41. Angelina to Sarah, [n.d.] Apr. 1826, quoted in Birney, *Grimké Sisters*, pp. 43-44, tells Sarah of her conversion.

42. Angelina to a sister, Mrs. Anna Frost, 17 Mar. 1828.

43. Angelina to Elizabeth Bascom, 23 July 1828.

44. From the early 1820s, when she became a Friend, and throughout the decade, Sarah's Diary is filled with her mental conflict and anguished struggle. For example, entries for 15 Jan., 20 Feb., [n.d.] Apr. 1823; 14 Sept., 31 Dec. 1825; 16 Feb., 23 Apr., 14 June 1826; 22 May, 5 June 1827.

45. Sarah, Diary, 22 Oct 1827. Also Angelina, Diary, 10 Dec. 1827: "My second sister [Sarah] is eminently pious but is a Quaker and instead of being a helper to my joy and the partner of my trials . . . she does not even countenance family worship by her presence . . . if she were anything but a Quaker."

46. Sarah, Diary, 23 Dec. 1827.

47. Angelina, Diary, [n.d.] Nov. 1827.

48. Sarah, Diary, 29 Nov., 1 Dec. 1827. "Oh Lord," Sarah wrote, "open the blind eye and [make] contrite the carnal heart, oh, break the false rest," referring to Angelina.

49. Sarah, Diary, 29 Nov., 1 Dec. 1827.
50. Angelina, Diary, [Dec.] 1827.
51. Sarah, Diary, 5 Feb. 1828.
52. Angelina, Diary, 10 Dec. 1827.
53. Angelina, Diary, 10 Jan. 1827; also Sarah, Diary, 10 Jan. 1827.
54. Angelina, Diary, 1 Feb. 1828.
55. Angelina, Diary, 24 Feb. 1828; also 10 Feb., 24 Mar. 1828, and other entries during March.
56. Angelina to Elizabeth Bascom of Camden, S.C., 18 Apr. 1828.
57. Angelina, Diary, [n.d.] Apr. 1828.
58. Angelina, Diary, 17 Apr., 16 Mar. 1828.
59. Sarah, Diary, [n.d.] Mar. 1828.
60. Angelina, Diary, 25 Apr. 1828.
61. William MacDowell to Angelina, 24 Apr. 1828.
62. Angelina to William MacDowell, 26 Apr. 1828. On 25 April she had written in her Diary, "Saw William MacDowell yesterday, conversed with him . . . we wept together."
63. Angelina to William MacDowell, 14 May 1828, and William MacDowell to Angelina, 23 May 1828; also Angelina, Diary, 28 Apr., 7 May 1828.
64. William MacDowell to Angelina, 30 May 1828.
65. Angelina to William MacDowell, 30 May 1828.
66. William MacDowell to Angelina, 3 June 1828, and Angelina to William MacDowell, 3 June 1828.
67. Sarah, Diary, 5 Feb. 1828. Sarah writes of how she shrinks from "being cast on the ocean of life, an alien" as she was leaving her home for Philadelphia.
68. Angelina, Diary, 11 Jan. 1828.
69. Angelina, Diary, 29 Jan. 1828. Angelina arrived in Philadelphia on her visit to Sarah on 19 July 1828 and returned to Charleston on 11 Nov. 1828.
70. Angelina, Diary, 29 July 1828.
71. Angelina in [Weld], *Slavery As It Is*, p. 53.
72. Angelina, Diary, 30 Nov. 1828.

Chapter II
1. Angelina to Sarah, 8 Mar. 1829.
2. See Frederika Bremmer, *Homes in the New World*, 2 vols. (New York: Harper & Brothers, 1853), 1:263, 264: "The city, like a great assemblage of villas, standing in their gardens"; and, speaking of the Battery, calls it "the place of promenade" for the city's "fashionable."
3. Angelina to Sarah, 7 Dec. 1828.
4. Angelina, Diary, 25 Dec. 1828.
5. Angelina, by this time, had visited Sarah in Philadelphia and had attended the prominent Arch Street Meeting with Sarah.
6. Angelina, Diary, 28 Dec. 1828.
7. Angelina, Diary, 21 July, 2 Aug. 1829; also Angelina to Sarah, quoted in Catherine Birney, *The Grimké Sisters: Sarah and Angelina E. Grimké, the First Woman Advocates of Abolition and Woman's Rights* (Boston: Lee and Shepard, 1885), pp. 60-61.
8. Angelina, Diary, 26 July 1829; Angelina to Sarah, 5 Aug. 1829.
9. Angelina to her sister, Mrs. Anna G. Frost, [spring] 1829.
10. Angelina to Sarah, 7 Dec. 1829.
11. Angelina, Diary, 20 June, 5 Oct., 23 June 1829.
12. Angelina, Diary, 6 May, 5 Apr. 1829.
13. Angelina to Sarah, 10 Mar. [1829]; Angelina, Diary, 12 June 1829.
14. Angelina, Diary, 12 June 1829.
15. Angelina, Diary, [n.d.] 1829.
16. Angelina, Diary, 4, 23 Apr. 1829.
17. Angelina, Diary, 24 June, 29 Mar. 1829.
18. Presbyterian Synod of South Carolina and Georgia, *Report of the Committee to*

whom was referred the subject of the religious instruction of the colored population of the Synod, at its late Session in Columbia, South Carolina. December 5-9, 1833 (Charleston: Charleston Observer Office Press, 1834).

19. [Theodore D. Weld, ed.], *In Memory of Angelina Grimké Weld* (Boston: Press of George H. Ellis, 1880), p. 37. Some of Weld's stories of Angelina's experiences, as he gives them in this booklet, were from his firsthand knowledge, others he must have learned from Angelina. Few stories from her childhood could be verified, but those from her adulthood, before he knew her, could usually be checked against contemporary records. It appears that Weld's accounts were often in error about precise time, place, and sequence of events, though he usually recalled the essence of the matter. An example of his inaccuracy is his account in this memorial booklet of Angelina's experiences with the Third Presbyterian Church of Charleston during 1828-29. Fortunately, the contemporary records are full for this period: Angelina's Diary entries at the time, her letters to Sarah, and her lengthy correspondence with the Reverend William MacDowell and the church elders.

20. Ibid., p. 37.
21. Angelina, Diary, 14 May 1829.
22. From Weld-Grimké Collection.
23. William MacDowell to Angelina, 19 May 1829.
24. Angelina to William MacDowell, 21 May 1829.
25. Angelina, Diary, 31 Dec. 1829.
26. Angelina, Diary, [n.d.] 1829.
27. Angelina, Diary, 27 Jan. 1829.
28. Angelina to Sarah, 21 Mar., 23 Apr. 1829; and Angelina, Diary, [n.d.] 1829.
29. Sarah, Diary, 2 Sept., 6 Jan., 14 July, 12 July, 12 Sept. 1829.
30. Angelina, Diary, 12 Sept. 1829.
31. Angelina, Diary, 17 Nov., 19 Dec., 30 Aug., 23 Apr. 1829.
32. Angelina, Diary, 30 Aug. 1829.
33. Rufus M. Jones, *The Later Period of Quakerism*, 2 vols. (London: Macmillan & Co., 1921), 1:461, 468-69.
34. Angelina, Diary, 11 Apr. 1829. In this period Angelina wrote frequently of her "calling" or "mission." For example, Diary, 2 Nov. 1827; 10, 14 Jan., 1, 10, 23 Feb., 24, 27, 29 Mar., 18, 20 Apr. 1829.
35. Angelina, Diary, 20, 26 July 1830.
36. Angelina, Diary, [n.d.], 1830, 9 Sept. 1830.
37. Angelina, Diary, [n.d.] 1830.
38. Ibid.
39. Birney, *Grimké Sisters*, p. 100, provides this description of Angelina's appearance at this period.
40. Angelina, Diary, 9, 8 July 1831.
41. Angelina, Diary, 12 July 1831.
42. Angelina, Diary, 3, 21 Aug., 21 Sept. 1831.
43. Angelina, Diary, 22, 24 Sept. 1831.
44. Angelina to Sarah, 8 Dec. 1831.
45. Angelina, Diary, 21 Nov. 1831.
46. Angelina, Diary, [n.d.] 1831; Angelina to Sarah, 24 Jan. 1832.
47. Angelina to Sarah, 24 Jan. 1832; Angelina, Diary, 18 June, 14, 15 July, 2 June 1832.
48. Angelina, Diary, [May] 1833.
49. Some seven months after young Bettle's death, Angelina wrote a lengthy and candid account of her devastating experience when Jane and Samuel Bettle, at the time of their son's death, rejected her by sending word that it would be better if she did not call on them. In this account, she confronted her wounded pride and came to terms with the Bettles' treatment of her. Angelina, Diary, [May] 1833.
50. Wendell P. Garrison and Francis J. Garrison, *William Lloyd Garrison, 1805-1879: The Story of His Life Told by His Children*, 4 vols. (New York: Century Co., 1885-89), 1:194-99, 203-4, quoting the *Philadelphia Inquirer*, 2 Sept. 1830.
51. Angelina to Sarah, in Charleston, S.C., 8, 19 Dec. 1831, 4 Feb. [1832].

52. William Sumner Jenkins, *Pro-Slavery Thought in the Old South* (Chapel Hill: University of North Carolina Press, 1935), pp. 96ff. Also, Garrison, *Garrison*, 1:251-52, 255, quoting from the Virginia newspapers of this period.

53. Angelina to her brother, Thomas Grimké, 1 Feb. [1832] and 3 May 1833. Thomas Grimké to Angelina, 1 Nov. 1832 and 20 Mar. 1833.

54. Samuel J. May, *Some Recollections of the Antislavery Conflict* (Boston: Fields, Osgood & Co., 1869), pp. 39-57. Samuel May was one of those who went to Prudence Crandall's aid.

55. Angelina may have read of the event in the local press. *The Pennsylvanian* (Philadelphia) had a news item on 4 Dec. 1833, the day the founding convention of the American Anti-Slavery Society opened. It denounced the leaders as "hair-brained fanatics" and predicted that the organization would cause "dangerous ferment."

56. Birney, *Grimké Sisters*, pp. 118-19.

57. Dwight L. Dumond, *Antislavery: The Crusade for Freedom in America* (Ann Arbor: University of Michigan Press, 1961), Chap. 26, deals with mob violence against abolitionists.

58. See Dumond, *Antislavery*, Chap. 18, "Lane Seminary."

59. Angelina to Weld, 11 Feb. [1838]. In Gilbert N. Barnes and Dwight L. Dumond, eds., *Letters of Theodore Dwight Weld, Angelina Grimké Weld, and Sarah Grimké, 1822-1844*, 2 vols. (1934; reprint ed., New York: Da Capo Press, 1970), 1:537. These two volumes contain most of the letters between Weld and the two Grimké sisters for the period covered; hence I have used them as needed for the late 1830s and early 1840s. However, some letters of this period remained unpublished, and I have also made use of a number of these from the Weld-Grimké Collection in the William L. Clements Library, University of Michigan.

By the early summer of 1837, a regular exchange of letters between Weld and the Grimkés was under way. Until February 1838, when Angelina and Weld became engaged, Weld usually addressed his letters to the sisters jointly, and Angelina and Sarah, while writing separate letters, usually wrote them on the same sheets of paper. In citing the Grimkés' letters to Weld, I cite each one separately—"Angelina to Weld" or "Sarah to Weld"—even though they were sent under the same cover.

60. Philadelphia *National Gazette*, 15 July 1834, quoting from the New York press.

61. *Liberator*, see July and August issues, 1834, where "pro-slavery riots" or attempted riots are noted in Philadelphia, Connecticut, New Jersey, Ohio, and in Boston after George Thompson arrived.

62. Birney, *Grimké Sisters*, pp. 121-23.

63. *Richmond Enquirer* and New York *Courier & Enquirer*, as quoted from the *Liberator* in Garrison, *Garrison*, 1:452, 456.

64. Garrison, *Garrison*, 1:453-67.

65. George Thompson, *Letters and Addresses of George Thompson During His Mission in the United States from October 1, 1834 to November 27, 1835* (Boston: Isaac Knapp, 1837).

66. Quoted in Birney, *Grimké Sisters*, p. 114.

67. See ibid., p. 123.

68. Unsigned letter from a Quaker in Charleston to Angelina, "Charleston, 3rd Mo 30th 1835," Weld-Grimké Collection.

69. Angelina, Diary, 12 May 1835.

70. Angelina to Sarah, 27 Sept. 1835; 25 July, 5 Aug. 1836.

Chapter III

1. Angelina, Diary, 15, 26, 30 June 1835.

2. One riot occurred in Philadelphia in July 1834, at which time a white mob raged through the Negro sections of the city. Litwack says Philadelphia experienced five major anti-Negro riots between 1832 and 1849. Leon F. Litwack, *North of Slavery: The Negro in the Free States, 1790-1860* (Chicago: University of Chicago Press, 1961), p. 100.

3. [Samuel Webb, ed.], *History of Pennsylvania Hall, Which Was Destroyed by a Mob on the 17th of May, 1838* (Philadelphia: Merrihew & Gunn, 1838).

4. Lydia Maria Child to Ellis Jay Loring, New York, 15 Aug. 1835, in Lydia Maria Child, *Letters of Lydia Maria Child* (Boston: Houghton, Mifflin and Company, 1883), pp. 15-16; also Wendell P. Garrison and Francis J. Garrison, *William Lloyd Garrison, 1805-1879: The Story of His Life Told by His Children*, 4 vols. (New York: Century Co., 1885-89), 1:488, 490-91.

5. Garrison, *Garrison*, 1:494-500.

6. Sarah, Diary, 15 Mar. 1835; also 27 Feb., 5 Mar. 1835.

7. Angelina to Sarah, 27 Sept. 1835.

8. Garrison, *Garrison*, 1:503-4.

9. Angelina to Sarah, 27 Sept. 1835.

10. Angelina, Diary, [n.d.] 1835.

11. *Liberator*, 19 Sept. 1835; also Garrison, *Garrison*, 1:518. The *Liberator* noted some three weeks later that Angelina Grimké's "Letter to Garrison" "is obtaining a wide circulation in various newspapers, both religious and secular. Its ultimate influence will be worth a thousand speeches," quoting from the *Vermont Telegraph* that "the antislavery cause and the world would have been greatly wronged by its [the letter's] suppression." (*Liberator*, 17 Oct. 1835).

12. Angelina, Diary, [n.d.] 1835.

13. Angelina, Diary. Her entries for the period May through August 1835 reflect her inner debate on abolitionism which culminated in her letter to William Lloyd Garrison of 30 Aug. 1835.

14. Angelina, Diary, [n.d., but late] Sept. 1835.

15. Sarah, Diary, quoted in Catherine Birney, *The Grimké Sisters: Sarah and Angelina E. Grimké, the First Woman Advocates of Abolition and Woman's Rights* (Boston: Lee and Shepard, 1885), pp. 129-30.

16. Angelina to Jane Smith, 18 Sept. [1836], written from Shrewsbury, N.J. For further information on Angelina's letters to Jane Smith, see note 32 of this chapter.

17. Angelina to Sarah, 27 Sept. 1835.

18. Angelina to Sarah [n.d.], written from Shrewsbury, N.J. and the contents date it summer 1835.

19. Sarah, Diary, 19 July 1836.

20. Theodore D. Weld, ed., *In Memory of Angelina Grimké Weld* (Boston: Press of George N. Ellis, 1880), pp. 44-46, gives Margaret Parker's account of Angelina's decision to write "Appeal to the Christian Women of the South." Angelina was staying in Mrs. Parker's home in Shrewsbury, N.J., at the time.

21. Birney, *Grimké Sisters*, pp. 146-50.

22. Angelina to Sarah, 1, 14 Aug. 1836.

23. Elizur Wright to Angelina, in 1836, quoted in Birney, *Grimké Sisters*, p. 147.

24. Angelina to Jane Smith, quoted in ibid., p. 152.

25. Weld's account of the reception given the "Appeal," as told in after years, ibid., pp. 149-50.

26. *Right and Wrong in Boston*, No. 1, "Report of Boston Female Anti-Slavery Society. With concise Statement of events, previous and subsequent to the Annual Meeting of 1835" (Boston: Published by the Society, 1836).

27. Angelina to Sarah, 14 Aug. 1836.

28. [Weld], *In Memory*, pp. 54-56.

29. Birney, *Grimké Sisters*, pp. 142-46, on Sarah's difficulties with the Quaker Elders and her state of mind concerning Angelina. Sarah's Diary at this time contains many entries concerning the elders' objections to her attempted ministry.

30. See Louis Filler, *The Crusade against Slavery: 1830-1860* (New York: Harper & Brothers, 1960), pp. 66ff.

31. Dwight L. Dumond, *Antislavery: The Crusade for Freedom in America* (Ann Arbor: University of Michigan Press, 1961), pp. 184-86, for information on the "Seventy."

32. Angelina to Jane Smith, 18 Sept. 1836. Angelina's letters to her Philadelphia friend, Jane Smith, cover a period beginning in 1835 and continuing until late in her life. The letters from 1836 to 1838, during Angelina's active public career as an antislavery

lecturer, are numerous and many of them are several pages in length. They are a valuable record of those important years, resembling a diary in detail. The earliest letters were written when Angelina was becoming an abolitionist and was staying part of the time in New Jersey. When she went to New York to attend the convention of the "Seventy" and began her "parlor" meetings on antislavery, the more significant record begins. The extensive and frequent letters written in Massachusetts from May 1837 to May 1838 are particularly interesting. By sheer chance, all of these letters to Jane Smith were preserved. An account of them appeared in *The Woman's Journal*, an organ of the woman's rights movement. "A few years ago, after the death of the late Mrs. [sic] Jane Smith in Philadelphia, with whom, in those perilous times Angelina Grimké found shelter and a home, the letters of Miss Grimké to Mrs. Smith were returned [presumably to the Welds]. These letters written in confidence and with the fulness of friendship, contain as no where else the history of the fiery trials through which these first steps were cut in the solid rock of custom and prejudice to make a highway for other women. Should they be given to the public, as they ought to be, those who read them can now be told at what a great price the enlarged sphere and assured rights for women have been earned." *The Woman's Journal* 10, no. 44. (1 Nov. 1879):348. Angelina Grimké's letters to Jane Smith are now in the Weld-Grimké Collection, William L. Clements Library, University of Michigan.

33. Angelina to Jane Smith, [n.d.] Sept. 1836.
34. Angelina to Jane Smith, [n.d.] Nov. 1836, 22 Mar. 1837.
35. Angelina to Jane Smith, 18 Nov. 1836.
36. Angelina to Jane Smith, 19 Nov. 1836.
37. Birney, *Grimké Sisters*, pp. 163ff., tells how frequently Weld was calling on Angelina and lending support at the time she began lecturing to women's groups.
38. Angelina to Jane Smith, [n.d.], 19 Nov., 17 Dec. 1836.
39. Weld to Sarah, 27 Mar. 1838, Gilbert H. Barnes and Dwight L. Dumond, eds., *Letters of Theodore Dwight Weld, Angelina Grimké Weld and Sarah Grimké, 1822-1844*, 2 vols. (1934; reprint ed., New York: Da Capo Press, 1970), 2:603-6. See also Sarah to Weld, 1 Apr. 1838, ibid., p. 616.
40. Angelina to Jane Smith, 20 Jan. 1837.
41. Angelina to Jane Smith, 22 Mar. 1837.
42. *The Friend* 8 (1835):166-67. An article headed "People of Colour" states that at the request of the editor, "our estimable citizen, James Forten, a man of colour" furnished information, collected about three years before, "on coloured people of Philadelphia." Some two pages of factual material follow.
43. Angelina to Jane Smith, 20 Jan. 1837.
44. Litwack, *North of Slavery*, pp. 219, 221.
45. Ibid., p. 220; also Barnes and Dumond, *Weld-Grimké Letters*, 1:275-76.
46. Angelina to Jane Smith, 22 Mar. 1837.
47. Litwack, *North of Slavery*, p. 218n.
48. Angelina to Jane Smith, 22 Mar. 1837.
49. Ibid. Angelina's letters to Jane Smith from Massachusetts began on 21 May 1837.
50. Angelina to Jane Smith, 17 Apr., 20 Jan. [1837].
51. Angelina to Jane Smith, 17 Apr. [1837].
52. Angelina to Jane Smith, 20 May 1837. For actions taken by the convention, see Anti-Slavery Convention of American Women, *Proceedings* (New York: W. S. Dorr, 1837), held in New York City, 9-12 May 1837.
53. Angelina to Jane Smith, 10 Aug. 1837.
54. *Right and Wrong in Boston*, No. I, 1836, and No. II, 1837.
55. Angelina to Jane Smith, 20 May 1837.
56. Ibid.
57. Sarah to Jane Smith, 11 Apr. 1837.
58. Birney, *Grimké Sisters*, p. 122. The Grimkés' friend Sarah Douglass of Philadelphia gives an account of her experience from childhood with the Arch Street Meeting "Negro pew." (Sarah M. Douglass to William Bassett, Dec. 1827, in Barnes and Dumond, *Weld-Grimké Letters*, 2:829-32.)
59. Angelina's letters to Jane Smith, which she wrote once or twice a week, giving a

full record of events, provide the principal source for her remarkable Massachusetts lecture tour that began in late May 1837 and continued until November, when she became ill. Accounts in local newspapers as well as in the *Liberator* supplement the record.

60. Angelina to Jane Smith, 6 June [1837].

61. Angelina to Jane Smith, 16 July, [n.d.] July 1837.

62. Angelina to Jane Smith, 10 July 1837.

63. Angelina to Jane Smith, 25 July 1837.

64. *Right and Wrong in Boston*, No. 2, 1837; see also Garrison, *Garrison*, 1:134-35.

65. Angelina to Jane Smith, 25 July [1837].

66. *Lynn Record* (Massachusetts) quoted in *Liberator*, 3 Aug. 1837, under the heading "Female Influence."

67. Angelina to Jane Smith, 20 Aug. 1837.

68. Sarah to Jane Smith, 26 Aug. 1837.

69. Catherine E. Beecher, *An Essay on Slavery and Abolition with Reference to the Duty of American Females* (Philadelphia: Henry Perkins, 1837).

70. Angelina E. Grimké, *Letters to Catherine E. Beecher, in Reply to an Essay on Slavery and Abolition, Addressed to A. E. Grimké*, rev. ed. (Boston: Isaac Knapp, 1838), Letter II, "Immediate Emancipation."

71. Ibid., Letter VI, "Colonization"; also Angelina to Jane Smith, 25 July 1837.

72. Ibid., Letter III, "Main Principles of Action."

73. Ibid., Letter VII, "Prejudice."

74. Ibid., Letter VI, "Colonization."

75. Ibid., Letter VII, "Prejudice."

76. Angelina to Jane Smith, 6 June 1837.

77. Angelina to Jane Smith, 26 Oct. 1837.

78. *The New England Spectator*, issues of summer 1837; also later published in pamphlet form. The *Spectator* was published by the Boston Evangelical Anti-Slavery Society. It was discontinued in 1838. (Garrison, *Garrison*, 2:252-53.)

79. Angelina to Jane Smith, 10 Aug. 1837, telling of Phelps's letter and the sisters' reply. Also, Angelina to A. A. Phelps, 17 Aug., 2 Sept. 1837 in Rare Book and Manuscripts Department, Boston Public Library (hereafter referred to as MSS, Boston Public Library).

80. Weld to Angelina and Sarah, 1 Oct. [1 Sept.] 1837, in Barnes and Dumond, *Weld-Grimké Letters*, 1:442-43.

81. *Right and Wrong in Boston*, No. 2, 1837, p. 70.

82. Angelina to Jane Smith, 10 Aug. 1837.

83. John Greenleaf Whittier to Angelina and Sarah, 14 Aug. 1837, Barnes and Dumond, *Weld-Grimké Letters*, 1:424.

84. Weld to Angelina and Sarah, 15 Aug. 1837, in ibid., 1:425-26.

85. Angelina to Theodore Weld and John Greenleaf Whittier, 20 Aug. [1837], in ibid., 1:428-32.

86. Angelina to Jane Smith, 10 Aug. [1837]. Various false rumors were circulated about the Grimkés. *The Emancipator*, 5 Oct. 1837, felt it necessary to take notice of one. "Falsehood Exposed. . . . A report . . . that [the Misses Grimké] are imposters, in pretending to be from South Carolina. The report is false, and was doubtless known to be by him who started it. We do not know that a clergyman originated this base calumny, but we have our fears."

87. Weld to Sarah and Angelina, 10 Oct. 1837, in Barnes and Dumond, *Weld-Grimké Letters*, 1:452, 457-58.

88. Weld to Angelina, 16, 10 Oct. 1837, in ibid., 1:459-64, 458.

89. Angelina to Jane Smith, 26 Oct. 1837.

90. Angelina to Jane Smith, 11 Nov. [1837].

91. *Liberator*, 1 Sept. 1837.

92. Angelina to Jane Smith, 15 Sept. 1837.

· 93. Angelina to Jane Smith, 6 Oct. 1837.

94. Angelina to Jane Smith, 15 Sept., 10 Oct. 1837.

95. Angelina to Jane Smith, 11 Nov. [1837].
96. The estimates given of the numbers attending Angelina's lectures are based on the figures she gave in her letters to Jane Smith for the five-month period June through October 1837. Apparently Angelina kept a record of estimated attendance (in round numbers—250, 900, etc.). She reported these estimates to Jane Smith by name of town and for each meeting. But at best the figures are rough approximation.
97. Angelina to Jane Smith, 26 Oct., 15 Sept., 26 Oct., 6 Oct. 1837.
98. Angelina to Jane Smith, 5 Jan. [1838].
99. Sarah to Weld, 7 Nov. 1837, in Barnes and Dumond, *Weld-Grimké Letters,* 1:475; also Sarah to Jane Smith, 8 Nov. 1837, in ibid., 1:475-77; Sarah to Sarah Douglass, from Brookline, [Mass.], 23 Nov. 1837, in ibid., 1:480-83; and Sarah to Anna Weston, 1 Dec. 1837, MSS, Boston Public Library.
100. One account of Angelina's illness, recorded many years later in [Weld], *In Memory,* states that Angelina had typhoid fever. I could find no mention of it in letters written at the time.
101. Angelina to Jane Smith, 5 Jan. 1838.
102, Angelina to Jane Smith, [7 Feb. 1838].
103. Sarah to Weld, 16 Feb. 1838, in Barnes and Dumond *Weld-Grimké Letters,* 2:552-53; and Angelina to Weld, in ibid., 2:553-54.
104. Angelina to Jane Smith, 22 Feb. [1838].
105. Angelina to Weld, 21 [Jan. 1838], in Barnes and Dumond, *Weld-Grimké Letters,* 2:520-25.
106. Weld to Angelina, 8 Feb. 1838, marked "Private," in ibid., 2:532-36.
107. Angelina to Weld, 11 Feb. [1838], in ibid., 2:536-38.
108. Angelina (and Sarah) to Weld, 12 Feb. [1838], in ibid., 2:543.
109. Weld to Angelina, 16, 18, Feb. 1838, in ibid., 2:555-58, 562-63.
110. Angelina to Weld, 21 Feb. 1838, in ibid., 2:564.
111. *Boston Daily Advocate,* 21 Feb. 1838.
112. Lydia Maria Child to Elizabeth Carpenter, 20 Mar. 1838.
113. *Boston Evening Transcript,* 24 Feb. 1838.
114. Lydia Maria Child to Elizabeth Carpenter, 20 Mar. 1838. The *Boston Daily Advertiser and Patriot,* 24 Feb. 1838, gave a full account of this debate.
115. Angelina to Jane Smith, 5 Mar. [1838].
116. Angelina to Weld, 21, 22 Feb. 1838, in Barnes and Dumond, *Weld-Grimké Letters,* 2:564-66, 567-68.
117. Lydia Maria Child to Elizabeth Carpenter, 20 Mar. 1838.
118. Weld to Angelina, 16 Feb. 1838; and Angelina to Weld, [Feb. 21, 1838], in Barnes and Dumond, *Weld-Grimké Letters,* 2:556-57, 564-65.
119. Angelina to Weld, [11 Mar. 1838]; and Weld to Angelina, [12 Mar. 1838], in ibid., 2:590-91, 601-2. Also, Angelina to Weld, 15 Mar. 1838.
120. *Boston Evening Transcript,* 21 Mar. 1838.
121. Angelina to Weld. 28 Mar. [1838], in Barnes and Dumond, *Weld-Grimké Letters,* 2:607-8.
122. Weld to Sarah, 27 Mar. 1838, in ibid., 2:603-6.
123. Sarah to Jane Smith, 24 Mar. 1838.
124. Sarah to S[arah] Douglass, [n.d.] Sept. 1838.
125. [Anna Weston], Boston, to Sarah, 4 Apr. 1838, unsigned copy, portions struck out and changed, apparently a draft of the letter that was sent. MSS, Boston Public Library.
126. Weld to Sarah, 27 Mar. 1838, in Barnes and Dumond, *Weld-Grimké Letters,* 2:603-6.
127. Angelina to Weld, 28 Mar. [1838], in ibid., 2:611-12.
128. Sarah to Weld, 1 Apr. 1838, in ibid., 2:616, also postscript to Angelina's letter, p. 612.
129. Samuel Philbrick, Diary, 23 Apr. 1838, quoted in Birney, *Grimké Sisters,* p. 230.
130. [Weld], *In Memory,* p. 24.
131. Ibid., pp. 28, 30.

132. Angelina to Weld, 29 Apr. 1838 (Sarah appended a postscript), in Barnes and Dumond, *Weld-Grimké Letters*, 2:646, 651; also Sarah to Weld, 12 Apr. 1838, in ibid., 2:632-33.

133. Angelina to Weld, 28 Mar. [1838], in ibid., 2:609.

134. Sarah to Jane Smith, 24 Mar. 1838.

135. *Liberator*, 27 Apr. 1838.

136. In Weld-Grimké Collection.

137. Charles Chauncey to Sarah, 1 May 1838, in Barnes and Dumond, *Weld-Grimké Letters*, 2:651-52.

138. Sarah to Elizabeth Pease, [20? May 1838], in ibid., 2:678.

139. Anti-Slavery Convention of American Women, *Proceedings* (Philadelphia: Merrihew & Gunn, 1838), held in Philadelphia, 15-18 May 1838.

140. [Webb], *History of Pennsylvania Hall*, p. 136.

141. Ibid., pp. 123-28, printed the text of Angelina's speech, interspersed with terms descriptive of the sounds and threats of the mob outside the meeting hall and building.

142. Anti-Slavery Convention of American Women, *Proceedings*, 1838.

143. From a "private letter" from a "lady of Boston," written from Philadelphia, 18 May 1838, published in the *Liberator*, and quoted in [Webb], *History of Pennsylvania Hall*, Appendix.

144. *Philadelphia Gazette*, 18 May 1838, quoted in ibid., Appendix.

145. Quoted in ibid., Appendix, from *New Orleans Times-American*, 26 May 1838, and Augusta *Chronicle and Sentinel*, [n.d.] May 1838.

Chapter IV

1. Weld to Sarah, 27 Mar. 1838, in Gilbert H. Barnes and Dwight L. Dumond, eds., *Letters to Theodore Dwight Weld, Angelina Grimké Weld and Sarah Grimké, 1822-1844*, 2 vols. (1934; reprint ed., New York: Da Capo Press, 1970), 2:604.

2. Weld to Sarah and Angelina, 10 Oct. 1837, and Weld to Angelina, 16 Oct. 1837, in ibid., 1:454-57, 459-67.

3. Angelina to Weld, 4 Mar. 1838, in ibid., 2:585-88.

4. Angelina to Weld, 22 Feb. [1838], in ibid., 2:568-69.

5. Weld to Angelina, 1 Mar. 1838, in ibid., 2:575-80; also 16 Oct. 1837, in ibid., 1:467.

6. Weld to Angelina, 16 Feb. 1838, in ibid., 2:556-58.

7. Weld to Angelina, 1 Mar. 1838, in ibid., 2:576-80.

8. Weld to Angelina, 12 Feb. 1838, in ibid., 2:593; also 1 Mar. 1838, in ibid., 2:577.

9. Ibid., 1:xviii.

10. Benjamin P. Thomas, *Theodore Weld: Crusader for Freedom* (New Brunswick, N.J.: Rutgers University Press, 1950), p. 220.

11. Weld to W. L. Garrison, from Perth Amboy, 8 Oct. 1862, saying he had not lectured for twenty-six years. In the 1850s Sarah had voiced her doubts "if he [Weld] ever again can be a public speaker, though generally comfortable . . . his throat is still delicate." (Sarah to Gerrit Smith, 6 July [1851].)

12. Sarah to Weld, 27 Feb. 1838.

13. Angelina to Weld, 15 Mar. 1838.

14. Angelina to Jane Smith, 27 Mar. 1838.

15. Angelina to Jane Smith, 26 Aug. 1838.

16. Sarah to Jane Smith, [n.d.] 1838.

17. Weld to Lewis Tappan, 4 Mar. 1844.

18. Sarah to Jane Smith, [n.d. 1838], quoted in Catherine Birney, *The Grimké Sisters: Sarah and Angelina Grimké, the First Woman Advocates of Abolition and Woman's Rights* (Boston: Lee and Shepard, 1885), p. 246.

19. Angelina to Jane Smith, [n.d.] 1838, quoted in ibid., p. 246.

20. Mary S. Grimké to Angelina, from Charleston, S.C., [n.d.] July 1838.

21. Angelina to Anna Weston, 15 July 1838, MSS, Boston Public Library.

22. Angelina to Weld, [27 Apr. 1838], in Barnes and Dumond, *Weld-Grimké Letters*, 2:649.

23. Angelina to Elizabeth Pease [1838], quoted in Birney, *Grimké Sisters*, p. 252.
24. Weld to Angelina and Sarah, 21 Nov. 1837, in Barnes and Dumond, *Weld-Grimké Letters*, 1:479-80.
25. Quoted in Birney, *Grimké Sisters*, pp. 257-58.
26. [Theodore D. Weld], *American Slavery As It Is: Testimony of a Thousand Witnesses* (New York: American Anti-Slavery Society, 1839), pp. 22-24, for Sarah's testimony, and pp. 52-57, for Angelina's testimony. After the publication of *Slavery As It Is*, Mrs. Anna Grimké Frost of Philadelphia wrote to her sisters Angelina and Sarah, 14 Aug. 1839, referring to the recent death of their mother and commenting, "Whenever I think of your last infamous publication, the language of my heart is, thank heaven!"
27. See Chap. III, pp. 109-22 passim.
28. For a full discussion of the schism in the antislavery movement, see Aileen S. Kraditor, *Means and Ends in American Abolitionism: Garrison and His Critics on Strategy and Tactics, 1834-1850* (New York: Pantheon Books, 1960), especially Chaps. 3, 4, and 5, on "The Woman Question," "Religion and the Good Society," and "Politics." See also Louis Filler, *The Crusade against Slavery, 1830-1860* (New York: Harper & Brothers, 1960), Chaps. 4, 5, and 6.
29. Kraditor, *Ends and Means*, p. 48.
30. Wendell P. Garrison and Francis J. Garrison, *William Lloyd Garrison, 1805-1879: The Story of His Life Told by His Children*, 4 vols. (New York: Century Co., 1885-89), 2:335.
31. Filler, *Crusade against Slavery*, pp. 134-36.
32. Dwight L. Dumond, *Antislavery: The Crusade for Freedom in America* (Ann Arbor: University of Michigan Press, 1961), p. 285.
33. Filler, *Crusade against Slavery*, pp. 129, 130-31, 133-34, 135-36.
34. Weld to Amos Phelps, 2 Aug. 1840.
35. Sarah to Elizabeth Pease, 14 Nov. 1840, in Barnes and Dumond, *Weld-Grimké Letters*, 2:852.
36. Angelina and Sarah to Sarah Douglass, 21 Mar. 1839.
37. Angelina to Gerrit Smith, 18 June 1840, in Gerrit Smith Collection, Syracuse University.
38. Sarah to Elizabeth Pease, 14 Nov. 1840, in Barnes and Dumond, *Weld-Grimké Letters*, 2:853.
39. Quoted in Filler, *Crusade against Slavery*, p. 156, from *Liberator*, 12 Aug. 1842.
40. Weld to Lewis Tappan, 14 Dec. 1841, "Confidential," in Barnes and Dumond, *Weld-Grimké Letters*, 2:871.
41. Angelina to Weld, [n.d.] 1842, and two letters [n.d.] 1843.
42. Angelina to Weld, [29 Apr. 1838], in Barnes and Dumond, *Weld-Grimké Letters*, 2:649-51.
43. Weld to Sarah and Angelina, 10 Oct. 1837, in ibid., 1:452-57.
44. Angelina to Weld, 26 Jan. 1843.
45. Angelina to Weld, 22 Feb. 1838, and Weld to Sarah, 27 Mar. 1838, in Barnes and Dumond, *Weld-Grimké Letters*, 2:568, 604.
46. Angelina to Weld, [n.d.] 1843; also Weld to Angelina, [n.d.] 1842.
47. Angelina to Weld, 11 Mar. 1838.
48. Sarah to Sarah Douglass, 21 Nov. 1844, Manuscript Division, Library of Congress, Washington, D.C. Also Sarah to Augustus Wattles, [n.d.] 1852.
49. Sarah to Elizabeth Pease, 11 Feb. 1842, in Barnes and Dumond, *Weld-Grimké Letters*, 2:920-21.
50. Angelina to Weld, [Jan. or Feb.] 1842.
51. Angelina to Weld, [n.d.] 1843.
52. Ibid.
53. Angelina to Jane Smith, [late 1844].
54. Angelina to Weld, [1842]; also Angelina to Weld, 15 Aug. 1842.
55. Sarah to Weld, 7 Feb. 1843.
56. Sarah to Sarah Douglass, [probably 1842], quoted in Birney, *Grimké Sisters*, p. 266.
57. Sarah to Dr. Harriot Hunt of Boston, 10 June 1851. Dr. Hunt, a physician and

prominent woman's rights advocate, was Sarah's warm friend and confidant during these years.

58. Angelina to Jane Smith, [n.d., but probably 1845].

59. Sarah to the Gerrit Smiths, 26 May 1848. Gerrit Smith Collection, Syracuse Univerisity.

60. Angelina to Weld in Washington, [Feb. or Mar.] 1842.

61. [Theodore D. Weld, ed.], *In Memory of Angelina Grimké Weld* (Boston: Press of George N. Ellis, 1880), p. 43.

62. Sarah to Dr. Harriot Hunt, 16 Dec. [1845], 10 June [1851]; Angelina to Sarah Douglass, [summer of 1849]; Angelina to Jane Smith, 31 Mar. [1842 or 1843], in regard to her miscarriage and general health. Also, Angelina to Weld, 30 Sept. 1849, written from a mineral springs in Orange, N.J. She had told an allopathic physician who was there for the "cure," how she earlier had "cured" her prolapsed uterus and was now there for her hernia.

63. [Weld], *In Memory*, pp. 43-44.

64. Ibid., p. 44.

65. Sarah to Weld, 8 Jan. 1843.

66. Angelina to Weld, [winter] 1843.

67. Angelina to Weld, [n.d.] 1842; also Sarah to Weld, [early 1842].

68. Sarah to Weld, 13 Feb. 1842. It is certain that Angelina had read this letter in which Sarah set forth Weld's "faults"; it was addressed in her hand, and she had appended a short, cramped note commenting that little space had been left for her.

69. Sarah to the Welds' son Theo ("Sody" she called him), [n.d., but early 1850s]; and Sarah to Angelina, 4 May 1843.

70. Sarah to the Welds' son Theo, 26 Sept. [n.d., but in mid-1850s.)

71. Sarah to Dr. Harriot Hunt [n.d., but apparently early 1850s]; also Sarah to Dr. Hunt, 8 Mar. [1856], from Eagleswood, commenting, "I have not given up the idea and desire to do something for the cause of Woman."

72. Angelina to Weld, [n.d.] 1849. This letter was probably written in the summer of 1849. Angelina wrote from Orange, N.J., from a mineral springs resort where she had gone with Julia Tappan to take the "cure" for her hernia.

73. The *New York Herald*, 20 June 1853, gives an extended account of plans for the Raritan Bay Union sent in by its "New Jersey Correspondent" from Perth Amboy, 20 June, 1853. Also, John Humphrey Noyes, *History of American Socialism* (Philadelphia: J. B. Lippincott & Co., 1870), pp. 487-511, describes the community. Henry David Thoreau, *Familiar Letters of Henry David Thoreau*, edited by F. B. Sanborn (Boston and New York: Houghton Mifflin Company, 1896), pp. 335-38, for a letter from Henry David Thoreau to Sophia Thoreau, 1 Nov. 1856, telling of Thoreau's visit to Eagleswood School and the Raritan Bay Union. Thoreau describes Weld, who was then head of Eagleswood, and also mentions Angelina and Sarah: "Mrs. Weld and her sister . . . the former [Angelina] in extreme Bloomer costume, which was what you may call remarkable. . . ." Various letters and documents in the Weld-Grimké Collection at Clements Library give descriptions of Eagleswood School and of life there.

74. Angelina and Sarah, [early 1854]. This letter must have been written in early 1854, after Angelina and Weld had decided to make the move to Eagleswood School in the Raritan Bay community. They moved to Eagleswood in September 1854.

75. Sarah to Dr. Harriot Hunt, 15 Feb. [1854]. Sarah had apparently received Angelina's letter, although she does not mention it directly. Later correspondence between Sarah and Dr. Hunt, who was a warm friend of Sarah's, and between Angelina and Dr. Hunt indicates the probability of Dr. Hunt's knowing about Angelina's letter to Sarah, at least enough to know that Sarah was unsure of continuing to live with the Welds.

76. Sarah to Dr. Harriot Hunt, 15 Feb. 1854.

77. Angelina to Sarah (writing from Eagleswood School), [n.d.] Jan. 1855.

Chapter V

1. Angelina to Dr. Harriot Hunt, [n.d., probably early 1850s].

2. Sarah to Abby Kelley Foster, [n.d., probably 1850s or early 1860s].

3. Elizabeth Cady Stanton, Susan B. Anthony, and Matilda J. Gage,. eds., *History*

of Woman's Suffrage, 6 vols. (New York: Fowler and Wells, 1881-1922), see Vol. I for history of this period.

4. Ibid., 1:470.

5. Quoted in Catherine Birney, *The Grimké Sisters: Sarah and Angelina E. Grimké, the First Woman Advocates of Abolition and Woman's Rights* (Boston: Lee and Shepard, 1885), pp. 281-82.

6. Sarah to Dr. Harriot Hunt, 15 Feb. [1854], discusses at some length Sarah's conception of the moment of "woman's rights and duties."

7. Birney provides various reasons for Sarah's not being able to adjust to the Raritan Bay community and her teaching in Eagleswood, stressing her reluctance to leave the Welds and settle elsewhere. She quotes Sarah: "A separation from the darling children who have brightened a few years of my lonely and sorrowful life overwhelms me when I think of it as the probable result of any change." (Birney, *Grimké Sister,* pp. 272-78).

8. [Theodore D. Weld, ed.], *In Memory of Angelina Grimké Weld* (Boston: Press of George N. Ellis, 1880), p. 43.

9. Mary S. Grimké to Angelina, 4 May 1839, now approves the plan for Stephen to go north to be with the Welds. Anna G. Frost to Sarah and Angelina, 31 July 1839, tells of word from Charleston that Stephen at times became "deranged." Angelina to Jane Smith, 8 Sept. [1840], "Stephen is the fourth slave we have emancipated." Angelina to Weld, [1846], from Philadelphia (Stephen was then living in Philadelphia), tells how she has arranged to help Stephen buy his own lot for a little house.

10. [Weld], *In Memory,* pp. 62-63.

11. Angelina to Gerrit Smith, 5 Jan. 1854, Gerrit Smith Collection, Syracuse University.

12. Angelina to Gerrit Smith, 10 June 1855, in ibid.

13. No doubt Angelina's hopes were also raised by a letter she had received from her brother Henry in 1844, asking for any material she could send that would show the working of emancipation in the West Indies and to send it in "as small a compass as possible." See Weld to Lewis Tappan, [n.d.] Dec. 1844, requesting certain pamphlets.

14. James Redpath, *The Public Life of Capt. John Brown, With an Auto-Biography of His Childhood and Youth* (Boston: Thayer and Eldridge, 1860), pp. 345-47, 171, 377, tells of Mrs. Spring's visit to John Brown after his capture. See also Oswald Garrison Villard, *John Brown, 1800-1859: A Biography Fifty Years After* (Boston: Houghton, Mifflin and Company, 1910), pp. 546, 549, 572-74, for more on Mrs. Spring. Benjamin P. Thomas, *Theodore Weld: Crusader for Freedom* (New Brunswick, N.J.: Rutgers University Press, 1950), pp. 537-38, tells of the burial of Stevens and Hazelett, both of John Brown's band, at the Raritan Bay community. See also Louis Filler, *The Crusade against Slavery* (New York: Harper & Brothers, 1960), pp. 270ff.

15. Villard, *John Brown,* pp. 548-49, on Mrs. John Brown's visit to Raritan Bay community.

16. Angelina to her son Theodore, 12 Dec. [1860], 3 Jan. 1861.

17. Angelina to her son Theodore, 3 Jan. 1861.

18. Sarah to Dr. Harriot Hunt, from Eagleswood School, 19 June 1861.

19. Weld to William Lloyd Garrison, from Hyde Park, Mass., 5 Oct. 1873, MSS, Boston Public Library.

20. Weld to William Lloyd Garrison, 8 Oct. 1862, MSS, Boston Public Library.

21. Angelina to Gerrit Smith, 30 Jan. [1862], although dated in Weld's hand as 1861, Gerrit Smith Collection, Syracuse University.

22. *Liberator,* 2, 16 Jan. 1863, rejoicing because of the Emancipation Proclamation by President Lincoln.

23. Angelina to E. J. Cutler, [n.d.] June 1863.

24. *National Anti-Slavery Standard,* 15 Aug. 1863.

25. Angelina to Weld, 25 Feb. 1864.

26. Sarah to the Welds' son Theo, 17 May 1863.

27. *Proceedings* of the Meeting of Loyal Women of the Republic, held in New York City, 14 May 1863, pp. 51-53.

28. This account is based primarily on the letters exchanged between Angelina and her nephews, Archibald and Francis Grimké, and also on my interview with Archibald

Grimké's daughter, Angelina Weld Grimké. (See "Interview" in Bibliography.) Birney, *Grimké Sisters*, pp. 289-95, has an account. Also biographical material is found in Angelina Grimké Weld, "A Biographical Sketch of Archibald H. Grimké," *Opportunity: A Journal of Negro Life* 3 (Feb. 1925): 44-47; and Carter A. Woodson, ed., *The Works of Francis James Grimké*, 2 vols. (Washington, D.C.: Associated Publishers, 1942), Introduction.

29. Angelina to Archibald and Francis Grimké, 15 Feb. [1868]; also my interview with Angelina Weld Grimké. At this time the Welds were living in Fairmount, Hyde Park, Massachusetts, near Boston.

30. Archibald Henry Grimké to Angelina, from Lincoln University, Oxford, Pennsylvania, 20 Feb. 1868. At the time of my interview with Angelina Weld Grimké, she showed me this original letter and permitted me to copy it in full. This letter, together with her father's other papers, were then in her possession. They are now in the Howard University Library, Washington, D.C.

31. Angelina to Archibald and Francis Grimké, 29 Feb. [1868].

32. This account is based on a series of letters exchanged between Angelina and Archibald and Francis Grimké during the spring of 1868 and on my interview with Archibald's daughter, Angelina Weld Grimké, in which she told me something of what her father had told her of these exchanges and of Angelina's visit to Lincoln University in June 1868. There are also letters of Sarah's to friends in which she tells of their newfound nephews: Sarah to Sarah Douglass, 1 Dec. 1868, [n.d.] Aug. 1869; Sarah to Julia [Tappan?], 10 Nov. 1863; Sarah to Gerrit Smith, 6 Dec. 1870, 19 Oct. 1873. Gerrit Smith letters in Gerrit Smith Collection, Syracuse University; the other letters in Weld-Grimké Collection, Clements Library. See also material cited in note 28 of this chapter.

33. [Theodore D. Weld, ed.]., *American Slavery As It Is: Testimony of a Thousand Witnesses* (New York: American Anti-Slavery Society, 1839), p. 52.

34. Angelina to Archibald and Francis Grimké, 6 Apr. [1868].

35. Angelina several times inquired about the mother of Archibald and Francis Grimké: "Please tell me all about your Mother" and "I want you to tell me all about yourselves and your dear Mother," 6 Apr. [1868]. Angelina Weld Grimké had known her grandmother well, and in my interview she talked at some length, and in glowing terms, of the grandmother and of her courage and ingenious efforts to prevent her sons from serving as slaves.

36. Angelina to Archibald and Francis Grimké, 29 Feb. [1868].

37. Several letters of Sarah's to her friends show her efforts in behalf of her nephews, telling of their need for funds to advance their professional education. For example, Sarah to Sarah Douglass, [probably summer] 1868.

38. I. N. Randall, President of Lincoln University, to Angelina, 16 Jan. 1870.

39. Sarah to Sarah Douglass, 1 Dec. 1868.

40. Sarah to Sarah Douglass, 1 Dec. 1868, [n.d.] Aug. 1869; and Sarah to Julia [Tappan?], 16 Nov. 1868.

41. [Weld], *In Memory*, pp. 56-57.

42. Thomas, *Theodore Weld*, p. 261.

43. Angelina Grimké Weld, "Address to the Soldiers," in *Proceedings* of the Meeting of Loyal Women of the Republic, held in New York City, 14 May 1863, pp. 51-53. Angelina also spoke two other times at length (pp. 10-14 and 22-23).

44. Angelina to Archibald and Francis Grimké, 6 Apr. 1868.

45. [Weld], *In Memory*, p. 37.

46. Sarah to Sarah Douglass, [probably summer] 1868.

47. William Lloyd Garrison to Weld, 1 Feb. 1875.

48. [Weld], *In Memory*, pp. 58ff., 65ff.

49. Ibid., pp. 19-32.

Bibliography

Manuscript Collections

Anti-Slavery Collection, Oberlin College Library. This collection had been catalogued when I used it. See Oberlin College Library Bulletin, Vol. II, No. 3, "A Classified Catalogue of the Collection of Anti-Slavery Propaganda in the Oberlin College Library," compiled by Geraldine Hopkins, ed. by Julian S. Fowler, 1932.

Anti-Slavery Materials, Fisk University Library.

Gerrit Smith Collection in the George Arents Research Library for Special Collections at Syracuse University Library, Syracuse, New York.

Manuscript Division, Cornell University Library.

Manuscript Division, Library of Congress. For miscellaneous letters to, from, or about Angelina Grimké and Sarah Grimké.

Manuscript Division, Massachusetts Historical Society, Boston.

Manuscript Division, Pennsylvania Historical Society, Philadelphia.

Manuscript Division, Philadelphia Public Library. A few letters from Angelina Grimké to friends. Also, the General Pleasant Diary, 1838-44, commenting on the burning of Pennsylvania Hall in Philadelphia 17 May 1838, following the mass meeting at which Angelina Grimké Weld addressed a large audience.

Manuscripts in Department of Rare Books and Manuscripts, Boston Public Library. Numerous letters to or from Angelina Grimké, Sarah Grimké, and Theodore Weld, or about them, written in the 1830s, 1840s, 1860s, and 1870s, some of them of special interest. The papers of William Lloyd Garrison and of Anna Weston were especially valuable to me.

Negro Archives Collection, Howard University Library, Washington, D.C.

Samuel J. May Collection, Cornell University Library. See Cornell University Library Bulletin I, "Catalogue of Samuel J. May Collection of Anti-Slavery Material," for contents of this collection.

Weld-Grimké Collection, William L. Clements Library, University of Michigan, Ann Arbor. Unpublished letters, diaries, and other papers. This is the principal source for the abundant letters, diaries, and other papers of Angelina Grimké (both before and after her marriage) and Sarah Grimké. Through the kindness of the curator of manuscripts, I was able to work in these unpublished materials extensively and with close attention.

Published Works by Angelina Grimké, Sarah Grimké, and Theodore Weld (principal writings on antislavery and woman's rights)

Angelina E. Grimké. "Address to the Soldiers" [of the Union Army], in the *Proceedings* of the Meeting of Loyal Women of the Republic, held in New York, 14 May 1863. *Proceedings* also includes addresses by Elizabeth Cady Stanton, Susan B. Anthony, and Lucy Stone.

———. *Appeal to the Christian Women of the South.* New York: American Anti-Slavery Society, 1836.

———. *Appeal to the Women of the Nominally Free States.* New York: W. S. Dorr, 1837.

———. *Letters to Catherine Beecher, in reply to an Essay on Slavery and Abolition, Addressed to A. E. Grimké,* rev. ed. Boston: Isaac Knapp, 1838.

———. "Letter to the Woman's Rights Convention, Syracuse, 1852." Woman's Rights Tract No. 8, 1852.

———. Letter to William Lloyd Garrison, 30 Aug. 1835. Published in the *Liberator,* copied in other antislavery and general publications, and reprinted as a broadside and distributed widely throughout northern and midwestern states.

———. *Slavery in America: A Reprint of an Appeal to the Christian Women of the Slave States of America, by Angelina E. Grimké of Charleston, South Carolina, with Introductory Notes and Appendix by George Thompson, Recommended to the Special Attention of the Anti-Slavery Females of Great Britain.* Edinburgh: Oliphant & Son, 1837.

Sarah M. Grimké, *An Epistle to the Clergy of the Southern States.* New York: n.p., 1836.

———. *Letters on the Equality of the Sexes and the Condition of Women.* Boston: Isaac Knapp, 1838. First published in a series in the *New England Spectator,* 1838.

[Theodore D. Weld]. *The Bible against Slavery.* New York: American Anti-Slavery Society, 1837. Although Weld was known to be author of this tract, his name does not appear on it.

———. *The Power of Congress over the District of Columbia.* New York:

American Anti-Slavery Society, 1838. Weld's name does not appear.

————, ed. *American Slavery As It Is: Testimony of a Thousand Witnesses*. New York: American Anti-Slavery Society, 1839. Much of the material was gathered by Angelina and Sarah Grimké, each of whom also wrote articles for this widely distributed tract. Weld was known to be the editor, but he did not permit his name to appear on the publication.

————, ed. *In Memory of Angelina Grimké Weld*. Boston: Press of George N. Ellis, 1880. Dedication, "To the Old Abolitionists," signed T. D. W. In this little volume, Weld put together various materials relating to the life and death of his wife. It includes a portion obviously by Weld himself (although unsigned), stories of certain events in her life, and remarks by various friends, both men and women, on the occasion of her death.

Documents and Reports

The American Anti-Slavery Almanac for 1836, Vol. 1, No. 1. Boston: Webster & Southard, 1836.

American Anti-Slavery Society. Executive Committee Minutes (especially those for 1834-38).

————. *The Anti-Slavery History of the John Brown Years*. New York: American Anti-Slavery Society, 1861. (Twenty-Seventh Annual Report of the Society)

————. *Proceedings*. New York: American Anti-Slavery Society, 1854. (Second Decade)

————. *Report of Annual Meeting*. New York: American Anti-Slavery Society, 1863. American Equal Rights Association, *Proceedings*, New York: American Anti-Slavery Society, 1867. (First Anniversary, 9-10 May 1867)

Anti-Slavery Convention of American Women. *Proceedings*, New York: W. S. Dorr, 1837. (New York, 9-12 May 1837)

————. *Proceedings*. Philadelphia: Merrihew & Gunn, 1838. (Philadelphia, 15-18 May 1838, with most of the meetings in Pennsylvania Hall, which was burned by a mob on 17 May).

Boston Female Anti-Slavery Society. "Report of Boston Female Anti-Slavery Society, with Concise Statement of Events, Previous and Subsequent to the Annual Meeting of 1835," *Right and Wrong in Boston*, No. 1. Boston: Boston Female Anti-Slavery Society, 1836.

————. "Annual Report of Boston Female Anti-Slavery Society, Meeting Held October 14th, 1837, with Sketch of the Obstacles Thrown in the Way of Emancipation by Certain Clerical Abolitionists and Advocates of the Subjection of Women," *Right and Wrong in Boston*, No. 2. Boston: Boston Female Anti-Slavery Society, 1837.

Friends of Women's Rights. *Report*, Second General Convention. New

York, 1852. (Convention met in Worcester, Mass., 15 October 1851. Angelina Grimké Weld was elected vice president and to membership on the Central Committee.)

Hamilton, James, Jr. *An Account of the Late Intended Insurrection among a Portion of the Blacks of This City.* Charleston, S.C.: Authority of the Corporation of Charleston, 1822.

Kennedy, Lionel, and Thomas Parker. *An Official Report of the Trials of Sundry Negroes, Charged with an Attempt to Raise an Insurrection in the State of South Carolina.* Charleston, S.C.: James R. Schenck, 1822.

Loyal Women of the Republic. *Proceedings* of the Meeting of Loyal Women of the Republic, held in New York, 14 May 1863. New York: Phair & Co., 1863. (Included in the proceedings are addresses by Elizabeth Cady Stanton, Susan B. Anthony, Lucy Stone, and Angelina Grimké Weld. Angelina was elected a vice president—there were eight. Various names were used for this organization: the one above; in the "Call" to the convention, "Loyal Women of the Nation"; on printed proceedings a note stated that copies could be obtained from "Susan B. Anthony, 20 Cooper Street, Office of the Women's Loyal National League.")

Massachusetts Anti-Slavery Society, Board of Managers. *Seventh Annual Report.* Boston: Isaac Knapp, 1839. In the same volume, *Proceedings* of the Annual Meeting, held in Boston, 23 January 1838, pp. i-viii.

New England and Massachusetts Anti-Slavery Society. *Reports and Proceedings,* 1833-44. (These include accounts of important events in abolitonist history, such as the Lane Seminary debates, the Lane Trustees' statements, and the Prudence Crandall case in 1834.)

Presbyterian Synod of South Carolina and Georgia. *Report of the Committee to Whom Was Referred the Subject of the Religious Instruction of the Colored Population of the Synod, at Its Late Session in Columbia, South Carolina, December 5-9, 1833.* Charleston, S.C.: Charleston Observer Office Press, 1834.

Philadelphia Female Anti-Slavery Society. Minutes for 9 Dec. 1833 to 4 Jan. 1838. MSS, Pennsylvania Historical Society.

———. Minutes, Board of Managers, for Dec. 1833 to 6 Jan. 1836; also for 26 May 1836 to Mar. 1839. MSS, Pennsylvania Historical Society. (Angelina Grimké was a member of this local society during a part of this period. After her public activities began, various entries in the minutes relate to her work.)

———. *Thirty-Third Annual Report.* Philadelphia, 1867.

Trustees of the Cincinnati Lane Seminary. *Fifth Annual Report,* November 1834. (Together with the rules of the institution and a catalogue; appended is a "Statement of the Faculty Concerning the Late Difficulties in the Lane Seminary.)

[Webb, Samuel, ed.] *History of Pennsylvania Hall: Which Was Destroyed by a Mob, on the 17th of May, 1838.* Philadelphia: Merrihew & Gunn, 1838. (Included is the historic address by Angelina Grimké Weld. The mob that later burned the building was gathered outside the

building when she spoke. This report gives a full account of events before and following the burning of the hall.)
Woman's Rights Convention. *Proceedings*. (Third National, Syracuse,
8-10 September 1852, at which Angelina Grimké Weld was again
elected to the Central Committee.)
———. *Proceedings*. (Fourth National, New York, 6-7 September 1853,
where Angelina Grimké Weld continued as vice president.)

Newspapers and Journals of the Period

ANTI-SLAVERY NEWSPAPERS

Anti-Slavery Standard
Published by American Anti-Slavery Society, following the split into
two organizations at the national convention of 1840. Vol. I, No. 1,
appeared 11 June 1840. This paper was covered extensively for the
1840s, 1850s, and 1860s. This was the paper Angelina Grimké was
reading during the 1860s, and perhaps before.
Emancipator
Official organ of the American Anti-Slavery Society before the split in
1840. It was then taken over by the Tappan wing of the Society. Issues
covered for the 1830s and into 1840s.
National Inquirer
Benjamin Lundy, editor, published Philadelphia.
Liberator
William Lloyd Garrison, founder and editor. The *Liberator* was covered
extensively for the 1830s, early 1840s, and the 1860s for events relating
to Angelina Grimké, Sarah Grimké, and Theodore Weld and for back-
ground materials on activities of the abolition movement.
Liberty Bell
Lydia Maria Child, editor for a time, published 1839-58. Selected years
were covered.

SELECTED GENERAL NEWSPAPERS

Boston Daily Advertiser & Patriot
Boston Daily Centinel and Gazette
Boston Evening Transcript
Boston Recorder (denominational)
Charleston (S.C.) Courier
Carolina Gazette
New York Herald

Interview

Interview with Angelina Weld Grimké, only daughter of Archibald
Henry Grimké, at her apartment in New York City in January 1955. Miss

Grimké died about three years later. Miss Grimké was a poet, and her verse appeared in several Negro anthologies.

I talked with Miss Grimké for several hours. She told me of her father, of much she had learned from him, and about his letters and papers which, at this time, she had stored (unsorted) in a closet. She permitted me to copy certain long-lost letters, in particular the first long letter her father had written to Angelina Grimké Weld in reply to Angelina's first letter to Archibald and Francis Grimké, at Lincoln University, Oxford, Pennsylvania, after she had read in the *Anti-Slavery Standard* in 1868 of the distinguished scholastic record of these two young men named Grimké. Angelina wrote to inquire who these young men were. Miss Grimké also told me at some length of her grandmother, Nancy Weston, and of her remarkable qualities.

While Catherine Birney, in her biography *The Grimké Sisters* (1885), told something of the story of the discovery of these young men, the discovery of these original letters exchanged between Angelina and Archibald and Francis Grimké adds much to the record that had been lost.

Books and Articles

Aptheker, Herbert, ed. *A Documentary History of the Negro People in the United States.* New York: Citadel Press, 1968.

———. *American Negro Slave Revolts.* New York: Columbia University Press, 1943.

Austin, George Lowell. *The Life and Times of Wendell Phillips.* Boston: B. B. Russell, 1884.

Barnes, Albert. *An Inquiry into the Scriptural Views of Slavery.* Philadelphia: Perkins and Purves, 1846.

Barnes, Gilbert H., and Dwight L. Dumond, eds. *Letters of Theodore Dwight Weld, Angelina Grimké Weld, and Sarah Grimké, 1822-1844.* 2 vols. 1934. Reprint ed., New York: Da Capo Press, 1970. For the late 1830s to 1844, these two volumes contain most of the letters between the Grimkés and Weld; hence they were used extensively for these years. However, some letters of this period remained unpublished and were also used.

Barnes, Gilbert H. *The Antislavery Impulse.* New York: D. Appleton Century Co., 1933.

Birney, Catherine. *The Grimké Sisters: Sarah and Angelina E. Grimké, the First Woman Advocates of Abolition and Woman's Rights.* Boston: Lee and Shepard, 1885.

Bowes, Frederick P. *The Culture of Early Charleston.* Chapel Hill: University of North Carolina Press, 1942.

Bremmer, Frederika. *Homes in the New World.* 2 vols. New York: Harper & Brothers, 1853.

Cash, W. J. *The Mind of the South.* New York: Alfred A. Knopf, 1941.

Child, Lydia Maria. *Isaac T. Hopper: A True Life*. Boston: John P. Jewett & Co., 1853.

———. *Letters of Lydia Maria Child*, with a Biographical Introduction by John G. Whittier, and an Appendix by Wendell Phillips. Boston: Houghton, Mifflin and Company, 1883.

Duberman, Martin, ed. *The Antislavery Vanguard: New Essays on the Abolitionists*. Princeton: Princeton University Press, 1965.

Dumond, Dwight L. *Antislavery Origins of the Civil War in the United States*. Ann Arbor: University of Michigan Press, 1939.

———, ed. *Letters of James Gillespie Birney, 1831-1857*, 2 vols. New York: D. Appleton-Century Co., 1938.

———. *Antislavery: The Crusade for Freedom in America*. Ann Arbor: University of Michigan Press, 1961.

Eaton, Clement. *Freedom of Thought in the Old South*. Durham: Duke University Press, 1940.

———. *The Growth of Southern Civilization, 1790-1860*. New York: Harper & Brothers, 1961.

Filler, Louis. *The Crusade against Slavery: 1830-1860*. New York: Harper & Brothers, 1960.

Fladeland, Betty. *James Gillespie Birney: Slaveholder to Abolitionist*. Ithaca: Cornell University Press, 1955.

Flexner, Eleanor. *Century of Struggle: The Woman's Rights Movement in the United States*. Cambridge: Belknap Press of Harvard University Press, 1959.

Garrison, Wendell P., and Francis J. Garrison. *William Lloyd Garrison, 1805-1879: The Story of His Life Told by His Children*. 4 vols. New York: Century Co., 1885-89.

Goodell, William. *The American Slave Code in Theory and Practice*. New York: American and Foreign Anti-Slavery Society, 1853.

Grimké, Angelina Weld. "A Biographical Sketch of Archibald H. Grimké," *Opportunity: A Journal of Negro Life* 3 (Feb. 1925):44-47.

Hart, Albert B. *Slavery and Abolition, 1831-1841*. New York: Harper & Brothers, 1906.

Henry, Howell M. *The Police Control of the Slave in South Carolina*. Emory, Va.: n.p., 1914.

Hinton, Richard J. *John Brown and His Men*. New York: Funk & Wagnalls Co., 1894.

Jay, William. *An Inquiry into the Character and Tendency of the American Colonization and American Anti-Slavery Societies*. New York: Leavitt, Lord & Co., 1835.

———. *Miscellaneous Writings on Slavery*. Boston: John P. Jewett & Co., 1853.

Jenkins, William Sumner. *Pro-Slavery Thought in the Old South*. Chapel Hill: University of North Carolina Press, 1935.

Johnson, William D. *Lincoln University: Or, The Nation's First Pledge of Emancipation*. Philadelphia: p.p., 1867.

Jones, Rufus M. *The Later Period of Quakerism*, 2 vols. London: Macmillan & Co., 1921.

Kemble, Frances Anne. *Journal of a Residence on a Georgian Plantation in 1838-1839*. New York: Harper & Brothers, 1863.

Koch, Adrienne. *The Maryland Historian* 3, no. 1 (Spring, 1972): 51-84. A special Memorial Issue for Adrienne Koch (1912-71), with tributes and selections from her works, including two articles on the Grimkés.

Kraditor, Aileen S. *Means and Ends in American Abolitionism: Garrison and His Critics on Strategy and Tactics, 1834-1850*. New York: Pantheon Books, 1969.

——, comp. *Up from the Pedestal: Selected Writings in the History of American Feminism*. Chicago: Quadrangle Books, 1968.

Lander, Ernest M., Jr., and Robert K. Ackerman, eds. *Perspectives in South Carolina History: The First 300 Years*. Columbia: University of South Carolina Press, 1973.

Lerner, Gerda. *The Grimké Sisters from South Carolina: Rebels against Slavery*. Boston: Houghton Mifflin Company, 1967.

Litwack, Leon F. *North of Slavery: The Negro in the Free States, 1790-1860*. Chicago: University of Chicago Press, 1961.

Lofton, John. *Insurrection in South Carolina: The Turbulent World of Denmark Vesey*. Yellow Springs, Ohio: Antioch Press, 1964.

Loveland, Anne C. "Evangelicalism and 'Immediate Emancipation' in American Antislavery Thought." *Journal of Southern History* 32 (May 1966): 172-88.

MacDonald, William, ed. *Select Statutes and Other Documents Illustrative of the History of the United States, 1861-1898*. New York: Macmillan Company, 1903.

Macy, Jesse. *The Anti-Slavery Crusade: A Chronicle of the Gathering Storm*. New Haven: Yale University Press, 1921.

Martineau, Harriet. *Society in America*. London: Saunders and Otley, 1837.

May, Samuel J. *Some Recollections of Our Antislavery Conflict*. Boston: Fields, Osgood & Co., 1869.

Noyes, John Humphrey. *History of American Socialism*. Philadelphia: J. B. Lippincott & Co., 1870. (See the account of the Raritan Bay Union written not many years after Angelina, Weld, and Sarah became members.)

Olmsted, Frederick Law. *A Journey in the Seaboard Slave States, with Remarks on Their Economy*. New York: Dix & Edwards, 1856.

O'Neall, John B. *Biographical Sketches of the Bench and Bar in South Carolina*. 2 vols. Charleston, S.C.: S. G. Courtenay & Co., 1859.

Phillips, Ulrich Bonnell. *Life and Labor in the Old South*. Boston: Little, Brown & Company, 1929.

——. "The Slave Labor Problems in the Charleston District," *Political Science Quarterly* 22, no. 3 (Sept. 1907): 416-39.

Pillsbury, Parker. *Acts of the Anti-Slavery Apostles*. Concord, N.H.: Clague, Wegman, Schlicht & Co., Printers, 1883.

Redpath, James. *The Public Life of Capt. John Brown, With an Auto-Biography of His Childhood and Youth*. Boston: Thayer and Eldridge, 1860.

Riegel, Robert E. *American Feminists*. Lawrence: University of Kansas Press, 1963.

———. *American Women: A Story of Social Change*. Rutherford, N.J.: Fairleigh Dickinson University Press, 1970.

Savage, Sherman. "Abolition Literature in the Mails, 1835-1836," *Journal of Negro History* 13, no. 2 (Apr. 1928): 150-84.

Stampp, Kenneth M. *The Peculiar Institution: Slavery in the Ante-Bellum South*. New York: Alfred A. Knopf, 1956.

Stanton, Elizabeth Cady, Susan B. Anthony, and Matilda Jocelyn Gage, eds. *History of Woman Suffrage*. 6 vols. New York: Fowler and Wells, 1922.

———. *Eighty Years and More*. London: Unwin, 1898.

Stowe, Charles Edward. *Life of Harriet Beecher Stowe Compiled from Her Letters and Journals*. Boston: Houghton, Mifflin Co. 1889.

Stringfellow, Rev. Thornton. *Slavery: Its Origin, Nature, and History*. Alexandria: The Virginia Sentinel, 1860.

Sweet, William Warren. *Religion in the Development of American Culture, 1765-1840*. Gloucester, Mass.: Peter Smith, 1963.

———. *Revivalism in America: Its Origin, Growth and Decline*. New York: Charles Scribner's Sons, 1944.

Thomas, Benjamin P. *Theodore Weld: Crusader for Freedom*. New Brunswick, N.J.: Rutgers University Press, 1950.

Thomas, John L. *The Liberator: William Lloyd Garrison*. Boston: Little, Brown & Company, 1963.

Thome, James A., and J. Horace Kimball. *Emancipation in the West Indies: A Six Months' Tour in Antigua, Barbadoes, and Jamaica in the Year 1837*. The Anti-Slavery Examiner, No. 7. New York: American Anti-Slavery Society, 1838.

Thompson, George. *Letters and Addresses of George Thompson During His Mission to the United States from October 1, 1834 to November 27, 1835*. Boston: Isaac Knapp, 1837.

Thoreau, Henry David. *Familiar Letters of Henry David Thoreau*. Edited by F. B. Sanborn. Boston and New York: Houghton Mifflin Company, 1896.

Villard, Oswald Garrison. *John Brown, 1800-1859: A Biography Fifty Years After*. Boston: Houghton, Mifflin and Company, 1910.

Williams, George W. *A History of the Negro Troops in the War of the Rebellion, 1861-1865*. New York: Harper & Brothers, 1888.

Woodson, Carter G., ed. *The Works of Francis James Grimké*. 2 vols. Washington, D.C.: Associated Publishers, 1942. In an Introduction by Woodson, the story of the life of the Reverend Francis Grimké is briefly told.

Woodard C. Vann. "The Anti-Slavery Myth," *American Scholar* 31 (Spring, 1962): 312-28.

Woodward, Helen Beal. *The Bold Women*. New York: Farrar, Straus and Young, 1953.

Index

Index

263

proclamation, 215; for woman's suffrage, 227
Phelps, Amos (antislavery leader), 117,
130, 140, 174, 175; protests Grimkés'
lecturing to "promiscuous" audiences,
118-19; Weld writes to, on "anti-
woman" stand, 178
Philadelphia Inquirer: on Garrison as a
speaker, 70-71
Philbrick, Samuel (retired Boston merchant, active abolitionist): has Grimké
antislavery meeting in Brookline
home, 109; invites Grimkés to home,
124, 129-30; entry in diary on Angelina's Odeon lectures, 145
Phillips, Wendell (antislavery leader),
205; on Angelina's powers as speaker,
145, 229
Prejudice: Angelina on racial, 102-5,
116-7; against woman's freedom,
105-6, 117-21
Presbyterian church: and evangelical religion, 21; in Charleston, S.C., 22, 24-
25, 50; Report of Synod of South
Carolina and Georgia on "religious instruction of slaves," 50-51; General
Assembly of, opposes antislavery petitions, 70
Prisons: Angelina's interest in, 64, 68
"Promiscuous" audiences: opposition to
females lecturing to, 99, 118, 121, 166;
Angelina's first lecture to, 101-2; pre-
vail from outset of Grimké Massachusetts crusade, 109; Grimké controversy over, with Amos Phelps, 118-19

Q
Quakers: discipline among, 28, 31, 45,
60-70 *passim*, 77; "plain" apparel of,
40-41, 58; in Charleston, S.C., 43-44;
Hicksite schism, 59, 77; on duty of
children to parents, 60. *See also*
Friends, Society of

R
Randall, President I. N., of Lincoln University, Pennsylvania: writes Angelina on promising future of Archibald
and Francis Grimké, 226
Raritan Bay Union, 242 (n. 73); Angelina
and Weld move to, 201, 203; social reform interests of, 206; abolitionist sentiment in, 210; women wearing
"bloomer" costume in, 206-7; Thoreau's visit to, 242 (n. 73); impact of
John Brown movement on, 212-13
Religion: evangelical, in southern states
from 1800, 20-21; and first "great

awakening," 21; Grimkés and revivals
of, 21, 22-23; Mary S. Grimké on,
23-24
Riots. *See* Mob violence

S
Seventy, the: also called "Anti-Slavery
Apostles," 95; Angelina's description
of training convention, 96-99
Slave insurrection: Denmark Vesey's, attempted in Charleston, 16-18, 71; Nat
Turner's, in Virginia, 71, 89
Slavery, 4-5; in Grimké family, 14-16,
41-42; Angelina on mistreatment under, 15-16, 42, 56; Mary S. Grimké
on, 23-24; as "sin," 38-39, 50, 52; and
the churches, 79; violence under, 116;
in District of Columbia, 130; Angelina
on corrupting power of, 200
Smith, Gerrit (wealthy philanthropist,
antislavery leader), 100; and Angelina's public lecturing, 101; Grimkés
visitors in home of, 101, 107; member of Congress, 1850s, 210; Angelina
writes to, on slavery and the national
crisis, 210-11
Smith, Jane (Philadelphia, life-long
friend), 115, 121; supports Angelina
concerning letter to Garrison, 87; Angelina writes to, on woman's rights,
118, 120, 121-22; Angelina's letters to,
on antislavery crusade of 1836-38, 128,
237 (n. 32); Sarah writes to, on her
Odeon lecture, 141-42; visits Weld
home in 1840s, 190
Spring, Marcus (wealthy merchant, a
founder of Raritan Bay Union), 212
Spring, Rebecca (reformer, wife of
Marcus, daughter of Arnold Buffum):
involves Raritan Bay community in
John Brown events, 212-13
Stanton, Elizabeth Cady (woman's rights
leader, wife of Henry): and husband
visit Welds at Belleville, 167; as leader
in early woman's rights conventions,
201, 205; and "bloomer" costume,
206; as leader in Loyal Women of the
Republic, 218
Stanton, Henry (antislavery leader,
Elizabeth Cady's husband), 80-81, 117,
130, 167, 174-75; helps Weld recruit
the Seventy, 95; supports Grimké lectures to mixed audiences, 119; ar-
ranges Angelina's addresses before
Massachusetts legislative committee,
130-31; on the Odeon lectures, 131-32
Stevens, Aaron D. (with John Brown at
Harper's Ferry), 212; buried at Raritan
Bay, 213